D0305652

HOW TO MANAGE A
VOLUNTARY
ORGANIZATION

THE ESSENTIAL GUIDE FOR THE
NOT-FOR-PROFIT SECTOR

**DAVID HUSSEY &
ROBERT PERRIN**

**KOGAN
PAGE**

First published in 2003

Kogan Page Limited
120 Pentonville Road
London N1 9JN
UK

British Library Cataloguing in Publication Data

A CIP record for this book is available from the British Library.

ISBN 0 7494 3780 4

Typeset by Jean Cussons Typesetting, Diss, Norfolk
Printed and bound in Great Britain by Biddles Ltd, Guildford and King's Lynn
www.biddles.co.uk

We dedicate this book to our wives, whose support, encouragement and active help have never failed.

Contents

Foreword

Voluntary organizations play a hugely important role in the fabric of our society. This is not only because of the services they provide but also because they act as a powerful source of social cohesion, bringing people into contact with one another, building a network of relationships in the community and thus creating the glue that holds society together.

They vary enormously in size and the nature of their objectives. At one extreme there are global organizations such as the League of Red Cross and Red Crescent Societies or huge national institutions such as the National Trust. At the other end of the spectrum there are thousands of local charities carrying out a very wide range of valued services to the community. These activities fill gaps in the state's provision of such things as medical research, child protection, the rehabilitation of ex-offenders, education and care of the elderly – the list is endless. Through fund-raising from the general public, grants from government, the Lotto and private foundations they consume a huge slice of the national economy. It is right that they should be held accountable for the resources that are entrusted to them and that they should demonstrably be efficient in the execution of their tasks.

I have been involved in the voluntary sphere in many different capacities – as chairman of the management committee, as volunteer, as fund-raiser and as consultant. In the course of this experience I have encountered a wide range of standards of performance. Some have a track record of outstanding success in achieving their goals, demonstrating very clearly that the profit motive is not a necessary factor in promoting efficiency. Others fall far short of the standard of performance that would justify their raising funds from the public. These differences in performance reflect a range of factors among which I felt the following to be most critical:

- Governance issues, including lack of relevant competence and commitment on the part of trustees. I have served on management committees that have been far too large and unwieldy to allow for proper discussion and decision making. As a chairman I have encountered lack of commitment on the part of trustees who fail to attend meetings or come to meetings not having studied the papers and so wholly unprepared in relation to the often complex issues to be resolved.
- The level of professionalism of paid staff – particularly in relation to their ability to inspire and lead volunteers. Managing volunteers is in many ways more challenging than managing paid employees and calls for a great deal of tact and powers of persuasion.
- The need to clarify precisely what is expected of volunteers and to obtain firm commitment to meet these expectations. No organization can function efficiently if it cannot rely on the attendance and punctuality of its key staff or does not have the ability to require them to undertake training.
- The importance of competent financial management and of cash flow management in particular. This requirement calls for much greater attention than the common practice of looking for a retired bank manager to act as treasurer.

These issues and others are well explored in this work by two very experienced consultants. I am sure it will be of great help to all those in the voluntary sector who are concerned to raise standards of performance.

Philip Sadler, CBE
Vice President, Ashridge Business School

Acknowledgements

We are grateful to all the people who have given us help and advice during our research for this book. We owe a particular debt to the many who have cooperated with us in the preparation of case studies, without which the book would have been much less practical and probably much less interesting. Although we hope we have made no errors of fact in interpreting the information, we have to accept responsibility both for these and for any conclusions we have drawn.

Organizations and the names of those who helped:

- Action Research – Rear-Admiral Simon Moore, CB;
- British Red Cross – Mike Adamson and Kate Lee;
- The Children's Trust – Sir Brian Hill and Andrew Ross;
- Coram Family – Dr Gillian Pugh, OBE;
- Enham Trust – Mark Maclay, Gail Pussard and Michael L Smith;
- Horsham Christian Centre (The Centre) – Doug Fletcher;
- National Society for the Prevention of Cruelty to Children – Kate Howard;
- National Trust – Briony Sutcliffe;
- Roffey Park Management Institute – Val Hammond;
- Royal National Lifeboat Institution – Andrew W Freemantle, MBE;
- The Ramblers Association – Nick Barrett;
- Z/Yen Ltd – Ian Harris and Michael Mainelli.

Individuals:

- Richard Brewster.

Other organizations:

- HM Treasury;
- Royal Philanthropic Society;
- The Cabinet Office;
- The Charity Commission;
- The Church Commissioners.

To this list we should add numerous colleagues and associates in various charities and church organizations in which we have had, or still have, an involvement, and from whom we have learnt much over the years.

Introduction

WHY WE HAVE WRITTEN THIS BOOK

Both of us have had involvement with a number of voluntary organizations over a long period. By involvement we mean something more than dropping money in a collecting box from time to time: playing a role in the foundation, management and other activities, always as volunteers. Some of the things we have done have been long term and significant, while others have been occasional and small.

It was our various foundation and management experiences in charities that first made us aware that there was a need for such a book: in particular Robert's long-term management involvement with the Prince's Trust, and the experience of both of us in establishing the Strategic Planning Society, to which each of us has given years of service on the board, on various subcommittees and in many other ways.

We were both aware that there are people whose whole career has been spent in the voluntary sector, and who are very experienced and capable. But in addition there are people who take staff roles in the charity sector later in their careers, and have to face very different problems and issues to anything that their past experiences have prepared them for. There are volunteers who become trustees, sometimes without really understanding all the issues that they have to face. Other volunteers may have to work closely with paid staff, and

1

sometimes the relationships could be better. Then there are people who are seconded to a charity or other voluntary organization for a period by a large organization, who can deliver great benefit provided their skills and motivation are up to the job.

Although much of the book includes material from charities, we believe that most of it has real relevance to other voluntary organizations for whom the legal background is different, such as churches, associations, trusts and many organizations registered as friendly societies, or industrial and provident societies.

SOME SPECIFIC PROBLEMS FACING VOLUNTARY ORGANIZATIONS

We started with the general intention of offering a basis from which people could improve their own capabilities when moving into a management or senior specialist role. However, we were also aware that there are some specific issues in managing voluntary organizations. For example:

- Voluntary organizations need to have a shared vision and clear supporting strategies.
- There is a periodic need to modify that vision because of changing conditions and the relevance of the original purpose.
- While leadership is always important, strong leadership from the top is vital in charity management, not only to inspire staff and volunteers, but also to maintain the high motivation that many have when they first join a charity or other voluntary organization.
- Voluntary organizations need to obtain high performance from paid staff and volunteers, and to overcome the reluctance that we have observed, among some of those running voluntary organizations, to clarify and measure their expectations.
- There is the issue of improving people management skills, including the particular problems that arise from time to time because of the conflicting priorities of staff and volunteers.
- Some organizations need to improve decision making.
- There is the whole issue of fund-raising and the potential implications for charities that become overdependent on grants.
- There is a need to strengthen accounting awareness among many staff and trustees.

These are the main things we have tried to cover. They led us to a concern over the long-term viability of some organizations, and into issues like mergers and the future of the voluntary sector.

WHAT WE HAVE NOT INCLUDED

There are four aspects that are important that we have not tried to cover in depth. First are the legal issues, although we have touched on a few of these from time to time, and second is the detail of the legal requirements for the annual financial returns. (Our two chapters on accounting deal with the basic concepts, the custodial role, and management accounting and decision making.) Although we have given attention to issues in managing people, we have not tried to cover the whole scope of human resource policies. Finally we have not dwelt in depth on the specialist subject of information technology.

These omissions are of matters that are important, but their complexity would have considerably lengthened the book. There are good sources of information, including some excellent publications that can be downloaded free of charge from the Charity Commission Web site, and we felt that we could add little to these.

WHO SHOULD READ THE BOOK?

We see several different types of reader:

- Firstly there are those involved in running medium-sized voluntary organizations, where some of the things we recommend may not be done. We believe that the book can help bring a real improvement to these.
- Secondly there are new employees in the large charities. Although the book may have little to offer the top management of those large charities that are already very well managed, we believe that it has relevance for those moving into charities either as new graduate employees or from careers in the private or public sectors.
- Our third target is trustees of voluntary organizations of any size who do not already have good, extensive experience in the sector.

- Fourthly we should recommend it to persons being seconded by their organizations to voluntary organizations of any size.
- Finally there are the numerous volunteers who are involved in aspects of the administration or management of voluntary organizations, and particularly those who are new to their role.

The voluntary sector

WHAT IS THE VOLUNTARY SECTOR?

All charities are in the voluntary sector, but not all voluntary organizations are charities. Among the numerous types of voluntary organization are trusts and foundations whose purpose is to fund work by others. We touch on these organizations, many of which are registered charities, and have included them in our chapter on fundraising, but we have not attempted to cover their complexities in any depth.

Although we have used charities as our point of departure for much of the book, the majority of the content is equally relevant for those organizations in the sector that are not charities. This is because our focus has been on management, and we have not tried to cover charity laws in depth, partly because this would have made the book less interesting to other voluntary organizations, partly because of the complexities, but mainly because there are excellent guides to much of the legislation that can be obtained free from the various authorities.

One of the complexities is that there is no standardized charity law across the whole of the UK. The largest number of registered charities are in England and Wales, governed by laws that are administered by the Charity Commission, which is also the registering authority. The legal framework is different in Scotland although, as in England and Wales, registration is an important part of the process, and the three

countries share a number of common principles, including a requirement to lodge annual reports. Registration in Scotland is with the
Inland Revenue, and the Scottish Charities Office has a monitoring
and controlling role. In Northern Ireland the registration is also with
the Inland Revenue and, although the legal principles are based on
English law, there is a less rigorous legal control: there is no requirement to make annual reports, but accounts must be produced if
demanded by the Inland Revenue.

The Scottish Executive Central Research Unit (1999: para 1.8)
makes the point:

> charities, that is voluntary organisations which fall within the technical
> legal definition of 'charity', make up one sub sector only of a much wider
> voluntary sector. In the UK charities are treated differently from other
> voluntary organisations in two important respects: they are automatically
> entitled, by virtue of their charitable status, to a wide range of tax reliefs,
> and they are subject to a special regime of supervision (differing in each
> of the three constituent jurisdictions of the UK) associated directly with
> their status as charities.

Not all voluntary organizations are eligible to be registered as
charities. The organization must be set up for purposes that are
entirely within the legal definitions of charitable purpose, and the
organization has to be exclusively devoted to these. To obtain
registration as a charity, an organization must have aims that
are exclusively charitable, that is they must be directed to
provide something of clear benefit to others in society, and
must not benefit individuals in a way that outweighs any benefit
to the public. Its activities must not be harmful to humankind,
and must be lawful. A charity must be independent, and cannot
exist for political purposes. Membership conditions must not
restrict the availability of facilities so as to prevent the organization
as a whole from benefiting the public (see Charity Commission,
1997).

Many voluntary organizations cannot meet all the requirements of
the charities legislation, and so cannot register. This may be because
they are not exclusively set up for a legally recognized charitable
purpose, or because the intention is to pay the committee members,
or because they cannot be shown to benefit a wide enough sector of
the public. Others, such as some religious denominations, may be
exempt from registration, but are required to observe certain other
aspects of the charities legislation.

There can be great variety in the legal structure of a voluntary organization, whether or not it is a registered charity. The unincorporated forms are association, society or club, trust, or friendly society registered under the Friendly Societies Act 1974. An incorporated structure is registered under the Companies Act (this will be a company limited by guarantee if charitable status is also sought), as an industrial and provident society (under the Industrial and Provident Societies Act 1965), or by Royal Charter.

To complicate matters further, friendly societies and industrial and provident societies that have an appropriate purpose and rules can register as charities through the Registrar of Friendly Societies, and are exempt from registration with the Charity Commission. For example, the housing association MOAT describes itself on its letterheading as a charitable company registered under the Industrial and Provident Societies Act.

THE SIZE OF THE VOLUNTARY SECTOR

The differences in legal structure, besides bringing a great variety in benefits, obligations and costs to the organization, make it much more difficult for the size of the voluntary sector to be measured. There are figures from various organizations that give an indication of its size and contribution to the economy, but there are none that can be taken as definitive. In a way this does not matter, because the figures we can get at are sufficiently large to make the point that the overall sector both is very significant and covers a great variety of activities and organizations of various sizes.

So let us start with what we have. There are three sets of figures from the Charity Commission, the National Council for Voluntary Organisations (NCVO) and the Scottish Council for Voluntary Organisations (SCVO).

The Charity Commission (www.charity-commission.gov.uk) data are derived from its register, and cover charities in England and Wales. In 2001 there were 160,778 main charities in England and Wales with a combined income of £26.71 billion. In addition there were some 27,000 subsidiaries or branches of other charities, whose results are consolidated into the main charity. Table 1.1 gives summary details for the past three years.

These figures conceal a great deal of variation. Table 1.2 illustrates

Table 1.1 *Number and income of main registered charities in England and Wales*

As at 31 December	Number of Charities	Annual Income (£ billion)
1999	163,35	23.740
2000	159,845	24.561
2001	160,778	26.708

(Source: Charity Commission © Crown Copyright)

the extremes. There are 42,000 charities (26 per cent) with less than £1,000 annual income, which represents 0.03 per cent of the total yearly income of all charities in the UK. At the other extreme, less than 400 charities have an annual income of over £11 billion, which represents 43 per cent of the total of the entire sector. The implications of this will be discussed later.

There is a valid argument that there may be some double counting in these figures. They are based on the returns entered

Table 1.2 *Breakdown of number of charities and income*

Annual Income Bracket	Number of Main Charities	% of Registered Main Charities	Total Annual Income (£ billion) of Charities in Each Bracket	% Income of Registered Main Charities
£0 – £1,000	42,012	26.13%	0.008	0.03%
£1,001 – £10,000	59,699	37.13%	0.268	1.00%
£10,001 – £100,000	41,097	25.56%	1.349	5.05%
£100,001 – £250,000	8,168	5.08%	1.305	4.89%
£250,001 – £1 million	6,164	3.83%	3.008	11.26%
Over £1 million – £10 million	3,266	2.03%	9.353	35.02%
£10 million and over	372	0.24%	11.417	42.75%
Total	160,778	100.00%	26.708	100.00%

(Source: Charity Commission © Crown Copyright)

into the register. However, where a charity exists in order to give grants, some of which go to other charities, in effect the income that enables the grants is counted in the income of the giving charity and also as income of the receiving charity.

The NCVO (www.ncvo-vol.org.uk), working with similar organizations in Scotland, Wales and Northern Ireland, produces estimates of the nature and scope of the voluntary sector at both UK and regional level (eg NCVO, 2002). Their estimate is that the voluntary sector had an annual income of over £14 billion in 2000, with 10 per cent of organizations having 90 per cent of the income. These figures need exploring because, although the voluntary sector includes organizations that are not registered charities, and the figures cover all four countries of the UK, they are in fact lower than those quoted from the Charity Commission. (Note: the source of the figures quoted here is NCVO, 2000.)

All statistics are collated for a purpose, and the purpose affects the definitions used. The NCVO uses a definition of general charities rather than registered charities. This excludes a large number of registered charities, such as public schools, housing associations and religious bodies. The NCVO estimates that 40 per cent of the registered charities in the over £10 million income band are excluded by this definition.

Fortunately we do not have to try to reconcile the two sets of data. The NCVO research gives two other order-of-magnitude figures that are helpful. The voluntary sector employs nearly 500,000 paid staff, and volunteers contribute £12 billion worth of unpaid labour (although, using different definitions, which would include many organizations excluded from the NCVO universe, the Institute for Volunteering Research, www.ivr.org.uk, puts the figure at £40 billion). It seems that for different reasons both the Charity Commission and the NCVO figures may be on the low side, but they are big enough to capture attention.

The third source of information refers only to Scotland, and uses similar definitions to the NCVO. The SCVO (www.scvo.org.uk) found that there were 44,000 voluntary organizations in Scotland in 2000/01, 23,907 of which were general charities. (The total number of registered charities was 27,347.) The sector employed 100,000 people, 80 per cent of whom were full-time employees, and was supported by 600,000 volunteers. The income of the sector was £2.01 billion, 67 per cent of which was produced by 5 per cent of the organizations (SCVO, 2001).

Northern Ireland has an estimated 5,000 registered charities, coincidentally about the same number as in Eire.

A PICTURE OF GREAT VARIETY

We may not know precisely what the income of the voluntary sector is, but there is enough evidence to conclude that it is large, with the overall figures concealing a great variety of differences. Some of the organizations are massive, and others are so tiny that their annual income would be insignificant were it not for the way it is obtained. Some are national, like the National Society for the Prevention of Cruelty to Children (NSPCC); some are local, like many hospices; others, like Oxfam, are international. Some, like the British Red Cross, are linked to a global charity. Some are well endowed, while others are in a permanent cash crisis.

The activities of these organizations vary across a wide spectrum. At first sight it is hard to see a connection between disaster relief in the world's trouble spots, the rescue and protection of animals, the teaching of music, the transcription and indexing of historical records, sheltering the homeless and the preservation of old buildings. Yet this is only the smallest indication of the immense range of activities undertaken by charities and other voluntary organizations.

So what is the common thread? We will use charities as the basis of this discussion, although much of what we say is equally relevant to other forms of voluntary organization. The common strand is that they are organizations that are philanthropic by design and, though staff may be adequately paid, there is no profit to those who provide the original endowment or ongoing funding, nor is there gain to those who supervise the charity as trustees.

The idea of giving to help others is by no means modern. Individual acts of charity, whether through money or services, are almost as old as humanity itself. Spontaneous collections of money for specific charitable actions, such as when many towns made collections for the relief of the London poor during the Great Plague in 1665, at a time when over 100,000 people in London died (out of perhaps 450,000). The government of the day fled the city and did not make any money available to help the city and its outlying parishes cope with what was a massive disaster. At a time when a high proportion of doctors and clergy also fled the disease, others remained and many gave their lives to help alleviate the suffering: a few even came into London from plague-free areas in order to help. The lack of government interest in a particular critical issue has long been the cause of the formation of many charities. Much of the early development and history of charities was linked to religious movements through which came many schools and universities, hospitals and almshouses. In Britain charities without the traditional religious backing were starting to appear in the 18th century and many of the most famous charities of today date back to the 19th century.

One example, for which more detail is provided in the case study, is now known as the 'Coram Family', founded in 1739, with the support of key figures in the world of art and music. Hogarth and Handel were two of its most famous supporters. This charity has had to refocus itself several times during its long history, which brings us to two related management issues that are common to many charities.

Management issues

1. *The need for voluntary organizations to have a shared vision and clear supporting strategies.* If the vision is unclear, not shared by those who play a key part in achieving it, or if no one quite knows how to implement the vision, the organization runs the danger of drifting and underperforming. This is a problem that is not restricted to the voluntary sector, but may be more acute here because of the governance and management of such organizations, the danger of schisms developing, and confusion between the charitable purpose and the actions the charity is free to take (see Chapters 2 and 3).

2. *A periodic need to modify that vision because of changing conditions and the relevance of the original charitable purpose.* Many charities have recognized this need and have recently undertaken far-reaching strategic reviews. During our researches we found the National Trust, Oxfam, The Prince's Trust, Ramblers' Association and the Coram Family who had recently done this or were in the process of doing it. We also found a few who should be doing this, but were not actually doing so (see Chapters 2 and 10).

Case study 1.1: Coram Family, a charity founded in 1739

Background

Thomas Coram established the Foundling Hospital for abandoned children in 1739. Fortunately it was well connected. Hogarth donated a number of paintings, and Handel performed the *Messiah* for the charity on a regular basis. For many years the charity was known as the 'Thomas Coram Foundation'. It is now known as the 'Coram Family'. The charity, based near King's Cross, now runs 30 projects, working with over 1,000 children and young people in the care system, as well as 800 families in local community projects. It has an annual income of £4 million, with fixed assets of £4.5 million. Its investments are valued at £12 million.

Its main fields of work include adoption and fostering services, a leaving-care service, a contact service, a family support service and a parent centre. It is controlled by a 'Court of Governors', 25 in number, who appoint the trustees. In addition there are patrons, honorary consultants and officers. There are also audit, investment and fund-raising committees as well as investment managers and investment consultants.

There is an exceptionally valuable collection of paintings given to the original Foundling Hospital. It has been the subject of controversy, including a cross-party debate in the House of Commons in March 2001. The issue has been whether these assets achieve the best financial advantage to the charity. The outcome has been to agree the refurbishment of 40 Brunswick Square in London to house the collection, and then to undertake to sell the pictures in situ over a 25-year period in order to realize their value for Coram Family's work.

The chief executive is Dr Gillian Pugh, OBE, a nationally known authority in childcare. Her appointment four years ago led to a successful shake-up and review, the results of which are now appearing.

This charity seems to be a model of how a charity should be run. It has not allowed its wonderful history to lull it into self-satisfaction. An example of the high management standard is found in the 'Framework for annual service reviews', which is appended to this case study. This might act as a template that other charities might follow, even if only on an informal basis.

In recent years, Coram Family has grown at a compound rate of 35 per cent a year largely on local authority funds, based on the provision of subcontracted services, and on grants from government and charitable trusts.

Issues the charity faces

In a short study of this charity a number of particularly interesting management issue became apparent:

● *Issue 1:* Given the scale of public sector funding, is there a danger of the charity becoming, or being perceived to become, a poodle of government or even of party politics?

Comment: The danger is fully appreciated, and the answer comes in seeking to ensure the maintenance of a balance between public sector funds and those from other sources.

- *Issue 2:* Is it possible to maintain the rate of growth? Where will the bottle-necks or limits to growth be first noticed?

  Comment: It is very difficult to recruit and build middle managers to run new services. This is particularly a problem in London. Above all it is vital the quality is not sacrificed for size. If signs of this appear, and it may happen, then growth must be restricted.

- *Issue 3:* Given the above, what can be done?

  Comment: The approach has been to establish a training and consultancy service. This will spread the know-how, expertise and standards to a wider community while not diluting the core.

- *Issue 4:* Could the solution be to 'mop up' or absorb a number of other regional charities in the same field, but which lack Coram Family's professionalism or funding?

  Comment: Though this seems a good idea in theory, in practice this has not to date been found feasible. Good fits are hard to come by, and the issue of local trustees can bring problems that are hard to resolve. It is felt best to husband resources within London, where control and supervision of quality can be maintained.

- *Issue 5:* Five years ago Coram as a major charity was in a certain amount of disarray. What did the new chief executive bring that could achieve so much in such a short space of time?

  Comment: The view of the staff is that she brought vision, leadership and a professional credibility, which in turn brought in major public sector contracts.

- *Issue 6:* How has this been achieved?

  Comment: The simple answer is the creation of a 12-point plan of action. But behind this lies an approach to empowerment and enabling that allows staff to get on with the job. It also involved knocking a few heads together to eliminate petty friction, and getting everyone to march to the 'same drumbeat'. The chief executive also undertook a simple but classic 'SWOT' analysis (strengths, weaknesses, opportunities and threats). This emphasized the basic strengths on which so much could be built.

- *Issue 7:* Is the ancient history of a 'Court of Governors' and a 'Board of Trustees' a structure with a potential for confusion?

  Comment: These two committees did need very clear terms of reference, which have now been agreed. The main role of the governors is to select the trustees and make key appointments both paid and honorary. The main role of the trustees has been defined as:

  - establishing the long-term strategy;
  - agreeing the annual budget;

- agreeing the capital budget;
- monitoring progress, with particular attention to the three-, six- and 12-month accounts, set against the provision of the quality of service.
● *Issue 8:* How are the prospective governors found?
Comment: A 'gap analysis' of the expertise and contribution existing governors and trustees could and did bring was undertaken. The aim was to ensure that there was an adequate spread of gender, age, ethnicity and background, as well as key skills and experience. The existing governors produced quite a number of names. However, there was an anxiety to ensure existing trustees did not just replicate themselves and for this reason Coram agreed in principle to advertise for applicants. This is exceptionally unusual for such a well-known charity.

The procedure for selection includes getting the court to agree in principle the names of the candidates. They are then interviewed by the chair, the chief executive and one other governor with relevant expertise. The appointment is ratified by the Court.

This whole programme seeks to match what skills are available with what is needed. This required expertise that included taxation, investment and accounting. It also required an in-depth expertise with hands-on experience in the various aspects of childcare. Important titles, or popularly known figures, are noticeable by their absence, although the charity also has six patrons.
● *Issue 9:* What really are the key criteria by which the work of Coram should be judged?
Comment: These are publicly set out as: 1) quality; 2) innovation; 3) replication.
● *Issue 10:* Given that the charity as a result of its history and origins owns such a massively valuable collection of paintings, is there a danger that the motivation to raise new funds is weakened, and a cautious policy of conservation of funds is enacted? Is there a fear that people knowing the wealth you have in the form of pictures will be less generous to Coram?
Comment: There is always a danger when running a charity that too cautious and conservative a financial policy is pursued. This is particularly true when large historic assets are owned. Coram is anxious to preserve on site its paintings as part of its heritage, yet it wants ambitiously to build on its traditions with new funds.

There is also an 'Old Coram Association' of former pupils ('foundlings') with more than 300 members. The 'Friends of Thomas Coram' separately promote cultural activities and invite donations. The marketing department organizes theatrical and musical events, to raise the profile of the charity as well as raise money.
● *Issue 11:* The charity has moved from being an orphanage, through becoming a school, to offering a range of services of adoption, nurseries, leaving care etc. The question needs to be asked as to how these have come about and where the future lies.

Comment: The charity has been sufficiently flexible to be able not to be imprisoned by its past. It has been able to move to what was needed at the time. At present, attention is being given to being able to offer 'preventive' support as well as continuing with intervention services. Cost-benefit analysis shows that often effort put in to prevent a problem is more cost-effective than seeking to remedy the problem after it has occurred.

Conclusion

This is a wonderful example of the best of management in a British charity. This management is on a par with any well-known public company. However, this exhibits not just efficiency, but human sensitivity to staff, coupled to a professional expertise in the needs of underprivileged children.

Appendix: Framework for annual service reviews

Aims and objectives:

- What are we trying to achieve?
- Are the current objectives still appropriate?
- On what theories are we basing our intervention?

Services provided:

- range and balance of project within service;
- outcome measures.

How well has the service been performed?

- How much service did we deliver?
- How well did we deliver the service?
- How much effect/change did we produce?
- What quality effect/change did we produce?

Resources:

- Staffing:
  - strengths and weaknesses of the current structure;
  - recruitment;
  - balance;
  - quality;
  - stability.
- Accommodation and equipment:
  - Is it adequate?
  - Do items need replacing/updating?

- Budget:
  - Is service within budget?
  - Do any elements require additional grant funding?
- IT:
  - Is it adequate/effective?
  - Are there systems for information collation/database?
- Professional support:
  - Is the advisory group effective?
  - Is other external support/consultants required?
- Quality assurance:
  - quality standards in place and being implemented?
  - policy and procedures up to date?
  - staff training requirements;
  - consumer responsiveness;
  - research commissioned;
  - equal opportunities.
- Lessons learnt:
  - What has been successful?
  - What have been the difficulties?
- Innovation and replication:
  - What aspects of the service are innovative?
  - What opportunities/strategy is there for replication?
- Priorities for the next year.

Among modern charities that were founded in the 19th century are Barnardo's, the Royal Botanical Gardens in Kew, the National Trust and the YMCA. Over the years a number have been based on the success and wealth of industrialists. These include the Wellcome Trust, the Nuffield Nursing Homes Trust, the Wolfson Foundation and the Leverhulme Trust.

The vast bulk of the charities operating in Britain today are of more recent vintage. Save the Children Fund, founded in 1919, and Oxfam in 1942, are each a reflection of one of the two world wars. Many others are also a reflection of new needs or perhaps more precisely a perception of the urgency of an existing need. New charities are being formed every year, and even those that start small can with energy and dedication grow to a point where they can make a significant difference. There are others that are shrinking, and some that stay small and should perhaps reinvent themselves, merge with other charities or wind up.

When forming a new commercial company there is always a problem of raising sufficient capital, having an adequate cash flow and being big enough very quickly to be on an economic scale to be viable. There has to be a critical mass if a charity is to be effective, although what this is will vary with the nature of the charity. Forming a new charity needs seed corn. It also must watch its cash flow, but it is answerable to the public, via the Charity Commission (or its equivalent in Scotland). Well-directed energy and dedication can turn small acorns into large oak trees.

THE VARIETY OF VOLUNTARY ORGANIZATIONS

Let us examine some of the key features that differentiate charities, and illustrate the variety of critical management problems each will face.

Scale

Of course the size of the charity makes a difference. The degree of expertise needed and available to run a multi-million-pound charity is of a totally different order of magnitude to that required for a small band of dedicated volunteers running a local charity with less than £1,000 a year income. The larger voluntary organizations may be just as complex as a commercial business of similar size and scope, with the added complication of having a mix of volunteers and paid staff. In the charity of under £1,000 a year, unless it is expected to grow significantly there is very little management needed, and only a modicum of administrative skill.

Our aim is not to provide new insights to the really large organizations, although it may still be valuable for new recruits to those organizations. And of course even the largest charities do run into rough patches from time to time. However, below these, but somewhat above the tiny minnows, lies an area where the management and administration of many charities could be run to better effect. It should be remembered that for many organizations income size measures only a part of the resources they can deploy to achieve their charitable purpose, as the labour supplied by volunteers can outweigh the impact of the money itself. Where volunteers are used to provide a skilled input, the value to the organization is greater than the figures in the surveys, as these generally use the minimum wage as the basis for the calculation. In the target size range lie many organizations that could achieve much more, and where trustees, paid staff and volunteers could all contribute.

Management issue

3. *An overwhelming requirement for leadership from the top, to inspire staff and volunteers, and to maintain the high motivation that many have when they first join a charity.* Leadership is critical. The mix of volunteers and paid staff, which is a feature of voluntary organizations, means that it is not enough to be a good administrator. Leading and managing people comes high on the list of essential requirements for success (see Chapter 2 for an approach to transformational leadership, and Chapter 5, where leadership blends with the management of people).

Scottish Executive Central Research Unit (1999), in a survey of charities, provides useful insight into some management issues. Among them was the lack of understanding about the need for accounts, and ignorance of the requirement to make accounts available to members of the public, on request. While the basic accounting issue is unlikely to occur in the larger charities, the information requirement was ignored by charities across the spectrum. The accounting issue is echoed in England and Wales, with too many charities periodically failing to meet their legal accounting obligations. It is also apparent that many of the mismanagement cases investigated by the Charity Commission or the Scottish Charities Office are caused by ignorance rather than fraud. Lack of financial control and accounting understanding are contributors to failure and the wastage of resources.

Management issues

4. *Improving decision making in some charities.* Not all decisions require a need to be able to use and interpret figures, and few decisions can be made sensibly on the basis of the figures alone. However, good management is not possible unless there is some understanding (see Chapter 7, which deals with management accounting and evaluation of decisions, and Chapter 3 for information about assessing the consequences of strategic decisions).

---

5. *The need to strengthen accounting awareness among many charity staff and trustees.* Accounting follows sensible principles, but one has to know what they are in order to begin to understand the figures. A basic understanding of accounting is essential if those involved in the management of voluntary organizations are to play their parts effectively (see Chapter 6,which deals with the purpose of accounting, the principles, some of the issues in financial accounting and the all-important financial control).

Level of capital base

Some charities have a very large endowment or an investment fund that produces an investment income that is reasonably secure. Their chief worry is to manage their funds wisely to try to ensure that falling interest rates do not drastically curtail their income. There is also a need to ensure that the investment base increases in line with inflation, so that it does not fall in real terms.

There are variations on this theme. For example, one charity draws much of its income from a separate trust, which is the main shareholder in a commercial company with aims that are related to the main charity. So although the charity benefits greatly from this source, it does not itself manage the trust.

Investment income fluctuates. The Royal National Lifeboat Institution (RNLI) found that its £11 million investment income fell by 20 per cent in the year ended 31 December 2000. Comic Relief's income, which is largely generated by television programmes, ran at £2 million, showing a rise of 13 per cent in the year ended 30 June 2000. However, those charities with a stable investment income base are usually in a better position over the long run.

Typically the RNLI investment income has originated from legacies. Many of the big charities earn quite a steady stream of legacy money year after year. At the Macmillan Cancer Relief charity, legacies rose by 30 per cent in the year ended 31 December 2000 to a total of nearly £20 million. Cumulatively, as legacies build the investment base year after year, the effect on the charity can be very considerable.

Such a scale and nature of funding can provide stability. Indeed in an emergency, a loss can be made, with the deficit being made up from the capital base. Minimal financial reserves can act as an inhibitor, causing trustees to be risk-averse and avoid experimentation. Trustees of a charity with adequate cash reserves are bound to think differently, compared to those of a charity that annually has to raise the funds it needs to spend and that does not have significant financial reserves. At the same time there is a balance to be struck, and the Charity Commission is always concerned when charities build up large reserves instead of using them for the purpose for which the money was donated.

Sources of income

The majority of charities do not have a large investment income, which makes the need to raise funds an ever-present issue. SCVO (2001) published some interesting figures about the sources of funds for voluntary organizations in Scotland (see Table 1.3). Although the percentages may not be typical of other parts of the UK, the sources of funds are, and in any case the figures are interesting.

Table 1.3   *Sources and types of income: Scottish voluntary sector 2000/01*

Sources of Income	%	Types of Income	%
Public sector	35	Grants	37
Self-generated	32	Trading, rents, investments	32
General public	19	Donations	19
National Lottery	7	Service agreements/contracts	1
Charitable trusts	6	Sponsorship	1
Other private sector	1		

(Source: SCVO)

It is when one looks at individual organizations that the differences become very apparent. Henley Management College, a management educational and research establishment, depends on the fees it earns from the services provided. Eton College, another charity, earns £25 million a year in grants and fees. The National Trust earns four times as much from grants and fees as it does from investments. Trading companies provide income for numerous charities. The Horsham Christian Centre, a small charity that is the subject of a case study in

Chapter 2, is wholly dependent on its income from its coffee shop and bookshop; the few donations it receives are a minute proportion of its funds.

The National Trust brings us to another type of fund-raising: membership. Having members is one way of stabilizing the income stream to a degree, although the number of members may go up or down. Membership also provides a source of volunteers, and a sympathetic address list that can be used for further appeals. In a few cases the benefits of membership are little more than a periodic newsletter (eg the Woodland Trust) and are more a way of securing a regular donation than anything else. Other membership organizations provide real benefits to their members, although if membership is too exclusive it is not possible to obtain charity status. Many membership organizations are very dependent on annual renewals of income for the main part of their funds.

Dresdner (2001) suggests that although income has increased by 30 per cent since 1996, and there have been minor fluctuations from time to time, the overall significance of the sources of charity income has been remarkably constant, as has the proportion of expenditure devoted to charitable ends (see Table 1.4). Although the percentages for each year are interesting, they should not be allowed to obscure the growth as the size of the total pot has risen. There is a health warning about the figures, as the results may well have been different had the analysis be done on the top 100 charities, or the whole universe.

There are vulnerabilities in the high proportion of income that comes from grants and fees from the public sector, which leads to the conclusion that to achieve success charities have to put is a lot of effort to voluntary giving and fees and charges related to charitable work.

Voluntary organizations should take a strategic view of the courses of action that are open to them. They should not assume that the way their income has come in the past has, of necessity, to be the only way forward in the future. The Church of England, whose financial problems have been well aired, is saying that the parishes themselves must become more responsible for their own finances, as the Church Commissioners have to devote more of their available funds towards the payment of an increasing pensions commitment.

The strategy of fund-raising will dictate the style and future of the charity. Nothing should be taken for granted, or regarded as unable to be changed.

Table 1.4   *The top 2,950 charities*

		2000	1999	1998	1997	1996
INCOME						
Legacies	% total income	6.28%	6.12%	6.59%	5.89%	5.53%
Donated goods, gross	% total income	1.85%	1.90%	1.94%	1.87%	1.70%
Other voluntary income	% total income	22.64%	23.26%	20.69%	19.31%	20.74%
National Lottery income	% total income	1.24%	1.27%	0.86%	0.39%	
Public grants, fees	% total income	23.36%	22.60%	24.01%	25.63%	26.11%
Fees and charges	% total income	31.41%	30.83%	31.81%	32.11%	31.27%
Non-charitable trading, net	% total income	1.15%	1.10%	1.11%	1.03%	0.89%
Interest, dividends, rents	% total income	12.07%	12.93%	13.00%	13.77%	13.76%
Total Income	Index 1996 = 100	130	125	114	106	100
GAINS						
Realized gains	% total gains	77.14%	66.23%	10.39%	47.99%	27.07%
Unrealized gains	% total gains	22.86%	33.77%	89.61%	52.01%	72.93%
Total Gains	Index 1996 = 100	86	47	76	75	100
EXPENDITURE						
Grants and awards made	% total expend	21.33%	20.87%	19.65%	20.09%	19.09%
Other direct charitable	% total expend	65.01%	65.14%	66.02%	64.85%	65.20%
Management and admin	% total expend	6.41%	6.57%	7.17%	7.62%	8.15%
Fund-raising	% total expend	4.18%	4.10%	3.99%	3.80%	3.49%
Sale of donated goods	% total expend	1.34%	1.36%	1.31%	1.21%	1.14%
Capital, unusual	% total expend	1.73%	1.96%	1.86%	2.43%	2.93%
Total Expenditure	Index 1996 = 100	134	123	114	107	100
ASSETS						
Land and buildings	% net assets	20.07%	21.08%	21.38%	22.26%	24.30%
Other assets	% net assets	2.89%	2.89%	3.19%	2.18%	1.51%
Investments	% net assets	74.64%	73.13%	71.96%	73.20%	72.34%
Debtors and stocks	% net assets	3.65%	3.87%	3.80%	4.04%	4.01%
Cash and deposits	% net assets	11.03%	11.12%	10.96%	10.15%	10.49%
Creditors	% net assets	−9.33%	−8.58%	−7.69%	−8.32%	−8.92%
Loans	% net assets	−2.94%	−3.44%	−3.42%	−3.51%	−3.73%
Total Net Assets	Index 1996 = 100	159	142	131	116	100

Notes: There is double counting in that the table is based on the addition of the reports of individual charities, and therefore includes inter-charity grant making. Because of the wide diversity of charity activities, the percentage distributions are unlikely to be typical of individual charities.

(Source: Our calculations on data in Dresdner, 2001)

Management issue

6. *The whole issue of fund-raising and the potential implications for charities that become overdependent on grants.* For a few charities, like Henley Management College, fund-raising is as much a business activity as it is for their competitors in the public and private sectors. For some membership organizations the main issue is the retention of old members and the gaining of new ones, which means that they need a great deal of information about their membership and its needs in order to make the right decisions. But for the majority of organizations, fund-raising is a multi-strand activity that requires careful choices to find the best options (see Chapter 8, which deals with the broader aspects of marketing, and Chapter 9, which is focused on fund-raising).

The nature of operations

Every student of business is aware that, while there are many common principles of management, many things have to be modified to fit the activities and situation of the specific organization. The two extremes of danger are those managers who apply principles blindly, without regard to the situation, and those who can only see the differences and never the common threads and so reject everything not stamped with the industry name. The voluntary sector of the economy also undertakes an immense range of issues and causes, has various styles of operating and works across various geographical canvases. These include:

- *Health.* There are organizations that give help, advice and support, and others that are involved in funding research into serious diseases. Others run nursing homes, particularly for the aged. We might also include hospices under this heading. As new diseases become prevalent, as AIDS did not all that long ago, so new charities spring up to give help to sufferers and relatives.
- *Environment.* Just about every aspect of conservation and the environment has an organization either campaigning or protecting it. Greenpeace and Friends of the Earth come immediately to mind, but so do aspects of the work of the National Trust, the Woodland Trust and the various nature conservancy charities.

- *Housing.* Many of the housing associations are registered under the Industrial and Provident Societies Act, and not all are charitable companies. There are organizations such as Shelter helping the homeless, the YMCA focusing on young people, and Methodist Homes, and examples of many organizations making provision for the elderly.

- *Education.* Eton College and Henley Management College have been mentioned earlier as two examples of educational organizations targeting very different needs. Henley, like other organizations of its type, also adds to knowledge through its research programme. The Royal College of Music provides another specialized type of education. Organizations like the Society of Genealogists, which among other things runs a major library and offers seminars, various societies that index and transcribe old archive records, and the Strategic Planning Society, which has a programme of workshops, all contribute to education in their different ways.

- *Art/culture.* Under this heading there are museums and art galleries, and broader-based organizations like the National Trust, which are the custodians of many unique, furnished buildings.

- *Employment.* The Prince's Trust – Business helps to reduce unemployment by helping young people to become gainfully self-employed. This is achieved by a mix of the provision of loans to help start a small business, and the mentoring service, which supports the emergent businesses over their first few years. Although many that survive will always remain one-person businesses, some have grown to significant size, employing other people. In addition, many young people who later find that they have to close down their businesses find it easier to gain employment afterwards because of their experience and growth in self-confidence.

- *Animals and birds.* Friends of the Earth, mentioned above, have an interest in the preservation of species. The Royal Society for the Prevention of Cruelty to Animals has a specific role indicated in its title. There are societies that campaign against the use of animals in research, or the conditions in which they are transported. There are societies to protect birds, and others to provide sanctuary for unwanted animals.

- *Overseas aid.* There are many societies that provide various types of aid, mainly to third world countries, but also wherever disaster strikes. Some concentrate on health, others on education and others on the essentials of life. In fact most of the UK expertise in dealing with the aftermath of natural disasters is within organizations like the British Red Cross and Oxfam.

● *Religion.* Many faiths are represented in this segment. Some are registered charities; others are exempt from registration for various reasons.

Although some voluntary organizations cover a specific need targeted at a specific group of people, others are broader in both what they do and whom they do it for. Some causes are more popular than others, which makes fund-raising and obtaining volunteers more difficult for those at the bottom of the popularity ladder.

There will always be new issues, new problems and new disasters to lead to new areas in which charities will work. It is a measure of society's compassion and resilience that a new topic can generate a big response. The question that this creates is whether new appeals increase the total level of giving, or whether one appeal beggars another. Does the success of the Lottery and the resultant charitable funds that become available mean that people feel exonerated from giving?

At the same time, there are organizations either that have outlived their usefulness to society or that face such an overpowering need that they could achieve more if they combined with other organizations with related aims.

It would certainly appear that the total amount given is influenced by wider issues of economic well-being, the level of taxation and social tradition. At a narrower level a new charity starting vigorously to raise funds for a particular illness may succeed in drawing off funds from other well-established charities, operating in the same field of medicine.

Two styles of operation

There appear to be two fundamental styles of operation. Charities can raise funds for a particular cause or need and then direct it to others to spend, or they may obtain funds and spend them directly on the services needed.

Provision of funds to other bodies

There is variety among these organizations. Many are trusts and foundations whose sole purpose is to provide funds for good works. The Wellcome Trust, for example, uses its massive resources to fund a

25

large number of university chairs of medicine. It also has a major programme of directly funding medical research across dozens of universities and research establishments.

Others may be broader-based charities, like the various cancer charities, which include the funding of research as one part of their activities.

Where the role of the charity is to raise funds or manage an investment portfolio in order to allow others to spend it, the style of the charity will be greatly simplified. It is after all likely that the investment will be in the hands of a fund manager – a professional outside the charity who has been appointed and rewarded accordingly.

A trust or foundation puts considerable effort into the evaluation and determination of the benefits from backing one grant application as opposed to another, and in monitoring the results.

The provision of services

The other style of operation is where the charity itself spends the funds it raises. It does this by the provision of facilities (eg residential homes) or the provision of human resources (eg counsellors, mentors, legal advice, social workers, missionaries etc), where much of the service may be provided by volunteers. In such cases, the recruiting, training, allocating, motivating and monitoring the support worker will be a major management effort.

The Children's Trust in Surrey, an offshoot from the rationalization of Great Ormond Street Hospital, is an interesting case in point. Left with minimum funds, it has aggressively, and with extensive local support, managed to raise funds and re-establish itself. It also encourages many neighbours to give their personal time in the care of the children who have long-term disabilities.

The charity not only provides the facilities and staff of the hospital, but also undertakes its own important research programme. The management issues involved in running and indeed greatly expanding such a programme will be far more diverse than for one that already has the investment and simply pays it out to others to perform.

In these cases there is a need to raise funds through voluntary donations, an endowment programme and contributions from the parents of the patients. Often in such cases grants and service contracts from the public sector (National Health Service and local authorities) are likely to be a critical factor that needs to be carefully negotiated.

Geographical spread

Another dimension of diversity is the difference between those with a local, national and international remit. Obviously the wider the span of service delivery, the greater the management problems involved. There are charities whose activities are confined to one locality, such as The Horsham Christian Centre. There are others that are multi-local, like the Prince's Trust and the Samaritans. There are others that are national, but are able to manage their affairs from one central point. And, as we have already seen, there are others that raise funds nationally, but deliver the service in other countries.

With local charities the need for good public relations in the immediate vicinity is of the utmost importance. At the other end of the scale, operating internationally brings with it a host of human relations issues (eg pay levels, selection of people, host country staffing, staff contracts and similar matters). The management of risk and financial control will be an order of magnitude greater in such situations. Establishing and maintaining good relations with overseas governments and institutions may be among the critical success factors.

The use of volunteers

Most voluntary organizations usually start by being governed and run by a small number of dedicated individuals. As the organization grows and becomes more complex, the number of paid staff will grow, and the role of the volunteer may change or be eclipsed. Historically, many voluntary organizations have tended to underpay their staff, relying on their commitment, enthusiasm and idealism for recruitment and retention.

Experience has shown that grossly underpaying staff may be short-sighted and injurious in the longer term. Setting pay levels too low right across an organization may be a false economy. Of course there may be excellent people who are willing to accept low pay, but having a more appropriate reward policy may mean that more high-calibre people will not only be attracted but will also be more likely to stay and will give better performance. Although most voluntary organizations will never be a haven of highly paid individuals, the need for professional expertise cannot always be satisfied by excluding some of the best people by pay levels that are too low. This is particularly true with regard to obtaining the right calibre of chief executive. Recruiting the wrong person for any key job is a recipe for failure.

There is often an inclination to accept lower standards from those who are volunteers or not well paid. This is most unwise. Just because someone is giving their time free should not be a reason to accept second best from a volunteer. People will respect the organization far more if they know that only the highest standard is tolerated. Sloppy standards lower the organization in the eyes of a volunteer.

Fund-raising is often a sensitive issue. Typically it is the least popular task to be undertaken by a volunteer. The question then arises as to whether there is a need to bring in professionals with the extra cost that this will involve. The issue should be addressed with an open mind, and trustees should weigh very carefully the cost against the benefits of paying for a true professional.

Sometimes the issue is how to maintain the enthusiasm and dedication for a charitable cause, as volunteers become less important, and paid staff work alongside those who are giving their time without charge.

Today we live in a litigious society, and a voluntary organization must guard itself from any claims that arise from accidents, poor standards of performance or misdirected handling of people. There are also legal obligations under various pieces of legislation that govern health and safety matters, and that can leave managers and trustees open to prosecution if there are serious failures. If many volunteers are needed, their level of skill or knowledge has to be addressed. This brings the issue of how to attract such volunteers. There are all the HR issues of selection, what training a volunteer will need and how will it be provided. Some volunteers, either from the start or at a later time, attain the required standard. Others do not, which brings the issue of how to drop a volunteer (often of long standing) without causing great offence to someone who may be well meaning but inadequate for the task.

The enthusiasm of volunteers is a very tender plant, which needs to be nourished. Volunteers need to be given recognition and thanks, however humble the job they perform. There is an ever-present danger that in the drive for efficiency and professionalism the spirit and enthusiasm of those who started the charity are gradually lost. Once lost, they are hard to recoup.

Management issues

Many of the issues already discussed apply to voluntary organizations whatever their activity although, as we show in Chapter 3, how the concepts should be applied will vary. But there are other issues that are virtually universal:

7. *The need to obtain high performance from paid staff and volunteers, and to overcome the reluctance that we have observed among some of those running a charity, to clarify and measure their expectations.* People management comes high on the list, and escalates rapidly as an issue as the numbers employed or working as volunteers escalate. Management can enable people at all levels to make a greater contribution, or if done badly can make it harder for the organization to achieve anything.
8. *Improving people management skills, including the particular problems that arise from time to time because of the conflicting priorities of staff and volunteers.*
9. *Improving decision making in some charities* (see Chapter 5, which is about the management of people).

ONGOING OR ONE-OFF

Our last area of diversity in voluntary organizations can be described as 'ongoing' or 'one-off'. The ongoing will be the organization whose specific remit or role will continue year after year, with no definite end in sight. This is the case with the majority.

Others will have an end in sight even at the start. An example might be a charity for the survivors of a particular disaster, or those injured in a specific war or battle. In these situations the beneficiaries may be cured or will eventually die. The closure may appear a long way off to those who found the charity. Ultimately it will be for the trustees to decide what to do with the remaining resources of the charity after their mission has been completed.

The Princess Diana Memorial Fund is an example of what is expected to be a finite life organization. Speed is not the critical factor, but trustees need to be seen to act resolutely and sensitively, and to avoid being trapped in a bureaucratic minefield. Donors become quickly disillusioned and resentful if they feel their gift is not being used with due diligence.

CONCLUSION

This chapter has sought to point out the vast variety within the world of voluntary organizations, a variety that calls into play many very different management skills. What is critical for one organization may not apply to another, which has its own critical requirements.

This shows how important it is for the trustees fully to understand what the important issues are, and what really makes a particular voluntary organization succeed or fail. This is essential if they are to ensure attention is focused on the key areas, that they have adequate expertise and that adequate resources are deployed. How can the trustees ensure they keep in touch with reality and know what operating in the field is really like in today's conditions? It is up to themselves and management to ensure they have such an opportunity. Sadly some of the biggest charities have trustees who do not take the time to know what is going on or to understand the real issues.

There is another trustee problem. Our own observations of real-life situations and press articles from time to time have thrown up many situations where people take on the role of trustee without understanding of the legal implications or what they should really be doing. There is some research evidence to support our observation, as the Scottish Executive Central Research Unit (1999) found in one of their surveys. The quotations come from their report:

> 2.40   Our research revealed that a number of those involved in the management of charities were unaware (until receiving our questionnaire) of the charitable status of their organisation and their consequent legal obligations. It was reported that this was most likely to occur where those in management at the time of our research had not been involved in management at the time of recognition [as a charity]. It is common within parts of the sector to have a high turnover of committee members and records are frequently lost as a consequence of this. This finding was supported by our interviews with local umbrella organisations, who said that many of the organisations they advised were

unclear about their legal obligations and because of frequent changes of office-bearers, committees often lost charity records and copies of their constitution.

2.147 Our postal survey pointed to just 63 per cent of those in management or control being in receipt of an up-to-date copy of the constitution or other founding document, and only 31 per cent were in receipt of a written statement outlining key roles and guidance on the legal responsibilities they have as committee/board members.

2.148 A number of charities were unable to locate their founding documents which had been lost due to changes of location and/or supervisory structure (for example, local government reorganisation). The lack of access to founding documents raises the issue of how those in management or control can be sure that they are meeting or staying within the objectives of the charity they are elected/appointed to manage.

This research applied to Scotland. Charity Commission (2002) includes summary information from a survey of England and Wales. Only 55 per cent of charities surveyed automatically supplied trustees with a copy of the governing document, and it was an issue that was not restricted to the smaller charities. It was found that 69 per cent provided copies of accounts to new trustees, which worryingly meant that 31 per cent did not. For these reasons, as well as emphasizing the role and duties of trustees in several chapters, particularly those dealing with accounting, control and people management, we have also included Chapter 4, which deals with governance.

REFERENCES

Charity Commission (1997) *Guide to the Charities Act*, Charity Commission for England and Wales

Charity Commission (2002) *Trustee Recruitment, Selection and Induction*, Charity Commission for England and Wales, London

Dresdner (2001) *Top 3000 Charities, 2001*, Dresdner RCM Global Investors, London (financial analysis provided by Caritas Data Ltd)

National Council for Voluntary Organisations (NCVO) (2000) The A to Z of the voluntary sector, *Research Quarterly*, 9, April

NCVO (2002) *UK Voluntary Sector Almanac*, 2002, Hamilton House Mailings, Corby

Scottish Council for Voluntary Organisations (SCVO) (2001) *The Voluntary Sector in Scotland*, SCVO, Edinburgh

Scottish Executive Central Research Unit (1999) *Scottish Charity Legislation: An evaluation*, Scottish Executive Central Research Unit, Edinburgh

2

Beginning with a vision

DEFINITION

When a new charity is formed, it is usually because one or two people are passionately committed to an issue and believe that they can do something to make things better, and this becomes the cause. It is enthusiasm and belief in the cause that is the driving force that gives a charity its vigour, creativity and originality. Other people become involved, and the founders infect them with the same passion for the cause and, as the organization is formalized, the circle of committed people increases. During the difficult times the members of the group reinforce each other's enthusiasm and dedication, as they seek ways to overcome problems.

However, to achieve any results there has to be more than a shared passion for a cause. There have to be detailed objectives, plans and actions to make the ideals an effective reality. The results of the actions taken have to be monitored, and the trustees, staff and volunteers given thanks and recognition for the role they have played.

Unfortunately the cause may change over time. The Coram Family case study in the previous chapter provided an example of how what we might term the 'vision' of the organization has changed since the charity's foundation as a foundling hospital.

It is a truism that an organization is more likely to achieve its aspirations if it has a clear vision of what those aspirations are and what they mean. Unfortunately organizations do not always have a clear vision even at start-up, or do not redefine or reconfirm the vision as situations change.

Clarifying vision will not guarantee success, but not doing so will increase the chances of relative or absolute failure.

Vision implies foresight, imagination and perceptive qualities, which are important for success. However, other dictionary meanings of the word give us warnings of the things that can go wrong. There is a link with fantasy, and a visionary may also be someone who is prone to impracticable schemes and out of touch with reality. We need the warnings hidden in the word because, although a sound vision, rooted in reality, is a foundation for success, a poorly considered vision may be seen as a joke rather than something through which to steer an organization.

'Corporate vision is: a clear mental picture of a future goal created jointly by a group for a group for the benefit of other people which is capable of inspiring and motivating those whose support is necessary for its achievement' (Johnson, 1999). The definition was devised specifically in the context of voluntary organizations. It was part of a study of the hospice movement, from which the author identified four key areas for assessing the feasibility of a vision:

- clarity of the vision;
- communicability;
- qualities in relation to the community;
- availability of suitable property (which would not apply to every type of charity).

In business organizations the argument for a shared vision within the organizations is tied to getting all employees to work in a way that supports the vision. It is about a culture within the organization that helps everyone to head in the same direction and to overcome obstacles that might lie in the path. Voluntary organizations have this need, but their nature means that they have at least four additional publics with whom the vision should be shared. Firstly there are the supporters from whom the funds to enable the organization to operate are raised. Secondly there are the volunteers as well as the employees: if the vision is not supported it will be much harder to recruit and retain the armies of voluntary workers on whom many charities depend. Thirdly, for many charities there are the communities/governments/local authorities from which the charity may need acceptance, support or planning permissions. Fourthly there are the clients of the organization, the people for whom it is working: this is a less clear-cut requirement, as it will vary with the organization and the nature of its activities.

The main factor not specifically stressed so far is leadership, something we will return to later in this chapter.

VISION AT DIFFERENT LEVELS

So far the emphasis has been on the overall vision of the whole voluntary organization, and this will certainly drive everything the organization does. But the concept of vision does not stop there. For example, some charities run trading companies, whose role is to generate funds for the charity. This is a key factor for a trading company, and certainly is important in the decisions of volunteers to work with it, but it is hardly a complete recipe for a good business. What is needed in addition is a vision for the specific business.

The message is that the concept of vision is important to the organizations operated by the voluntary organization, and may take a different shape from, although still be related to, that of the organization as a whole.

Pause for reflection

We have given some of our views about vision. How do you think they apply to your organization? How clear is the vision of your organization? Does it bring the purpose and values to life, in a way that is stimulating and exciting? Does everybody buy into it?

A MODEL FOR TRANSFORMATION

At the beginning of this chapter we gave a brief outline of how the passionate commitment to a cause by the founders of a new charity becomes converted to action.

The stages of the vision process can be outlined in a more formal way:

1. envisioning;

2. activating;
3. supporting;
4. implementing;
5. ensuring;
6. recognizing.

This is a model for transformational leadership, and is particularly helpful in that it combines the processes of formulating and implementing a vision. Our focus is on using the model to develop and use a corporate vision for a voluntary organization, but it is worth mentioning that the same steps are appropriate for managing any change of significance, such as a new strategy, a different organizational structure, a new way of working or a new IT system. The vision in these situations would be related to the change and its effect, but the concept is similar.

The model describes three stages with a strong behavioural element, and three that are more about systems and control. Of course the envisioning process should have an analytical content, just as the systems and control methods will also influence behaviour. But the first three steps are mainly about developing a shared vision, and the last three about the management actions to turn it into reality.

The initial letters of the labels spell out the word 'easier', as an aid to memory. This does not imply that the process itself is easy. In fact it may be very difficult indeed. The model needs a brief explanation before we look at things in greater depth.

Behavioural elements

These three elements embrace the actions to define the vision. Typically the process will start with one or two people who put in the intellectual thought, drive and energy to start the process. As things develop the three elements may become an iterative process, with a widening circle of people committed to and involved in the vision. In the early stages the process may result in some modification of the vision, but eventually the vision hardens and becomes the driving force of the organization:

● *Envisioning.* Developing a vision requires initiative. It is tempting to think that once the job is done the vision will last for ever. In reality it rarely does, as voluntary organizations, like businesses and governments, have to change and adapt to new situations. The task that loomed as large as a mountain when the organization was formed may, as it evolves, be seen as a springboard to even more testing endeavours. Some of the things the organization was set up to do may no longer be needed. Despite the need for periodic change, a vision should be something that will remain relevant for a reasonable length of time.

- *Activating* is about bringing more and more people on board. It involves communication and discussion, and the creation of a snowball effect so that enthusiastic supporters help to bring conviction to others. It is also about actions as well as words: it is counter-productive for managers to talk one message and demonstrate a completely different one by their behaviour. Supporters may defect if it appears that what the charity actually does, and how it does it, is different from the vision that inspired it.
- *Supporting* means the help and encouragement given by the leaders of the vision process to those involved in implementing it. Mentoring, coaching, motivation and the removal of obstacles all play a part.

Systems and control

In the context of the corporate vision, these elements of the model would relate to the strategies and plans for turning the vision into reality. It is possible to fire a whole organization with enthusiasm for a vision, only for it to fail because inadequate attention is given to the actions that enable the vision to be realized. Because the vision is for the longer term, there will usually be a need for a sequence of new strategies over the period that the vision remains valid:

- *Implementing* involves developing a thorough understanding of the implications of the vision, and preparing the detailed plans for the actions that have to be taken to implement it. It may be a business plan, budgets, a critical path analysis, or one or more of many other management tools.
- *Ensuring* covers the monitoring and controlling process that ensures that the necessary action steps have been taken, at the right time, and checks that the results of that action are as expected. Into this step comes any remedial action that is needed.
- *Recognition* may be related to the performance management system and monetary recognition of employees through the reward system. However, it is also about demonstrating in

various ways that the roles of key players in helping to make the vision happen are appreciated. It can take many forms, of which the simplest, and often the most appreciated but the most over-looked, is to say thank you.

Although some of the steps in this model should properly be left until later chapters, the model should be borne in mind as we look at some examples from practice, and some of the principles that underlie the concept of vision.

THE CASE STUDIES

The case studies chosen to facilitate the discussion come from three very different charities: the National Trust, The Ramblers' Association and Horsham Christian Centre. In each case we have focused only on certain aspects of vision, and do not mean to imply that we have summed up the whole vision process in any of the char-ities. A final case study, the Royal Philanthropic Society, gives another example of a charity that has had to rethink its role and develop a new vision.

Case study 2.1: The Ramblers' Association

Background

The Ramblers' Association (RA) is a registered charity with 130,000 members in the year ending 30 September 2000. It is an unincorporated organization, first registered as a charity on 5 June 1967. Its history is longer than this. In 1931 a National Council of Ramblers' Federations was formed, from a move-ment that had seen individual walking clubs group together on a regional basis. The RA succeeded the National Council in 1935.

The annual report for 2000 shows that its geographical coverage is Great Britain, where it has a network of 53 areas and 423 local groups. At area and local level all work is done by volunteers, coordinated by democrat-ically elected committees. Throughout the three countries the local groups, among other things, organize regular programmes of walks, lead walks, undertake work to promote walking and the Association, and draw the atten-tion of county councils to blocked footpaths. Where the county council allows, volunteers work on signposting paths, clearing paths and building bridges.

Aims

The constitution defines the charitable objectives as:

- To help all persons especially those of limited means, to a greater knowledge, love and care of the countryside.
- To work for and assist in: (i) the provision of, preservation of, and the prevention of obstruction to public rights of way over footpaths and other ways used mainly for footpaths; (ii) The preservation and enhancement for the benefit of the public of the beauty of the countryside; (iii) The provision and preservation of public access to open country (freedom to roam); (iv) With the object of improving conditions of life for the persons for whom the facilities are intended, namely the public at large, and in the interests of social welfare to encourage the provision of facilities for and the organizing of healthy open-air recreational activities in the countryside and in particular rambling and mountaineering.

The literature of the Association summarizes these objectives in four aims:

- Encourage walking in Britain.
- Protect public paths.
- Campaign for freedom to roam over uncultivated open countryside.
- Defend the beauty of the countryside.

Membership has grown, from 79,000 in 1990 to 130,000 in 2000, which is small compared to the very large number of people in the population who claim to walk regularly for pleasure.

There was a large financial deficit in the 2000 annual report. In recent years the charity has put most of its money and efforts into campaigning, but the main interest of the active portion of the membership is the local walking groups (which is the main benefit offered to members), which receive much less attention.

In May 2001, Nick Barrett, the recently appointed chief executive, began a strategic review of the organization with the intention of producing a strategic plan by October 2002. Included in his thinking is the need to review the Association's mission, values and overall objectives within the context of the constitution. A consultation exercise has started among the area and group officers, as well as a sample survey of members and other research.

The Ramblers' case draws attention to something that all charities have as part of their registration under the charities legislation: a statement of charitable purpose. Legally this is important as it confines what actions a particular charity can take. However, the legal statement would rarely qualify as a statement of vision, although it is related to it. For example, we might imagine a legal statement of charitable purpose for a new hospice that does little more than describe what a hospice is and states the community it is intended to serve. A vision for the hospice might well encompass the details of the building required, the number of people it will hold, the environment that will be created in the building, the standards of care, the values of compassion and caring that the founders see in the vision of what the hospice will be, and the all-important issue of why the hospice is needed. It cannot conflict with the legal statement of purpose, but it can interpret it in the context of the organization and the task.

The Ramblers' Association's vision is not clear, and the four headings and the actions reported under them show what it does and has done, but not what it wants to achieve, nor is there much idea of the values of the Association.

There is also an issue about two roles of the organization, campaigning and walking groups, in relation to the motivation of supporters (members), the size of the membership and therefore the availability of resources to pursue both roles well.

The need for a clear vision and its supporting strategies now appears to have been recognized so, although the RA currently does not give an example of a coherent vision, we hope that by the time this book is printed the situation will have changed.

Case study 2.2: The Centre, Part 1

The Centre occupies an attractive old building in the centre of the Sussex town of Horsham. It consists of a café with 32 covers, a Christian bookshop and meeting rooms, and has been operating since September 1994, and in its present premises since March 1995. To the casual observer it is just a pleasant place for a light meal or a cup of tea, which happens to have a bookshop upstairs. Yet it is much more than this, and the business operations are a means to fulfil a much wider vision. The pleasant atmosphere and friendly staff make it a nice place to be, and the clue to why this is so can be read by anyone from the back of the menu (see Part 2 of the case study later in the chapter).

The business is operated by a limited company, HCC Trading Ltd, which is owned by a registered charity, Horsham Christian Centre Ltd. The charity holds the lease on the building. A number of Horsham churches are nominal shareholders in the charity, whose liability is limited by guarantee.

The vision and its origins

The business project plan (5 January 1993) for The Centre described the origins of the charity and its vision. There are minor alterations to the text quoted below to make the sequence of dates clear:

> Over recent years there have been a series of ecumenical house groups during Lent, promoted by the British Council of Churches (now known as 'Churches Together in England'). These have encouraged Christian people to question their place and role within the community.
>
> The Churches in Horsham have taken part in these courses. At Easter 1990 reports to the Horsham Council of Churches from these groups urged the Council to provide some kind of Christian Centre to fulfil aims along the lines now agreed.
>
> The Council, under the Chairmanship of Reverend Eric Maynard, believed it to be right to follow up these recommendations...
>
> In May 1991 Horsham Churches Together held an open meeting at which the great majority of the 80 people present expressed an enthusiasm for opening a Centre and offered their support.
>
> From the information thus gained the Council gave its approval for the setting up of a feasibility group to do the necessary work and research and report back with proposals.

The feasibility group was able to present a statement of aims, very similar to those that were ultimately in the business plan, for agreement by the Council of Churches in September 1991. The feasibility group then became an action group to take the project forward.

Initially 12 churches, of five denominations, supported the concept. Others joined later. Although the initial concept emerged from the house meetings, and was endorsed later in the wider meeting, in between the translation of the idea into a practical vision was the result of the hard work and dedication of various representatives to Horsham Churches Together. The investigatory work included drawing on the experience of a number of churches and charitable organizations across the country.

One such source of inspiration was the Beaconsfield Churches Christian Trust, which had been operating for 10 years. As this scheme had developed, more churches had become involved. New activities were added: a temporary shelter for women and children; a 'Hospice at Home' scheme; and the purchase of property adapted to accommodate handicapped people. Visits to organizations such as this helped the council to see the practical issues behind the possibilities.

The action group examined the issues of premises, legal structure and finances in depth, as well as working on the further development of the vision, or statement of aims, of the venture. These grew from all the earlier work, and the plan itself was discussed and agreed by the Council of Horsham Churches Together, and ultimately by each of the participating churches.

The aims, which of course have an overarching religious content, are taken from the business plan. They are to:

● provide worthy premises in the Centre of Horsham to symbolise and promote Christian unity;

- enable Churches and individual Christians to work together in service to the community in Christ's name;
- provide a place where Christians and others within the community can meet and establish relationships of friendship and trust;
- promote a loving and accepting environment out of which the Gospel may be heard and received, thus enabling the Centre to be a stimulus for evangelistic outreach in the community as a whole;
- provide such facilities as will help meet the needs of the community for Christian literature, information, support and counselling, and to make available resources for use by the Churches;
- promote and encourage a ministry of prayer, both by and between the Churches, at every step in the establishment and ongoing life of the Centre, in supplication to God that it will further His saving purposes in Christ, and be to His glory.

The intention is for the Christian Centre to be a place where people can meet informally and share the love of God. It will be a witness to the unity of the Churches as well as a place where that unity can grow through having Christians of different backgrounds working together. It is believed that the Centre will enhance the spiritual well-being of the town and enable people to discover Jesus in an informal setting.

Part 2 of this case study deals with the implementation of the plan and the sustaining of the vision.

This case study illustrates one process for developing a vision. Awareness of a felt need came out of a series of meetings between members of different local churches. It could very easily have been something that withered, except that there was a nucleus of people who wanted to make The Centre happen, and who had the energy, initiative, skills and leadership abilities to move the project along. The case study shows how the involvement of additional people was brought about, and how the initial idea became a working vision that through widespread active involvement gained widespread commitment.

Two stages of the vision process model described above merged here as commitment was built and the vision became firmer. Attention was given to practicality, to ensure that the vision was realistic, including the visits to similar centres, investigations of available premises and the preparation of a business plan. All these also became steps in the process of building further commitment.

The vision statement (called aims) shows why the charity was formed and what its intentions are, and includes values as well as actions. The plan containing the final statement of aims and an action plan and financial assessment was agreed by the sponsoring organization on behalf of all the churches involved, but by this time the vision had become a shared commitment, and only the costed strategy required agreement through the approval of the plan.

The business plan is one action under the implementation heading of the vision process model. Other actions to realize and sustain the vision will be described in Part 2 of the case study.

Case study 2.3: National Trust

The National Trust is a registered charity, founded in 1895. It owns more than 612,000 acres of countryside, 600 miles of coast, 200 historic houses and gardens, and 49 industrial monuments and mills.

A summary of its strategic plan 2001–04 is available on its Web site (www.nationaltrust.org.uk), and describes the long-term vision and its related values. The plan is the result of widespread consultation.

The vision is stated as:

To inspire present and future generations with understanding and enjoyment of the historic and natural environments through exemplary and innovative work in conservation, education and presentation.

In realising our vision and objectives, our staff, volunteers and supporters will be guided by our values, which are to be:

- relevant
- actively involving
- outward looking
- professional
- innovative
- inspiring

The summary lists objectives under four headings: inspiring support; improving conservation and environmental quality; managing our affairs effectively and efficiently; developing our people and knowledge.

An important aspect of the National Trust plan is that it incorporates values into its vision statement. The information (not reproduced here) given under the four objectives reinforces the vision and values. The development of the strategic plan involved wide consultation and discussion, which itself was a step towards building commitment.

The public availability of the summary plan through the Web site is intended to influence supporters and volunteers and extend commitment to the vision and values. The summary is a communication document, and the strategies are described only to the policy level. The summary is well set out and well illustrated to capture the attention, and is quick and easy to read.

Pause for reflection

We have had a quick look at the vision and values statements of three charities. Contrast the various statements of vision. What do you think of their implications in the context of the definition of vision with which we started this chapter? How would you set about defining and implementing a vision in an organization?

SOME POINTS ABOUT VISION

We can now introduce some checklists for the vision process. The summaries were adapted from Hussey, 2000, and are written as advice to the persons leading the development and implementation of the vision.

Envisioning

1. *Is the vision credible?* To be credible, it must be grounded in the reality of the external environment, and the need. Are there sound reasons for believing that there will be enough supporters to finance a new charity or go on a new track with an established charity? Why should volunteers want to give their services to it? Does anyone really need the service the charity offers or hopes to offer? Do the resources that the organization can command or expect to obtain match the needs of the vision? If the vision is unrealistic the strategies may fail because they cannot be achieved. If it cannot be seen as relevant by others in the organization, their lack of acceptance may cause failure.

2. *Is it challenging?* To be too challenging may be to lose credibility; not to be challenging enough may be to lose the emotional appeal that the vision should have. Words such as 'inspiring', 'stretching' and 'exhilarating' have been used by various authorities to describe this aspect of the vision. Something that can excite

the organization is more likely to succeed than a boring statement that looks as if it will not inspire anything that will take the organization to a worthwhile future.

3. *Does it have internal integrity?* By this we mean: do the various elements of the vision fit together without contradicting each other? In a complex situation this may be much more difficult to achieve than it may appear at first sight.

4. *Is it clear?* A vision that lacks clarity may be difficult to communicate to others, and may also mean that the wrong strategies will be formulated to achieve it. The vision should be complete enough to ensure that it is sound, and should leave people in no doubt of what the organization will be like if it achieves the vision.

5. *How does the vision relate the past, present and future?* A new vision usually implies some discontinuity with the past trends, and often it is the discontinuity that justifies all the actions that have to be taken to achieve it. At the same time, denying the past may create a situation where longer-serving supporters, volunteers and employees feel resentful. If it is possible to build a bridge from where the organization is now to where it needs to be, praising past successes while emphasizing the need for change, the vision may be much more acceptable to the organization.

6. *Do you believe in the vision?* If you do not believe in the vision to the point where achieving it is the most important task you face, you will have difficulty in both holding on to it yourself and convincing others.

Activating

1. *Demonstrate your own belief in the vision and feeling of excitement* about it all the time. Although the grand occasions, like holding internal conferences, may provide platforms for the set speeches, remember that judgements are formed not on what you say but on how you behave. Think for a moment about how we view the policies of the national political parties: the grand speeches are important, but the real views we form are based on something more than rhetoric. It is what the day-to-day actions mean. Now extend this to all organizations. What percentage of those company chairmen who have stated 'Our people are our greatest asset' are stating something that those inside the organization see as credible? The vision is reinforced not only by your day-to-day actions but also by the opportunity you take to

45

mention aspects of it in the numerous regular contacts that you have with staff, volunteers and supporters.

2. *Extend personal contact as far as possible* through the organization, to communicate your own sense of excitement and to explain the vision. Most successful major changes have involved a high degree of 'managing by walking about', ensuring that everyone understands the vision or those aspects that relate to their job, and building a sense of trust in management and of belonging. Do this even though you may be relying on others in the organization to share the activating task.

3. *Workshops of key people are a valuable way of building commitment* and allowing those people to participate in the process. If the vision is defined, a typical workshop might find opportunities for people to test the vision, help define its implications and decide how to build commitment at lower levels. Such workshops may provide an element of education in the tools and methods needed, and should result in action plans. The best advice we can give for planning a workshop is to ensure that the participants have plenty of opportunity to work on the issues of the workshop; just listening to others talking about the new vision is unlikely to build commitment.

4. *Ensure that there are opportunities for two-way communication.* If all the communication is downwards, you may never know of serious concerns that people may have, which could have been dealt with had you known. There may also be information that would affect your thinking if it were shared with you. This means that you should be willing to admit errors when they exist (although if the vision has been properly thought through, these will be errors of implementation, not of direction). Never display anger if the vision appears to be criticized.

5. *Supplement the personal messages with other media,* such as any newsletters of journals published for supporters or staff, videos for internal use, personal letters to employees and key volunteers, the Web site, e-mail and voice-mail. Ensure that policy memos prepared by others reflect the message you are trying to put over. Think through the whole communications strategy at the outset for, although it will not be possible to forecast every action, this will put you in a position to exploit every opportunity and maintain consistency in all communications.

6. Use the everyday meetings to emphasize the message. These opportunities may arise in various forms: strategy review meet-

ings, periodic meetings to review progress against budget, routine management meetings and making time to speak at internal training sessions.

7. *Consider how external public relations might aid internal communication* and communication with the influencers outside, such as customers. This is essential for charities if they are to attract supporters and new volunteers.

8. *Seek out examples of success that reinforce the vision.* These do not have to be the major strategic successes; for many people simpler, everyday events may have more meaning.

9. *Select your team members with care* and do not be afraid to take tough decisions to sideline or remove those who you fear might obstruct the wider commitment to the vision (but do this in a dignified and humane way). Be willing to empower the team, so that it can make a genuine contribution. The vision will never be shared if all issues have to be referred upwards. Trust has to be built between the proponents of the new vision and the key members of the team that will help to implement it.

10. *Audit the nature and content of internal training* to ensure that the key changes are reflected in the courses and that appropriate skills are provided for those who are affected by the changes.

Pause for reflection

Use the checklists as a basis of thinking about your own organization. Are there things on the list that your organization does? If there are things that it does not do, do you know why it does not do them? Is it right in its judgement? What, if anything, would you add to the list if you were preparing a checklist for your organization?

MAINTAINING COMMITMENT TO THE VISION

A vision may be expected to last for a number of years, but maintaining commitment to it is a process that must continue for the whole of its life. When a charity is new, as in the case of The Centre, the period of risk is once it becomes active and the excitement of creation gives way to a feeling, 'Well, that's done'. Similarly when a charity reviews its vision, and in a sense recalibrates itself against the present and future needs of its clients, the people connected with it will probably feel relieved that a problem that has been obvious for some time has been tackled. There may well have been considerable interest and participation, but once the final document is produced there can easily be a 'Let's get back to work' feeling.

Case study 2.4: The Centre, Part 2

Getting started

Doug Fletcher is the manager of The Centre. He first became involved as a representative of the United Reformed Church at the end of 1993, as a member of a group looking at the bookshop side of the project. He had experience in publishing. There was an opportunity in August 1994 to take a short lease in a building in East Street, while negotiations were still going on for the premises in South Street. This meant that the bookshop could open in time for the Christmas trade. Coincidentally Doug was made redundant at about this time and was invited to become temporary part-time manager of the bookshop. It opened on 1 September, staffed by Doug and some volunteers.

In 1995 the lease of the present building was signed and the coffee shop opened and was joined by the bookshop in March. The initial idea was that the whole operation would operate with a paid manager and volunteer staff. Doug applied for the job of centre manager, and has been there ever since.

From a business viewpoint the timing was good. There had been a family-owned Christian bookshop in the town for many years, but it had closed some time before, leaving a vacuum that the new venture would fill. There were other cafés in the town, but it was not oversupplied. Indeed several more have opened since The Centre began operating.

Doug said:

> The initial problem was managing. We had a group of people who were willing to give their time and we obviously had to use that time as effectively as we could. When we had just the bookshop it was not so much of a problem. We only had two or three people working. It was a whole new ball game when we opened as a coffee shop. We used to have four great big charts on the wall with the weeks, days and the times and we used to write people down in pen if they were regular and in pencil if it was just for that particular week. It took a lot of phoning around to get people to slot into particular spaces.

At that time much more food was bought in. Sometimes in the very early days, when a volunteer was unable to attend and no replacement could be found at short notice, it was impossible to attend to any tasks beyond serving customers.

Solving the teething problems

The Centre now has about 120 volunteers, although the number fluctuates and the commitment that each person can give varies. One key volunteer is the administrator, who comes in every day. One of her tasks is to produce a daily spreadsheet where each job is divided into quarter-hour slots between 9 am and 5.30 pm. If people drop out, the administrator phones round for a replacement. A key factor is that she knows all the volunteers, and has a feel for what each can be asked to do. She is also aware of personalities, and works closely with the paid staff so that conflicts are avoided when the schedules are made up. Many volunteers like to come in at a regular time for each spell of duty, so that they work with the same colleagues and meet the same regular customers; conversely, some of the customers choose to come in at a particular time because they know who will be on duty.

It was not long before it was recognized that the ratio of paid staff to volunteers was inadequate and that there were specialist requirements in running a café that were not adequately available among the volunteers. A paid catering supervisor was recruited, through an advertisement in the local press. Doug said:

> She is wonderful, with a great rapport with the volunteers with whom she is very patient. This is very important as some begin with no idea about what they are doing, and others will choose what they will do. She works from 8 am to 2 pm and has brought professionalism to the work, and also enables us to cook all our own food.

Later two more paid part-time staff were recruited for the kitchen, and when this case study was being written attempts were being made to recruit a part-time paid supervisor to provide coverage on Saturdays. The nature of the volunteers is different on a Saturday, as most of the weekday people have other commitments. Most Saturday staff tend to be teenagers. Initially they are expected to volunteer, but those who do the job well are offered the opportunity to apply for a paid position. Saturday operations are therefore staffed very differently from those at other times.

Volunteer training

The business is important, but Doug has to balance the need to be operationally successful with the other elements of the vision. The vision is not just to run a business, but to provide a focus where people from various churches can meet and from which some service can be offered to the community. Both the café and the bookshop have a friendly ambience where the volunteers demonstrate their commitment to their beliefs by the way they behave, and try to spend time to develop a friendly relationship. Of course many customers go to their favourite pub, café or restaurant partly because they like the people who work there, but what makes The Centre stand apart is the consistency with which this is achieved.

Volunteers are drawn from the member churches, which means that there is a basis of shared values. However, this by itself would not be enough and another important action is training for volunteers.

An induction course is run every six to eight weeks. 'We have always had listening training,' observed Doug.

> This is an important part of what we are about and sets us apart from an ordinary coffee shop. It is not just about how to get involved with people, but also to know when not to get involved. We used to have an evening session on listening training. Now the first part of this is incorporated into the induction programme.

Other subjects covered include customer care, the aims of The Centre, and health and safety. Volunteers attend the induction training within a few weeks of joining. Two to three weeks later there is a follow-on to the listening training, which goes into it in more depth. After that anyone who is interested has the opportunity to receive further training in listening, the aim being to have people on call for particular situations.

Periodic food hygiene training is arranged through Horsham District Council, so that those who need it for the job they are doing can obtain a hygiene certificate.

The ability to listen

The menu makes it clear what The Centre offers by way of listening:

> Time allowing, any of the volunteers will be pleased to offer a listening ear to those who wish to share a problem or concern; alternatively we are happy to set aside a mutually convenient time to provide a more relaxed time of sharing. Please speak to any of the staff if you wish to take advantage of the confidential service.

There are around four or five occasions each year when people have a need to make an appointment, and some have had more than one session. The Centre does not offer a counselling service and has clear boundaries to what it can do. Where counselling is needed the person is referred to a specialized person who can help. Doug is convinced that for these few people who have faced real problems the listening service has been critical.

For the most part the listening skills are used to create a friendly atmosphere, to empathize with people who are lonely and to give an extra degree of friendly service beyond what would normally be expected from a coffee shop.

Volunteer issues

The reasons why people volunteer may be complex and are not the same for everyone, and Doug admitted that he did not always know the real motivation. 'We ran a small survey a year ago. Reasons given were things like fellowship, getting to know about other churches, a way of serving the community and the church, getting out of the house and a sense of purpose.'

There is considerable churn among the volunteers. 'We need a constant flow of new volunteers here, and skills too. People leave as they get older and find it too taxing, or they leave the area or there are other personal reasons.'

Volunteers are recruited from the member churches, which has the advantage of their being easy to reach through the ministers and the various church magazines. However, finding volunteers and maintaining commitment to The Centre is not a passive activity. Doug explained:

> We are now coming into a time where people are coming in who are not aware of what went on in the early years. We always try to meet with new ministers and share with them the vision of The Centre. Otherwise it is just a shop in town. They need to be envisioned with the same sort of excitement that we had in the beginning. I meet with them and go through it all with them, so that they in turn can sell the idea to their parishioners.

Remembering why we are here

Among the activities that take place on the premises is a weekly prayer meeting, held in one of the second-storey rooms, which are unknown to the casual customers in the shop. These rooms are used also for other church-related purposes. In addition The Centre has been able to give financial support to local projects: in 2000 it supported three community church projects.

'Probably the most difficult thing is remembering why we are here,' said Doug:

> It is very easy to get caught up in the objectives of the coffee shop and with the idea that we need to increase our sales – to forget that it is only a vehicle. It is so that we can afford the premises. We are actually here to serve and reach out to the community. We could not do this unless we had the income.

Many volunteers share this vision, but some have lost track of it. Those who have become more oriented to the business have said they only like it when the shop is busy. Others prefer it when it is slacker because there is more opportunity to talk to customers and to each other than in the busy times.

Performance of The Centre

The combined accounts of the charity and the company show a steady increase in business performance (see Table 2.1), to the extent that in 1999 the trustees were beginning to think about how to use the growing surpluses, a question that became more pertinent in 2000. Equipment, furnishings and decor have been improved each year, and in 1999 all loans were repaid.

Table 2.1 *Horsham Christian Centre: combined accounts (charity and company)*

	1994	1995	1996	1997	1998	1999	2000
Turnover Index	19	77	100	111	130	140	153
% Growth over Previous Year 1996 = 100		21	17	11	17	8	9

Notes: 1996 was the first full year of trading. In 1994 the bookshop operated for four months. In 1995 the bookshop operated for 12 months and the café for nine months.

The Centre case study touches on many things that are outside the scope of this chapter as the strategy to support the vision is implemented, the initial problems overcome and attention turns to the management of the operations. We have included it here because it contains not only a recognition that the vision remains the driving force of the activity, but also indicates some of the ways in which this can be done. One has only to talk to Doug Fletcher to realize that he lives that vision, and the case shows that balancing growth of the business against fulfilling the overriding vision behind the charity is something of which he is always aware. Among the methods he uses are induction training for volunteers, periodic discussions with the ministers of the participating churches and (not mentioned in the case study) the regular management meetings of the trustees.

In some ways his task is easier than that of the chief executives of many other charities. Doug has a modest operation and is able to talk to his volunteers and paid colleagues every day and in a very informal way. His main source of volunteers is easily reachable, and he has access to congregations through the ministers and the church newsletters.

Another important point is that he recognizes that the fact that there was wide commitment in the beginning does not mean that this continues automatically as ministers and congregations change and as new volunteers are recruited. He is active with new ministers to make sure that they know what The Centre is for, and among other things the induction programme helps create commitment among the new people.

For many national charities the issue is more complex. However, the principles that are visible in the case study are valid.

A VISION DOES NOT LAST FOR EVER

Most organizations will outgrow the original vision. This can be because the organization changes, it no longer has the capacity to do more or external events bring a need for change. Our final case study in this chapter is the Royal Philanthropic Society, and in addition to providing an example of where vision had to change it also makes a neat bridge to our next chapter, which is about the strategies needed to implement a vision.

Case study 2.5: Royal Philanthropic Society

In 1788 a small group of men met at a St Paul's coffee house in London to discuss a problem. They were worried by the increasing number of homeless children infesting the metropolis, and keeping alive by begging and dishonesty. Sometimes such children were imprisoned, whilst others were transported to the colonies. The group formed a committee, secured the interest of the Duke of Leeds and developed an income. A small house was acquired to provide shelter for some children, and a matron appointed. Increasing numbers of children were cared for, and substantial premises acquired in St George's Field.

Dormitories were built and workshops established in which to teach tailoring, shoemaking, printing, bookbinding and rope making. In a separate building girls were trained for domestic service, laundry-, kitchen- and needlework. In 1806 the Society was incorporated by an Act of Parliament. The Society grew rapidly, and in 1848 opened its farm school at Redhill in Surrey. At first this provided for 100 boys and girls.

There was little change until 1933 when the Children and Young Persons Act was passed. This set standards for 'reformatory schools', and the Home Office exercised control and supervision. The Society gained fame for its work and was cited as a model. This was recognized in 1953 when the Queen awarded the title of Royal Philanthropic Society (RPS).

In 1969 a new Children and Young Persons Act was passed, which transferred responsibility from the Home Office to the Department of Health and Social Security. Day-to-day management of the school was handed over to the London Borough of Wandsworth (LBW).

In 1973 the Society had virtually no role to exercise at the school, and it no longer had any control of the operations. LBW had free use of the Society's assets, which included five boarding houses, four community homes, two boys' prisons, two gymnasia, a kitchen block, various classrooms, a sanatorium, a chapel for 300 worshippers, workshops for industrial training, two office blocks, a 300-acre farm, 30 houses for residential staff and a cemetery. This estate and community of some 200 people was the property of the RPS – worth in excess of £5 million – but of no use or value to the Society.

In 1981 LBW found that it was losing money on the farm, and began to look for ways to reduce costs. A dialogue was opened with the Society, and eventually it was agreed to diminish the undertaking by half. In addition the Society took advantage of an obscure regulation, under which the Society wholly avoided any betterment charges in relation to the diminution.

Meanwhile the farm school was deteriorating. Most of the buildings were no longer in use. Sadly only 30 boys were in residence, there were serious staff difficulties and there was very little training. Understandably LBW looked for alternative uses for the property, and began to use it for remand custody. As remand was far from being consistent with the RPS's mission, the Society took advantage of another overlooked regulation and gave LBW two years' notice to quit. In retrospect this seems to have been a very daring and courageous move by the trustees.

New horizons

The next few years were largely spent in recovering the estate and turning it into cash. This was a very complex and arduous exercise made more difficult by the arrears of maintenance of some £1.5 million. For some years the RPS had made a practice of retailing its problems to the local and county councillors, their MPs, members of the House of Lords and selected ministers. This practice paid off in that the final settlement of RPS's affairs was a very favourable one. It allowed RPS to recover its property and to restart its charitable work with a handsome endowment.

The recovered endowment would provide an income and, within the terms of their founding Act, the trustees could decide how to use it. The committee worked singly and in pairs visiting a large number of children's charities, institutions and individuals to get their advice. Their views can be summarized:

- The need for support to young people is huge and continuing.
- Any work would need to be in partnership with local authorities, which have statutory responsibility.
- There was no future for residential care except for criminal custody.
- The locus of problems changed with time, as did the exact needs.

Taking this advice the RPS decided to concentrate its activities on prevention rather than cure, though the latter would not be totally neglected. They also sought to create mobile projects, not to build a treatment centre, but to deploy teams of specialists as and where they were wanted. It also decided to use its resources as 'seed corn' to develop new approaches and to disseminate these widely. To avoid having 'too many eggs in one basket', it decided to develop four or five areas of expertise with appropriate geographical spread.

Practical steps

The first step was to face the constitution. The Society was incorporated in 1806 and the Act of Parliament was very much out of date. The Charity Commission had power to provide a new constitution, but quoted a waiting list of six years. The RPS could not wait that long, so it drafted an appropriate document and approved it at a general meeting of the membership.

Another step was to change the committee. During the years of decline the more active members had resigned, leaving a group of mixed talents. Rebuilding the committee took many years. Understandably the best people were often not keen to join what appeared to be a failing organization. New recruits included an expert in property, an authority in the field of social work with children, an authority in penal matters, an outstanding finance officer and a group of dedicated businesspeople.

The Society's patron, the Duke of Edinburgh, had been appointed in 1953, but there had been no communication with him in the intervening 30 years. Contact was established, and the RPS explained its plans and hopes. The royal patron was most valuable with advice based on his wide experience of charities, and in the amount of time he gave to attending seminars and other functions. The Society's president had been in post for over 30 inactive years, and gave way to an outstanding new president, the Right Reverend Wilfred Wood, Bishop of Croydon. His help and guidance were invaluable.

The vision and real dynamism behind the liquidation of assets and their redeployment has clearly come from the leadership of Alan Fogg. As chairman at this critical period he masterminded the major decisions that transformed the nature of the society. Significantly he remained chairman for only four years. This was because of his belief that it was essential to encourage and develop a flow of new blood to the trustees. However, it is notable that Alan Fogg remained on the board for many years, and continued to play a pivotal role.

The next step was to appoint a director. They sought a man or woman who would be willing to join an unknown organization and this was advertised accordingly. There were many applicants, and eventually the committee had full interviews with four of them. The successful candidate, Don Coleman, had ideal experience as the Director of Dr Barnardo's in Northern Ireland. His manifest ambition led to nine members ranking him their first choice with the other two members placing him second. Starting with a clean sheet allowed the director to develop working practices and principles without too much 'baggage'.

Don stayed with RPS for 12 years, and deserves immense credit for his implementation of the vision. This illustrates the vital importance of taking trouble to make the right appointment. It was a key post at a critical time in the charity's history.

Where possible the aim was to appoint young staff, to encourage and facilitate personal development and to give progressive increases in responsibility.

From the beginning the accounts and budgets were immaculate, comprehensive and up to date. Operating staff could and did rely with total confidence on the financial information. The Society avoided being mesmerized by its charitable status. The only impact of this status was that part of the Society's income came as tax reliefs. In every other respect the society was a normal business.

The Society encouraged volunteers to give their services, with the proviso that volunteers were subject to the operating structures of the Society: there were no uncontrolled prima donnas. The committee members were a special class of volunteer; every committee member has a job in the Society, and there are very clear boundaries between them and management.

The RPS's own resources of £350,000 per annum would only support between 70 and 100 young people a year – a small fraction of those in need. The Society has recently appointed a very experienced fund-raiser. She heads a marketing and fund-raising department. Most of the donations come from children's charities and educational trusts. However, such fund-raising requires the confidence of management to commit to a long-term programme. Such trusts typically work on a two- or three-year cycle. There is little opportunity to get a quick donation on the spot! There is therefore a need to establish and develop contacts. The hope is that the RPS will be added to the list of donations of such charities over the next few years.

Most of the funds come from contracts from commissioning local authorities. To win these contracts often requires a major amount of work on a proposal, with no guarantee of any benefit at the end. At RPS this proposal is typically prepared by a senior executive who specializes in the specific field. However, the chief executive has to be closely involved, together with the finance director. Of particular importance is the cash flow, and where possible a front-end load is proposed to help fund the start-up costs.

As with many charities there are often difficulties in getting central core funding. Too often the use of donations is defined and restricted. What is needed is unrestricted funds as every organization must have some overheads. For this reason RPS puts an 'on cost' typically of 12 per cent on all contracts to meet this problem.

This charity could have collapsed as its role had become redundant, its assets tied up and no longer relevant. The initial moves needed courage, risk taking and an attention to the small print of old agreements. It is also an excellent example of how vision and leadership with strong management discipline have transformed this charity. It now employs 350 staff, tackling projects such as leaving care, young offenders, training for employment, young mothers and housing. It manages some 70 youth projects a year affecting several thousand young people.

This shows what can be done to exploit underused assets and the good will of a wide network of well-wishers.

In recent years several small charities, also focused on young persons, have approached RPS. They were attracted by its strong management and tight financial discipline. The advantage of spreading overhead costs on a wider base has also been particularly attractive to these charities. The outcome to date has been three mergers, and a further one in the pipeline.

The charity field has much to learn from what RPS has achieved. In particular many small charities might benefit if they could also find an appropriate charity in which they could share an exciting future helped by the benefit of synergy and first-class management (the subject of Chapter 11).

REFERENCES

Hussey, D E (2000) *How to Manage Organisational Change*, 2nd edn, Kogan Page, London

Johnson, M (1999) A feasibility test for corporate vision, *Strategic Change*, 8.6, September–October

3

Strategies and policies

CONCEPTS AND REALITY

In concept the vision establishes what the organization is striving to become and the values that are important to it. This leads to the development of strategies made in the context of the vision. Management policies, procedures and systems are then put in place to support the strategies and maintain the values of the organization. Unfortunately life is not as tidy as this. Even when a strategy is new, incremental development will mean that all the policies and systems cannot be developed in advance, and in established voluntary organizations much of what has developed is a matter of history and the reaction to issues as they have arisen. So everything is not marching in step.

Although the sequence of topics in this chapter follows the concept, we are not pretending that it is always possible or desirable to do everything in this order. However, we will stress the need to look carefully at the overall context when any changes or additions are considered.

STRATEGY AND THE NATURE OF THE CHARITY

Terms used in management literature tend to shift their meaning with the author. Our definitions of three much-used terms are:

- *strategy:* the means by which an organization moves to attain its long-term vision;
- *strategic planning:* detailed specification of the long-term vision and the means of attaining it;
- *strategic management:* the process by which the long-term vision, the strategy and the implementation are managed.

There are other terms in use. Some charities use the term 'strategic review', which is basically the same as strategic planning as we define it, but carries the implication that it is revisiting an existing vision and strategy. 'Corporate planning' is still used in some organizations, although it is somewhat out of fashion, and can be taken as approximating to strategic management.

Every reader of this book will have a specific voluntary organization in mind. Our case studies are from charities, but the models and methods are valid for all types of voluntary organization.

Later we will give some examples to illustrate some of the differences between certain voluntary organizations, which affect both how they develop strategies and the scope they have for strategic variation. It is probably reasonable to suggest that all charities need strategies for the raising of funds and the delivery of the charitable activity, and that many of them also need strategies for attracting volunteers. There are connections between these three strategy areas, and often the volunteers are also a source of funds.

There are a number of good reasons for advocating what effectively is a process of strategic management. The rewards depend on how well the organization tackles all the tasks involved, and will only come after reasonable effort:

- *Better strategic decisions.* Strategies that are carefully thought through, take more facts into account and relate to the vision are on average likely to be better than strategies that just emerge and that are never clearly articulated.
- *Future-oriented approach.* The aim is for strategy to be forward-looking, trying to anticipate and deal with problems. If the vision can be likened to the destination, strategy may be seen as the course that has to be plotted to get there.
- *Faster response to change.* The ability to react quickly to change depends partly on the flexibility built into the organization and partly on using information to detect early warning signals.
- *Reduction of uncertainty.* Forethought can reduce uncertainty, and additional information brought into the decision process may

help us to develop strategies that already take account of potential threats and opportunities. Unfortunately we can never remove all uncertainty.

- *Better coordination.* In any organization, particularly as it becomes larger, it is hard to ensure that everyone is pulling in the same direction. When key decisions are made on an ad hoc basis, there is a real danger that not all people will allow these to change what they are actually doing. When the decisions are out of step with the structure, processes and systems, people may be receiving conflicting messages about what they should do. These issues may be compounded in organizations that rely heavily on volunteers.
- *Basis for control.* Strategic management offers a basis for control that has a longer-term orientation than the traditional annual budget.
- *Wider consultation and involvement.* There is value in involving supporters, volunteers and staff, and sometimes clients, in the process of deciding strategy. This can add insights and ideas that would otherwise be missed, and help to build commitment. For most voluntary organizations consultation and involvement are essential. How to do it, and to what extent, is something we will return to.

Most voluntary organizations are programmed to cooperate rather than to compete. Cooperation with others in the same field and with other agencies and the public sector is second nature, which means that consultation and involvement often go well outside the borders of the organization. There is a penalty to this, in that the timescales for developing a new strategic plan may extend beyond what would be reasonable in a commercial organization.

A STRATEGY MODEL

Our model is a generalization, which will require adaptation to particular circumstances. The strategic situation is by no means the same in every voluntary organization. Some are in effect in business and charge fees at market rates to the people who use their services. At the other extreme there are numerous charities whose service to the client is free. In between there are those that take some income from clients, but at less than market rates. Others are membership organizations, where members join because they perceive a personal value by so doing. Some are highly focused on doing one thing or working in one local area. Others may be very complex in terms both of their services and of their geographical sphere for delivering it. After discussing the model, we will illustrate some of the modifications needed to fit particular circumstances.

Figure 3.1 looks at the elements of a strategy. It covers the 'what to do' rather than the 'how to do it', and can be used informally or as the basis of a detailed corporate plan. The white boxes show the various steps in the process, and the grey boxes show the types of information needed in order to work out the strategy. Those on the left relate to external and those on the right to internal factors. We have used the term 'strategy' here, but the same steps are valid when, as is often the case, there is a need to think through several linked strategies.

The steps in the process

- *Vision* is a concept already discussed. It is a projection of what the organization is working to become and the values by which it will operate. A vision may of necessity take several years to attain, and after that it has to be maintained until it is time to develop a new vision.
- *Objectives* are the key elements of the vision that the strategy or strategies will be designed to achieve. There may be varying time spans, as not all strategies can be implemented at the same time, some will not deliver the full range of expected benefits in one year and some may continue as an enabling framework for many years. The time dimension needs to be defined, as objectives that are unrelated to dates tend to lose their meaning.
- *Gap analysis* compares the objectives we want to achieve compared with our expectations if we carry on as we are. It highlights the difference for which we need to develop new strategies. It can be applied to many different subjects, including fundraising, volunteer needs and minority groups served.
- *Strategic options and risks* are an examination of the choices we might reasonably make. In the process of thinking through the options there is a need to balance the resources we can muster, the expected outcomes of each path and the risks to which each is subject.
- *Selected strategy* is what we have decided to commit to.

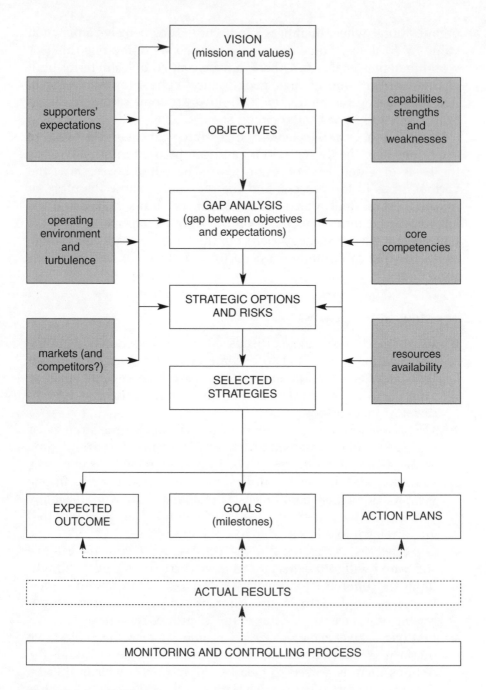

Figure 3.1 *Outline components of a strategy*

- *Expected outcomes* take the work done earlier and look at what we expect the strategy to achieve over each year as it is implemented, in both financial and non-financial terms.
- *Goals* are the firm targets along the route to help us measure our progress.
- *Action plans* are the very detailed plans that enable the broad strategy to be broken down into tasks so that it can be implemented.
- *Actual results* are what happens as we implement the strategies, and whether all the actions are taken on time.
- *Monitoring and controlling* is the process of comparing results against the goals and action plans so that action can be taken if necessary.

The external factors

- *Supporters' expectations* are those held by persons or organizations who contribute money and voluntary work. Equally relevant is the degree to which these expectations are met. Those running the voluntary organization may have opinions on these issues, but it is best if they can be supplemented with facts.

  Internal information can be obtained from a simple management information system that captures the numbers and turnover of volunteers, the ease or difficulty of recruiting new ones and the success of different approaches to fund-raising. If volunteers leave at a faster rate than is desirable, it is possible to find out why by informal interviews or more formal exit questionnaires. Staff who work closely with volunteers can also provide information.

  External information may come from published national surveys, from focus group discussions or from surveys of supporters and/or non-supporters.

- *Operating environment and turbulence* is what is going on in the world outside and how it affects the voluntary organization and its work. Turbulence is the speed at which things are changing, although this is only relevant to a specific organization if it affects its operations. Although it would be unrealistic to expect any voluntary organization to set up a vast scanning activity, there is a need to think about those changes in the business environment that may affect what the organization does, how it operates and how successful it can be. There may be threats, for example if a change of government reduces the number of public sector contracts, or opportunities, as when the Lottery became a new source of funds.

Internal information is of limited help, except that experience of what happened when a similar change happened in the past can be of value in making judgements.

External information at first seems daunting in the volume of things that could be studied. What we suggest here is an aid to help identify the trends and issues that might affect the organization, so that attention can be focused on these. A list of factor headings helps:

- demographic (eg population age structure, life expectancy, health issues);
- social (eg attitudes, culture, expectations, poverty);
- economic (eg inflation, economic growth/recession, employment levels);
- political (eg likely changes in government, pressure groups);
- ecological (eg global warming, conservation, waste disposal);
- technological (eg new materials, new fuels, new applications: communications, e-business, computers);
- legal (eg charities legislation, employment law);
- infrastructure (a concern mainly when operating in countries where it is inadequate).

Think of the subheadings that are important to the organization's activities and strategies under each of these headings, and then assess the possible effect that each factor could have for the charity. There are rating and scoring systems that can be used, and validity can be increased if a number of reasonably informed people can work together to reach the conclusions.

- *Markets and competitors* apply in the normal meaning of the terms for the business activities of charities. However, for a majority there is a need to modify it to suit the nature and extent of the need the charity is meeting. For many charities this part of the model will relate to how well they are serving their clients. Competitors in the normal commercial sense may be non-existent, although there remains a need to understand what other organizations in the same field are doing, to avoid duplication and foster cooperation.

Internal information includes the trends in the number of clients served, and in some situations the degree of success achieved. For some organizations it is possible to include a system that measures the client's level of satisfaction against expectations. The organization's own staff and some volunteers are likely to have some knowledge of how things really are at the coalface, although this information may be biased and unless supported from other data can breed a false complacency.

External information will probably involve some form of survey activity. There may be published surveys that provide some relevant information, but it is often desirable to survey current clients, as well as non-users of the service. It is impossible to generalize here, because of the enormous range of activities performed by the sector. In situations where surveying clients is too difficult or too costly, it may be worth surveying other people or organizations who are in a position to comment, such as over-seas partners for charities giving emergency help after disasters, or doctors if the service is in support of patients with certain clinical conditions, or their relatives. For example, relations of current patients may be in an excellent position to give feedback to a hospice.

There are published statistics on many aspects of performance of the larger charities (eg see Dresdner, 2001), which may be used to compare competitive performance on fund-raising and the control of costs. Discussions with other voluntary organizations may also be helpful.

The internal factors

- *Capabilities, strengths and weaknesses* relate to the current situation of the charity: part of the strategy might be about how to resolve any problems that have been identified. The most common way this is done in business, SWOT analysis, is also grossly deficient. SWOT analysis asks managers, individually or in group discussions, to identify and discuss the strengths and weaknesses of the organization, and the opportunities and threats facing it. It is deficient because it ignores the things that managers do not know about or that they do not believe to be important (see Jenster and Hussey, 2001). So SWOT should be used as a supplement to a more rigorous analysis, which looks into every corner of the charity and compares what is found against the original vision and strategic plans and where possible against the performance of comparable charities.

- *Core competencies* are the blend of skills and competencies that the charity needs in order to succeed, but looking forward to where it wants to be rather than backwards at its past. To assess the current core competencies requires considerable knowledge of employees and volunteers in relation to the current activities, which is supplemented by a performance management system. For small charities much of this may be an informal process, and is seeking an answer to the questions:

- What are the critical things we have to be good at?
- How good are we at these things?
- How serious is the gap to our performance?
- How can we plug the gap?

● *Resource availability* covers all resources, finance, volunteers, paid staff and physical. Uncertainty over what will be available, or knowledge that there are severe shortages, may limit the strategy that can be followed or stretch out the time needed fully to implement it. Some financial analysis is helpful here, including sensitivity analysis, which looks at areas of vulnerability through what-if questions.

Case study 3.1: A comparison of different situations

(Note: these examples are our assessments drawn mainly from published materials. Their only purpose is to illustrate differences in strategic situations as we assess them; they may not necessarily reflect the views of the organizations.)

Henley Management College

Background

It is effectively a university, with degree programmes at various levels, as well as shorter development and educational programmes for managers. It also undertakes research into various aspects of management. It competes with public sector business schools, other similar charities and private sector organizations. Income is around £20 million per year, and comes from its clients, which are usually organizations. The rates it charges are related to market expectations. The college is set in large grounds, and offers high-standard residential accommodation, with recreational and library facilities. Staff and faculty are paid, and roles and rewards are similar to those in business schools. It has a worldwide reputation, and attracts business from many countries.

Strategic issues

Although an educational charity, it has to operate as a business in a competitive environment. It needs to think continuously about the products it offers, the content of its research programme, its pricing and future expansion, as well as managing and maintaining the physical facilities.

Testing Figure 3.1

Every part of the figure would be relevant to this organization. Where for some charities we have to reinterpret the term market, with Henley survival depends on identifying and meeting market needs at a realistic price, and understanding the strategies of key competitors. Internal and external information is critical. Apart from its need to work within its charitable purpose, as a professional service organization it has legal responsibilities to its clients, and has to work within its capabilities. As a business it is affected by the business climate, and has to be able to develop strategies to respond when this changes.

Strategic Planning Society

Background

The purpose of the Society is to promote the practice and understanding of strategic planning and management in all sectors of the public, private and voluntary business communities. It is a membership organization, with some members providing voluntary work on the executive and the various policy committees, supported by a small paid staff. The 1999–2000 report showed that about half of its income came from membership subscriptions, and most of the balance from events and activities, publications and advertising.

Strategic issues

For many years the issues the Society has had to deal with have largely been operational, such as the management of the meetings of its specialist and regional groups, its workshop and conference programme, and the attraction of new members. Now it has a different challenge. Firstly changes in the contract with the publisher of its journal have meant a very large reduction in income from royalties, probably the main cause of the fall in revenue. Secondly it is facing an attrition of membership. These two issues mean that it can no longer follow the previous strategy and has had to undergo some fundamental thinking about how it can continue to meet its vision.

Testing Figure 3.1

In this case the supporters are the members, corporate and individual, who generally have joined the Society because of the benefits they receive. Much of the income from events and activities also comes from members, although these are open to a wider public. So in a sense the members are in both the market and the supporters' boxes. Competition is important although in a different way to Henley. There are other organizations that exist now, but that were not around in 1967 when the Society was formed, that compete for the members of the Society, so at the least there should be knowledge of these and their competitive offerings. There are competitors to the workshops. Until the changes to the journal royalty arrangement were visible, the Society had been more or less following the same strategy over several years, with occasional minor changes. Now it faces a new situation, where loss of income can lead to reduction in costs, and reduction of costs reduces the benefit to members, which in turn causes members not to renew. The whole of the model is very relevant to the Society at this time, as the strategic task it faces is both difficult and complex.

Suffolk Family History Society

Background

Suffolk Family History Society is typical of the county family history societies. It has no paid staff, and relies on volunteers for its management and for all its activities. It is supported by membership fees (£32,000 in 2001) from its 4,000-plus members, of which 700 are in Suffolk, and by the sale of publications and services (£21,000 in 2001). Typical of its work is the indexing and transcribing of various historical archive records, such as parish registers and coroners' reports. These are published in various media, and there are also various look-up services on a fee basis to find information from the various indexes it has created or obtained from other sources. There is a quarterly journal. Although based in Suffolk because of the need to access the county archives, it has members from the whole world who are interested in their Suffolk ancestry. Volunteers are drawn from the membership, and are enthusiastic about their work.

Strategic issues

The society is still following the basic strategies from its early years, and the issues it faces are mainly operational, such as which new indexing projects to undertake, the organization of evening meetings and whether to attend various family history fairs.

Testing Figure 3.1

At its present state the Society probably has no need to do more than make annual budgets and action plans to support the continuation of its existing effective strategy. The outcomes of its various projects give it one form of feedback on whether it is meeting the needs of members, so going through every part of the model every year to validate its strategy would be hard to justify. There are so many unfilled indexing and transcription needs that it is unlikely to run out of projects. The danger is that circumstances may change, but the risk of this is low for the foreseeable future.

Oxfam

Background

Oxfam had an income of some £125 million in 2000. It works in over 70 countries. Although having its highest profile in its emergency work resulting from war and natural disasters (in 1999/2000 its emergency relief programme was active in 41 countries), it has numerous development initiatives seeking lasting solutions to poverty. In addition it campaigns on development and trade matters that affect the poor countries.

Strategic issues

The charity faces a number of very different issues:

● Development work involves decisions about what, when and where to set up new projects, and the continuing management of existing ones. So although the overall strategic direction may be long-lasting, there are many strategic decisions to be made within this framework.
● Emergency relief is about being ready to react quickly, and involves considerable logistics skills. Six full-time staff are on call 24 hours in every day, and the logistics warehouse holds equipment worth £1.7 million. A new emergency is a trigger for a new appeal to the public for funds.
● Oxfam shops had sales of £43 million in 2000, compared with £44 million the previous year, but the net contribution to funds of £8.8 million in 2000 was down by about £5 million on the previous year.
● About 20,000 volunteers work in the shops, and there are many other volunteers in other fields. There is an ongoing issue to maintain the right number of dedicated volunteers.
● Fund-raising is a permanent strategic issue.

Testing Figure 3.1

Oxfam undertook a strategic review of all its activities in 1998, and as a result of this recognized a need to survey its stakeholders to assess how well it was doing. A survey was completed in 2000, covering project partners, supporters, staff and volunteers, and was discussed by an assembly meeting held in January 2001, and its council meeting in June 2001. The survey explored how various strategies were perceived to be working, in a sample of overseas operations and by various groups in Great Britain. There was particular emphasis on Oxfam's effectiveness and efficiency in the use of resources (funds, people's time, information and equipment). Information from the pilot for the survey had contributed to the establishment of a subcommittee of trustees and management to pursue a number of specific actions.

So although the different activities require different approaches to strategic thinking, Oxfam recognizes that there is a need for regular information on how it is doing, which will in turn affect strategy. The surveys help to uncover the key issues so that performance can be improved.

At one end of the spectrum there are the shops, and the model fits this activity almost without change. Indeed it is interesting to note that Oxfam 'has responded to customer demand by opening a number of specialist shops which are proving to be an increasingly popular part of our network of 850 High Street stores'. There are now separate shops (or shops within shops) for books, fair trade, bridal, originals (designer labels), furniture and super savings. A business of this size requires continuous attention to its strategy.

At the other extreme is the emergency relief activity. Although some disaster situations can be forecast if the right information is analysed, many cannot. The strategy behind the relief efforts is unlikely to require regular changes, and the most important top management decisions are likely to be about providing the resources to maintain the flexibility to react.

The Samaritans

Background

The Samaritans offer 24-hour confidential emotional support to those who are experiencing feelings of distress and despair, including those that may lead to suicide. It has 18,700 volunteers. Its largest activity is the emergency phone service, and 96 per cent of appeals for help are received through this service. It is also possible to contact the charity by e-mail, letter or visit to a branch. The number of volunteers is at its lowest level since 1975. There are other services, such as a scheme where prisoners are trained to befriend other prisoners ('befriend' is the term used by the charity for providing emotional support). It also commissions research into suicide and aims to be 'the number one source for information about suicide'.

Strategic issues

The main ongoing issue is more operational than strategic. Unless there is a dramatic fall in the number of people needing help, the key issue is the maintenance and expansion of the telephone support system and possibly the expansion of call centres. There may also be a need to upgrade equipment from time to time. This means constant attention needs to be given to fund-raising, and obtaining and retaining volunteers. There are problems of high volunteer turnover because of the particularly stressful nature of the phone calls they take.

Testing Figure 3.1

The model has little relevance to the operational aspects of the emergency service, for as long as the need continues to exist. However, fund-raising and attracting volunteers are areas where much of the model might be useful, and where it should be used regularly. It is also useful to question at least annually whether the charity should be undertaking different strategic initiatives, and the model is helpful as a process for doing this. A strategic question that might be raised is about the effectiveness of the various initiatives.

Trading companies of any voluntary organizations

The model is valid for the trading companies of all voluntary organizations, although common sense should be used in deciding how much information is needed on some of the headings we have suggested.

Pause for reflection

When did your organization last undertake a strategic review? Which elements of Figure 3.1 are appropriate for your organization? How often is the strategy reviewed? How frequently should it be reviewed?

KEY SUCCESS FACTORS FOR STRATEGIC SUCCESS

Business organizations are by no means perfect in the way in which they formulate and implement strategy, and there is considerable research that shows that for one reason or another a high proportion of strategies are never implemented. But there are lessons that can be learnt from the business world, and five key factors were derived from a study of numerous research projects and management consulting experience with many organizations. Neglect of any one of them can cause the strategy to fail:

1. *Careful analysis.* There is always a need for considerable analysis, including the collection and examination of information, because:
   - Analysis helps clarify the current situation and the way this is changing. It is also important for understanding the various strategic options, their risks and expected results. Analysis uses and manipulates information to provide insights into various situations.
   - No organization, charitable or otherwise, can afford to spend an infinite amount of money on information and analysis, which means that there is a great need to think carefully about priorities.
   - However, developing strategies without any analytical under-pinning is asking for trouble.

2. *Creative strategic thinking.* Analysis may lead to an understanding of a situation, but will rarely be enough to deliver a good strategy:

    - Without a creative input, strategies are likely to mirror those of other organizations. In business this is why so many companies within an industry seem to be making exactly the same strategic moves, and why in the end the results are often disappointing. The same copycat approach to strategy can be observed among many voluntary organizations.
    - Although some individuals possess creative insight, good ideas are often stimulated if groups of people are involved in thinking through the options. Techniques such as brainstorming and focus groups are useful in stimulating creative thinking.
    - Good strategies will be copied, whether they are for raising funds, attracting volunteers or fulfilling the charitable task, but there are often real benefits for the organization that is the pioneer.

3. *The strategic decision process.* There are several issues to consider:

    - Turbulent situations may make speed of response the main priority, which in turn constrains the length of time that can be spent on developing strategy. This may limit the amount of consultation and the depth of involvement that is possible.
    - The traditional idea of developing a new strategic plan every year may be wrong for many organizations. The Suffolk Family History Society is not changing fast enough to justify this, but some other charities may face a faster rate of change and need to monitor strategy continuously and be willing to adapt and think again where necessary.
    - Consultation both inside and outside the organization (for example, the National Trust plan and the actions being taken at the time of writing by the Ramblers' Association described in Chapter 2) may help build commitment as well as bringing new facts forward for consideration. The depth and scope have to be balanced against the time and cost.
    - Although it is possible to obtain information from a wide number of sources, genuine involvement in the strategy decision process can only occur when it is compatible with the style of the key decision makers. If the organization is generally managed in a command and control manner, it may be both impossible and undesirable to widen involvement.

4. *Implementation*. This is where it so often goes wrong. The elegant strategy just does not get turned into reality. The reasons may be complex and we will return to this topic in some detail later in this chapter.
5. *Quality of key decision makers*. Having the appropriate skills, personal qualities and experience is critical. Inappropriate management usually means that the wrong decisions are made in every aspect of the model. Again we have to emphasize the importance of high qualities of leadership.

CONSULTATIONS AND INVOLVEMENT

We have several times mentioned consultation and involvement. There are stakeholders in every type of organization. The nature of voluntary organizations means that there has to be a closer relationship with more of the stakeholders than may be the case in businesses. We have already mentioned some of the benefits of this, but there is a downside, in that it takes much longer, sometimes between one and two years, for a charity to undertake a strategic review, and after that, as we saw in the National Trust case, there is the issue of getting it all implemented. One clear danger is that a need arises for a new strategic review before much progress has been made on implementing the previous one. Fortunately many charities do not face the same level of turbulence in their operating environments as do most businesses. A second danger is if the process of consultation is used as a way of postponing unpleasant decisions. A third is if there is poor leadership from the top, and management hopes that somehow a strategy will emerge from talking to a lot of people.

Stakeholders

Who are they? Although the generic headings may be similar for all, there are differences underneath them, in terms of both the nature of the stakeholders and the ease with which they can be involved. We should also not forget that in the end someone has to make decisions: it is the trustees who are ultimately responsible at law, and the chief executive, where there is one, is responsible for implementing the decisions and should therefore play a large part in making those decisions. The stakeholders include supporters (who may be particularly important for a charity receiving grants or contract work), staff, volunteers, clients and the organizations with which the charity has to work to deliver the service to its clients (for example, a home for the elderly requires a close association with social services; the friends of a hospital can hardly do anything without close collaboration with the hospital).

Leading and managing the strategic review process

Consultation and involvement will not just happen. Once the stakeholders have been thought about, the nature of the involvement has to be decided and methods determined for how to do it. There are costs to be calculated and budgeted. The whole process has to be timetabled, and it must be clear who is responsible for what. There has to be a mechanism for pulling together all the elements of the process. Throughout, top management has to take action to hold the interest of everyone involved. There has to be communication about what is going on.

Four levels of involvement

Involvement may take many forms:

● At the most basic level it may be the use of surveys, forums, focus groups and other means to obtain opinions and information from certain groups of stakeholder. We have mentioned this aspect when going through the planning model. In effect such methods can tap into specific groups of stakeholders, on a sample basis. The resultant reports may be published to give the opportunity for comment; for example, Oxfam's survey can be downloaded from its Web site. Information is vital for effective strategy making and, if the process is managed well, can help stakeholders see that some effort has been made to bring them into the loop. When the numbers are large, everyone knows that it is not possible to consult everyone individually. Where there are a few important stakeholders, such as a foundation that gives grants to a charity, or an organization with which the charity has to work closely to deliver its services, face-to-face interviews and discussions are desirable and manageable.

● The next level is consultation, where stakeholders are invited to give their ideas and opinions about the issues facing the organization and the strategies it should follow. The process might be started by a discussion paper, but typically would involve a sequence of meetings, with the outcomes being funnelled into the process. Individual people might also be asked to write papers on particular aspects of the situation, or there may be some working parties formed to provide recommendations on particular issues. These processes may be done within specific stakeholder groups, or there may be forums of different types of stakeholder. It clearly is not possible to consult everyone, but it is possible to develop a number of representative groups that can help the process.

● Consultation can move on to the opportunity to consider and comment on the first draft of a plan, as part of the process of reining in thinking. Although a business may be inhibited in how freely it should spread its drafts because of commercial confidentiality, a voluntary organization rarely suffers from the same problem and can be much more open. Our recommendation is that when such a document is prepared for consultation, there should also be a summary of the information on which it is based. Otherwise there is a danger that those discussing and responding will do so from a parochial point of view and without seeing the broad picture. As part of this level of consultation, there has to be a mechanism set up to discuss and consider the feedback. For example, if the whole of a regional and district network were to respond as requested, there could be several hundred narrative comments to examine and analyse, and it is unlikely that they would all be making the same points.

● The final level of decision making is co-determination, where the stakeholders play a part in taking the final decisions. In all but the smallest of organizations this is not a practical option, and for a very large organization would be impossible. However, again it is possible to create a planning working group, which includes stakeholder representatives, to produce a final agreed plan for approval by what in most cases is the board of trustees. In the final event, although much may be gained from the various levels of consultation, it is those with ultimate legal responsibility who must have the final right of decision.

Anyone managing a process of extensive consultation as part of a strategic review must expect to face frustrations. It can also be very difficult to ensure that really creative and revolutionary ideas are considered, as many of those in the process may be very happy with the way things are. This is why an organization might be wise to include surveys of non-active supporters and the community at large, as part of its information gathering, so that it can do more than just balance the views of staff on the one hand and representatives of active volunteers on the other.

We cannot overstress the amount of work that has to go into the design of a process of consultation. Much depends on the quality of the staff work and the documentation produced to facilitate the process. If this is weak, it is easy to become bogged down in a morass of biased views and wishful thinking, without any clear view of how to make sense of it all.

Pause for reflection

Define the stakeholder groups and sub-groups of your organization. Are some more important than others? If you had to develop a strategic review for your organization, how would you go about designing a process of consultation? Would there be any real benefit in going down this route, or should the strategy be left to the chief executive and the board of trustees, without a much wider involvement of others?

Case study 3.2: National Trust – implementing the strategic plan

Background

The National Trust finalized its strategic plan early in 2001. Widespread consultation meant that the process took 18 months to complete. A summary of the plan was made available through the National Trust Web site, so that supporters and volunteers could understand the vision and the broad supporting strategies. The detailed corporate strategic plan is supported by plans from the 15 regions.

In January 2001 Fiona Reynolds was recruited as Director-General, and in March Briony Sutcliffe joined as Planning Manager, along with two new colleagues to form a planning department. The case study covers the planning department's first six months.

An initial priority was to implement the strategic plan, a task complicated by the fact that a key group of strategies would involve consolidating the three principal offices to one, reducing the presence in London, changing the structure from 15 to 11 regions, restructuring the management board and changing culture from a bureaucracy to something with greater flexibility.

The organizational review

Briony and her team have the task of helping the organization to move from the broad vision and initiatives to actions and projects that are capable of being executed. The organizational review was the first priority, because of its effect on managers at all levels, and on the respective roles of head office functions, regional managers and those managing the various properties.

'The National Trust has to run like a business,' Briony observed, 'and the basic business unit is a property. One step in making the vision and broad strategies actionable is to ensure that effective property plans are developed. An early priority for the planning department has been the development of guidance for the preparation of property plans. Our properties are key.'

An early action document states:

> Plans are only worthwhile if they are acted on and delivered. This will need close collaboration between Properties, Regions and Departments. The next steps will be to define in more detail who is doing what, where and when to deliver the priority actions, recognizing the dependencies between different parts of the Trust.
>
> The delivery of the priority actions will be weighed up against the day-to-day work. Territory directors will play a key role in getting the right balance between 'business as usual' and creating time to deliver the priority actions. The balance will need to be reflected in Property, Regional and Departmental Plans.

Property managers are asked to think from three basic principles:

- Understand what they have.
- Understand the wider context in which the property has to operate.
- Develop a vision for the property.

There are two area managers under each regional manager, and each area manager is responsible for 10 to 15 property managers. It is the area managers who will oversee the development of the plans by the managers who report to them. The planning department avoided arranging any special meetings to talk about the new guidance, but instead spent time at normal area and regional meetings to brief area and property managers.

Capacity planning

One of the internal problems had been the rain of initiatives that had come from the various head office departments without consideration of what other departments were doing, and without fully understanding the time implication for properties and regions. Three actions to correct this are under way:

1. Projects already in the plan are being classified and prioritized. Briony uses an analogy with aeroplanes, each one of which is under independent command but whose destinations are controlled by the airline, and each

flight is under the instructions of air traffic control. Following this analogy the National Trust is using a radar approach (see Figure 3.2). The radar separates three types of project at head office and for each region. Firstly there are national priority actions, most of which require some interaction between head office and the region. Secondly there are projects initiated at head office or a region where there is a measure of mutual dependency. Finally there are all the projects at various levels that can fly independently. In relating priorities to capacity, consideration has to be given to the core work that has to continue at all levels regardless of the number of new initiatives.

2. Planning meetings used to be held at the level of each region and head office department. This resulted in 23 such meetings that had to be attended by the planning team, and inevitably stretched out the time needed for the process. This year one meeting is held attended by the departmental directors and regional managers, which gives an opportunity for more coordination. The emphasis will be to focus on the priorities and pin down the actions needed to support them.

3. A commitment has been given that when new initiatives are considered this will be done in the context of the capacity of the properties and regions.

Briony said, 'The key words are what, where and when. We intend to treat all actions as projects, and have a much clearer idea of which are the big projects in the regions. The radar plan will be completed by December.'

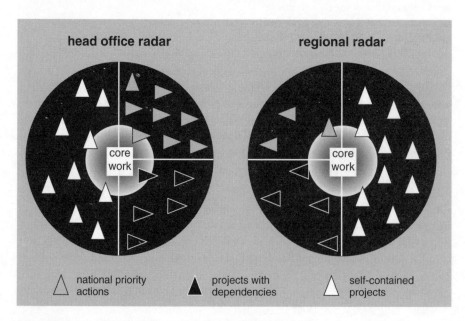

Figure 3.2 *National Trust outline radar chart*

The balanced scorecard

When the plan was being developed the National Trust were aware that the traditional approach of monitoring performance only by financial figures would be inadequate. The balanced scorecard approach was seen as one way of ensuring that broad visions and strategies became actionable, and that there was a balance in the performance measurements that included all the important variables that needed to be controlled.

Figure 3.3 shows the perspectives and performance dimensions that are being used. It gives an example under each of the four major strategic perspectives. The top-right box includes an explanation of the various headings, and applies in concept to all the other boxes.

perspectives, objectives and priority actions	
Inspiring support	*▶Conservation and environment*
	perspective ▶ *top priority in bold*
Broaden appeal	*Customer development strategy*: CRM, New sources of income/support
Properties	*Up-to-date property management plans*
Quality Visitor experience	Education and lifelong learning strategy, Customer service strategy. *Refresh interpretation at properties*
▶Countryside leadership	Implement 'Farming Forward'
Lead by example	*Align policy, advocacy around three key themes: countryside, heritage, lifelong learning*
objective	*priority action*
Managing our affairs	*People and knowledge*
Decisions	*Implement change programme*
Managing staff	Performance management system, Reduce long hours, Staff consultation, Pay/reward strategy
Resources	*New policy and planning process*, Risk management, Sustainability Principles
Information	New information systems
Training	Training and development strategy
Income	Long/medium term financial plan

Figure 3.3 *National Trust balanced scorecard concept*

The key performance indicators that arise from this work will change the management information system. 'What we will establish', Briony observed, 'is who is responsible for the performance indicator, how the data will be collected, its source and who will comment on it. The board will use a traffic light system to help them review performance on a regular basis, so that they can give attention to the things that are not going according to plan.'

IMPLEMENTATION

The National Trust case study illustrates one truth about strategic planning: that the effort given to implementing the strategies will frequently have to be greater than the effort that went into formulating them. Renaissance Worldwide 1996 found in a study of business organizations that there were four main barriers to implementation:

1. The vision barrier: strategy is not understood by those who have to implement it and not translated into objectives.
2. The management barrier: management systems are designed for operational control and tied to budgets, not strategy.
3. The operational barrier: key processes are not designed to leverage the drivers of business strategy.
4. The people barrier: personal goals, knowledge building and competencies are not linked to strategy implementation.

(As summarized in Creelman, 1998)

The National Trust case study shows how this organization is beginning to tackle at least some of the barriers. Unless visions and strategies are converted to action plans of some sort, the chances that they will be implemented are very small, so clarifying priorities, working out who does what and when, has been a necessary early step for the National Trust. Along with this, the National Trust is giving some attention to the second and third barriers, using the medium of the balanced scorecard.

Kaplan and Norton (1996, 2000) are the originators of the balanced scorecard approach. They developed it to offset the short-term orientation of conventional financial reporting. It consists of four perspectives. Three of these – customer, innovation and learning, and internal processes – contain the causal factors that lead to the fourth, the financial results.

It begins with the setting of clear objectives for the whole organization. The strategy for achieving the objective is built around the four segments of the scorecard, so that there is a part of the strategy that relates to each. From this, performance targets can be developed.

Monitoring the process requires an information system that can report back to management on progress against each part of the scorecard, thus giving the opportunity to take action before any errant element begins to affect results.

Although the perspectives chosen by the National Trust differ from these, the principle is the same, which is to make strategy part of the day-to-day management task. The balanced scorecard is only one way of ensuring that the right things are considered, and many other approaches are possible. However, the principles behind the approach may be said to apply to all of the successful methods.

The fourth barrier is only partly tackled in what is reported in the case study, although the need for culture change has been recognized. For the management of culture change, we would refer you to the vision process model, which appeared in Chapter 2. The same model can be used to help implement a change of an organization structure. There is something additional that should be said about the fourth barrier, which also provides a bridge into thinking about policies, systems and procedures. For this reason we look at it under a different heading, although it is a key tool in the implementation of strategies.

THE INTEGRATED ORGANIZATION

Many people, if asked to describe the workings of the organization, would begin with its structure, the organization chart with which we are all so familiar. Although almost everyone knows that organizations also have policies, systems and procedures, the interconnection of these is often blurred. The fact that there is a connection was argued some 35 years ago by Harold Leavitt, who introduced his diamond, a four-point model with the headings structure, task, people and technologies. From this beginning sprang many more detailed models, of which ours is an example.

The description that follows is adapted from Hussey (2000).

The vision and supporting strategies can be frustrated because different drivers in the organization are pushing people in different directions, and in these situations the strongest wins. An intention to

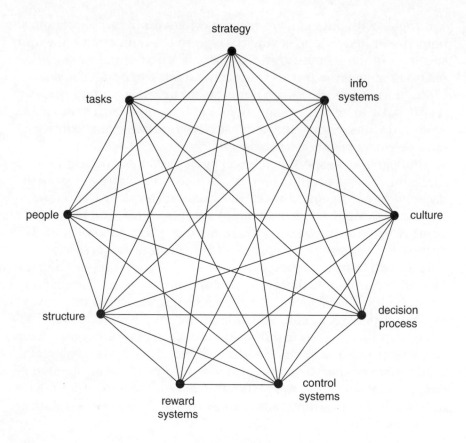

Figure 3.4   *An integrated view of organization*

emphasize teamwork could, for example, be frustrated if the rewards in terms of recognition and commendation were based on individual performance.

Figure 3.4 provides one way of thinking about those integrated aspects of the organization that have to pull in the same direction if strategies are to be implemented. An important point is that changes in any one of the factors can affect performance in all or any of the others. All the factors have to work in harmony, and if even one gets out of tune it may frustrate the intentions behind the others.

It makes most sense to use the vision, values and strategy as the force that drives the other factors, although if another factor is out of tune it may well force the strategy to change.

The organization requires people to perform certain tasks. These tasks are affected by technology. We have had accountants for several hundred years, but personal computers only began to be widely used in the 1980s and did not become commonplace until the 1990s. Now there can be few accountants whose tasks have not changed through the access they now have to PCs. Tasks are also affected by the manner in which the strategy requires them to be performed. A simple example is the commitment to customer care and relationships, which might be seen as important by a charity that either itself or through a trading company is engaged in selling products or services. An example was given in The Centre case study in Chapter 2.

Tasks are influenced by people through their experience, competencies, attitudes and availability. Sometimes it is possible to train people to fulfil the new requirements, but in others it may be necessary to recruit new people with the required skills. In most charities there are particular issues in the use of volunteers, whose motivations may be very different from those of employees. An expansion strategy may be delayed or frustrated because of difficulty in obtaining people with the competencies needed. The skills of people affect how tasks are drawn together to make jobs.

The structure is the way jobs are grouped into units for management and control purposes, and the various levels of management that are deemed to be needed. An existing structure may have to be changed because it prevents the organization from dealing effectively with certain types of client. A rigid multi-layered structure may be great if the organization is in a stable business environment and there is a need to ensure that every person does precisely what he or she is told. The same structure may stifle initiative and may be totally inappropriate if its rigidity prevents it from adapting to new challenges.

What makes a structure work is something more than the people. It is the way the processes and systems in the organization operate. Decision processes are about how power is distributed and exercised. They reflect the style of the organization and the depth and nature of empowerment throughout. Too much bureaucracy may stifle initiative and creative thinking and prevent a fast reaction to events. A laissez-faire situation can be dangerous for another reason, in that, if there is no control whatsoever over the types of decisions that may be taken at each level, opportunities for fraud may be created or resources squandered. Each charity has to find its own balance. Frequently this can be found through sensible policies that establish the rules within which delegated decision making can take place. For example, the Prince's Trust for Youth – Business loans money to enable small businesses to be established. The decisions about making specific loans are made by regional boards of directors (volunteers); the policy framework that sets the maximum amounts that can be lent to an applicant, and the rules for eligibility are set centrally.

Information systems affect the ability of managers to make good decisions and to manage their units. If the flow of information is not adjusted to a change in structure, the new structure may become unworkable. The nature of information required may also change as strategy changes.

Control systems relate closely to decision processes and affect behaviour. The way the budget system works in many organizations inclines managers to take actions that put short-term expediency ahead of the longer-term strategy. If a strategy requires new capital expenditure as well as operating costs, and the system will release only the latter, it is likely that the strategy will be frustrated. Necessary training might not be provided because no one provided for it in the budget, despite the fact that without it the employees and volunteers may lack the competencies to make a new strategy effective.

Reward systems were mentioned earlier. It is usually a fair assumption that people will assume that the reward and control systems indicate what the organization really wants, and will act accordingly, even when they agree with the vision, values and strategies, and the exhortations of management that might require them to behave differently. Charities in particular can rarely offer monetary rewards, although the larger organizations can provide promotion opportunities.

The final element of the model is culture. This is influenced by the way the decision, control and reward processes work, plus some very important additional factors, including the style and values of top management, the history and evolution of the organization, the business of the organization, the speed of change in the business environment and the nature of those changes. It can be very difficult deliberately to change culture quickly, and then only if there is strong leadership.

How decision processes work in the organization is both an effect of the culture and a way in which the culture is shaped within the organization. There are many causes that become effects, and effects that become causes. The strongest influence on culture is top management, and this is reinforced by the way each manager in the organization performs the task of management. There are differences in culture between different parts of any organization, but these are normally linked by some all-pervading shared values. Below top management it is very difficult for anyone to change the culture, partly because the rebels tend to be forced out of the organization and partly because so many of the other elements in Figure 3.4 drive behaviour so that it fits the culture. Usually, new people gradually adapt to the culture of the organization, or leave early because they feel uncomfortable.

Checklist for applying Figure 3.4

- Does each factor shown in the model contribute to the implementation of the visions, values and strategy?
- If not, which sub-factors require attention in order to enable implementation to be effective?
- If any factors require change, how will this affect the other factors in the model, bearing in mind the integrated nature of the model?
- Do the changes needed to any sub-factor have an impact on other operations of the organization? (Eg would a change needed to support a new activity have adverse effects on existing operations?)
- Is it possible for the person managing the particular strategy to bring about the modifications to the sub-factors that are necessary?
- If it is not possible, should the proposed strategy be abandoned or approached in a different way?
- If it is possible, what actions have to be taken to bring about the organizational changes that will be part of the overall implementation of the strategy?

It is not easy to attune the organization so that it enables a new situation to be implemented, partly because the integrated nature of the factors makes it difficult to make anything but the smallest of piecemeal changes to any one factor. Solve a structural problem without attention to the other factors and all that happens is that a new problem is created. There are also many hidden elements. For example, a chief executive may have produced a culture statement that states that decisions will be delegated to the lowest possible level in the organization, but his or her own behaviour may make this difficult. What is said and what happens can be two very different things.

Pause for reflection

Use the description of the model to think about your organization. Is everything pulling in the same direction or are there tensions between different policies that are frustrating progress? Why not use the model to undertake a simple audit of the organization?

THE IMPORTANCE OF A FRAMEWORK OF POLICIES

From the discussion so far it is clear that an organization has to have policies as well as strategies. In turn the policies lead to detailed procedures. Some of them may arise from the things we have already covered, but the need for others comes from different pressures. Policies and procedures are essential if the organization is to function effectively and within the law. There is a need for a sensible integration of all the policies, although we would stress that, if there is a conflict between the requirements of the strategy and the requirements of the law, the law has to win.

There are five main drivers of the need for policies and procedures:

1. *Vision and values.* We have already seen how vision and values help to shape the strategies of the organization, and ideally everything else that happens within it. While it is easy to think this way as a new organization is formed, in an existing organization many operational actions will continue. Some may be unaffected by any repositioning or new strategic initiatives; others may be given a different slant to how they are managed. The National Trust will continue to run its houses and gardens, even though the strategic plan brings many changes to how it is organized and many of the things it does through those properties.

The values of the organization may be brought to life through the way management manages, and through the policies that influence the procedures that have to be followed. They may in part be supported by specific strategies: for example, the value of being professional, which was among those listed by the National Trust in Chapter 2, could result in specific training strategies. They are just as likely to become incorporated into a number of general HR policies, such as recruitment, training and performance management.

2. *Strategy.* Much of what constitutes a strategy is about actions, such as cost reduction, expansion of facilities, changes to priorities and allocation of resources.

3. *Legal requirements.* All organizations are subject to a variety of legal requirements and voluntary codes of conduct. A charity must have policies and procedures to deal with health and safety issues, which may be relatively simple if the main activity is running a help line, or complex if the charity runs hostels or houses and gardens to which the public come in large numbers. A trading company like that which runs The Centre, with a number of volunteers, needs policies and procedures to cover the requirements of the environmental health legislation.

Although it is not mentioned in the case study in Chapter 2, The Centre, a relatively small charity, has written policies and procedures that cover these types of issues and those to do with the employment of paid staff and volunteers, which are available to all those who work there.

Employment legislation brings a need to put various policies and procedures in place, while leaving considerable discretion over the actual content.

Charity and company law means that trustees have duties to act within the terms of the charitable purpose and manage the financial affairs of the organization effectively. A number of policies and procedures are needed in the accounting area, for the areas where there is discretion on how things are treated in the books, to prevent fraud and to maintain clear lines of responsibility over financial commitments.

4. *Need for good order.* There are many policies and procedures, the need for which arises from common sense and a need for good order. They may come from a need for staff and volunteers to have clarity over their roles and boundaries of responsibility. They may give clarity over things like the class of rail travel staff

may use to travel on business, or whether volunteers can obtain reimbursement for expenses incurred in performing the charity's business. They may cover complex issues, or quite mundane things like how the mail is dealt with.

5. *Conditions attached to income sources.* Money sometimes comes with strings attached. Gifts and legacies are often made to a charity for a specific purpose, and can only be used for that purpose. Grants may bring more than restrictions on the use of money. They may bring a requirement to provide specific information on a regular basis, or to be able to prove that something that was critical to the grant has actually been done. An example is that a recent EU grant to the Prince's Trust for Youth – Business required continuing proof that a significant amount of time was spent on the mentoring element, which is a condition of all loans made. In turn this meant that there had to be a policy to measure the amount of time spent on behalf of clients by staff and volunteers. A procedure then had to be put in place for everyone to record and report monthly on what time was spent, and for the regional offices to collate and report on this information.

Practical application

Unfortunately there is not a 'one size fits all' approach to policies and procedures that can be used by every voluntary organization. There are three main factors that affect the decision of how much policy, how many procedures and whether it all has to be written down: size, complexity of structure and complexity of operations.

It is easier to explore this with a few examples:

● Suffolk Family History Society is small, its structure is simple and its activities are straightforward. The main areas where it needs documented policies and procedures are in the areas of governance and finance. The former may well have been set out in its constitution. It has no employees. It does not need extensive policy documents or numerous written procedures.

● The Ramblers' Association is of moderate size, and its main area of complexity is its structure. Its three offices, 53 areas and 423 local groups give it a complexity that is much greater than its size, particularly as all the areas and groups are run by volunteers. Each area and each group has its own elected board and a bank account, and also takes on roles such as publicity and representing the RA on various boards and committees. If there were no policies and procedures, national coordination would be impossible, activities could stray from the charitable purpose and there could be legal problems. The RA task is not whether they need well-defined policies and procedures, as it is clear that they do, but how to keep these clear and simple so that volunteers do not feel demoralized by the amount of red tape and cease to serve on the local boards.

● The National Trust is near the top on all three dimensions, and has extra responsibilities because of the public access to land, gardens and buildings. While we can imagine that the Suffolk Family History Society, where lines of communication are short, could operate very effectively with a minimum of written policies and procedures, for the National Trust such an approach would be chaos.

The message for every organization is to think very carefully, in relation to the five main drivers, where it needs policies and supporting procedures. Make the procedures as simple and concise as is compatible with their purpose. Think through the implications of the policies in relation to each other and the overall visions, values and strategies. Think too about the implications for volunteers. Finally make sure that everyone who needs to understands the policy and procedures that are relevant to the role that he or she is asked to play. This may require induction and other forms of training, because the one certainty is that there are few staff or volunteers who have the time and inclination to read through an enormous policy and procedures tome; therefore other means have to be found to ensure that key matters are understood and applied.

REFERENCES

Creelman, J (1998) *Building and Implementing a Balanced Scorecard*, Business International, London

Dresdner (2001) *Top 3000 Charities, 2001*, Dresdner RCM Global Investors, London

Hussey, DE (2000) *How to Manage Organisational Change*, 2nd edn, Kogan Page, London

Jenster, P and Hussey, DE (2001) *Company Analysis: Determining strategic capability*, Wiley, Chichester

Kaplan, RS and Norton, DP (1996) *The Balanced Scorecard*, Harvard Business School Press, Boston, MA

Kaplan, RS and Norton, DP (2000) *The Strategy Focused Organisation*, Harvard Business School Press, Boston, MA

Renaissance Worldwide (1996) *Translating Strategy into Action*, Survey, Renaissance Worldwide/Business International, London

FURTHER READING

Bate, P (1996) *Strategies for Cultural Change*, Butterworth-Heinemann, Oxford

Hussey, D (1999) *Strategy and Planning: A manager's guide*, 5th edn, Wiley, Chichester

McHugh, M (2001) *Managing Change: Regenerating business*, CIM Publishing, Maidenhead

4

Matters of governance

LEGAL FORM OF ORGANIZATION

In Chapter 1 we mentioned that voluntary organizations can take a variety of legal forms. Not all are eligible to register with the Charity Commission or the Scottish and Northern Irish equivalents, and some are exempt from registration. Organizations may be incorporated or unincorporated, the former limiting liability. An incorporated organization becomes a separate legal persona, which is not the case with unincorporated bodies. Those that register both as charities and as companies have to comply with both charity and company laws.

When a new voluntary organization is being established, an early task of the founding trustees is to decide what its legal form should be. In fact it cannot really do very much until they have made this decision, because it will affect the way in which the organization can run itself. Depending on the legislation, it needs a governing document, which may, depending on the legal form of the organization, be called the constitution, the rules, or the memorandum and articles. These all do roughly the same job, in that they set out what the organization is empowered to do and how it will be governed.

Although there is a free choice between an incorporated and unincorporated form, as we saw in Chapter 1 there is not the same freedom about whether to register as a charity. Some activities can only be performed by a registered charity or an organization specifically exempted by the charities legislation. There are some organizations that could function without registration, such as membership associations like the Society of Genealogists or local playgroups, where money is not solicited from the general public. For these, one of the advantages traded off against coming under an additional regulatory authority is the tax exemptions and concessions. (NAO, 2001 state that in tax year 1999/2000 these amounted to £2 billion for the UK.) However, the organization has to comply in all respects with the requirements of the law, and many would not be allowed to register because of the mix of activities undertaken or the nature of the activities, or because the organization allows some element of personal gain to individuals. Many that are ineligible never apply, but not all those that do apply are successful. We have figures only for England and Wales, where NAO (2001) gives the latest annual rejection rate as 27 per cent of those organizations applying for registration. Despite this some 6,000 new charities were registered.

For most members of the governing bodies of voluntary organizations the issue is not one of choice, as they are appointed to an existing organization. There is evidence, referenced in Chapter 1, that a significant number of trustees of charities are not aware that their organization is a registered charity and that not only had they never seen a copy of the constitution but the charity no longer possessed any record of this. It is easy to understand how this can happen in small charities, particularly those with no full-time staff or premises of their own.

Trustees change regularly, and files are handed on as people relinquish office. As many important documents are spread around people's houses, it is not surprising that they can disappear. New people, many of whom may have no real understanding of the role and responsibilities of being a trustee, may decide that only what is current is interesting, and dump old files. It is difficult to see how trustees can fulfil their responsibilities unless they are aware of the legal status of the organization, and understand the details of what the governing document empowers them to do.

It is possible to change legal status. For example, Suffolk Family History Society, a registered unincorporated charity for many years, became a limited company in 2001, after its annual income passed £50,000. Apart from the personal protection this form gives trustees in the unlikely event of the insolvency of the charity, it means that the charity can own assets in its own right, instead of their being held in trust by an individual trustee. For an organization that is expanding its range of activities to fulfil its charitable purpose this change of status gives much more flexibility, and makes it easier, should the charity wish, to move from a 100 per cent volunteer organization to one with a fixed office and some paid staff.

The Strategic Planning Society was incorporated in the second half of the 1960s, but did not immediately apply for registration as a charity. This took place after several years of operation, one reason being that it allowed access to different sources of funds. A sequence like this is not uncommon for membership societies.

The regulatory authorities also have power to deregister charities under certain circumstances. Chapter 10 deals with issues such as charities that need either to wind up or to revitalize themselves in some way because of changing circumstances.

Most charities in the UK conduct their affairs reasonably well, with most transgressions being technical (like late lodging of annual returns) rather than criminal. Despite this there were 212 formal enquiries by the Charity Commission in 2000/01, and irregularities were found in 90 per cent of these. This figure applies only to England and Wales, and there are additional investigations undertaken in Scotland. Additionally the Charity Commission each year visits 300 charities with a yearly income of over £100,000 to undertake a routine inspection (NAO, 2001). The chances of having a routine inspection are therefore small (see Table 1.2), but there is also a scrutiny of the annual returns, which if NAO (2001) recommendations are followed will result in the development of standard control ratios related to the specific nature of the charity.

Charities and other voluntary organizations are regulated by various other bodies, including Companies House, if a limited company, and the various tax authorities. Charitable foundations and the Lottery generally monitor the use of funds that they have contributed. The nature of the activity means that certain voluntary organizations are inspected or regulated by other bodies, such as the Housing Corporation for those in the housing sector, social services for organizations providing homes for the elderly, and environmental health when the activities include running restaurants. In other words, being a voluntary organization does not exempt the trustees from ensuring that any other relevant laws and regulations are observed.

Whatever the additional checks and balances, the prime responsibility for the proper conduct of a charity lies with its trustees, and for other voluntary organizations with their equivalent, whatever they may be called.

THE CONSTITUTION

Every voluntary organization requires a constitution, although it may be called something different. This is the document that describes the purpose of the organization, how it is to be governed, how the governing bodies will be appointed, and such items. It is advisable always to include the power to amend the constitution; otherwise this becomes more complicated later. Under the Companies Act the memorandum of association describes the purpose, and the articles the other matters.

It is not lawful for an organization to act outside the powers given it in its constitution (we will stick with this word for a while, although as we have said it may have other names), and doing so can create a personal liability for the trustees or directors. With a registered charity there is the added dimension that to be *ultra vires* could mean that the charity is no longer eligible to be registered. The moral is to think very carefully about the purpose and the governance, and build in as much flexibility as possible without making a nonsense of the purpose, or making the governance rules impossible to interpret. For example, if the purpose of a charity were to help homeless people in the City of London, it would not be empowered to do anything outside this narrow boundary. To say Greater London rather than the City of London would give scope for manoeuvre, without destroying the geographical focus.

There are organizations that offer a model constitution for voluntary organizations, which can be easily modified to suit many different purposes. This may be a very cheap way for a new, uncomplicated charity to ensure that nothing important is missed out. The National Council for Voluntary Organisations (www.ncvo-vol.org.uk) can supply such a model, and also has a legal service to provide more extensive help should this be needed.

The easiest way to give a flavour to what a constitution might contain is to illustrate the discussion with a real example. The detail will be different for another charity, but the sort of things to cover will be similar. Our headings sometimes group a number of more detailed headings, as our purpose is to indicate what is in the constitution, not to reproduce it.

Name

We have chosen The Ramblers' Association, partly because of some pre-existing knowledge of it but mainly because of its extensive network of area and group activities, which makes for a complex constitution. It obtains its capital letter in front of 'the' because this is part of its name and appears as the first clause of the constitution.

Objects

The second clause describes the objects of the association. There are reservation phrases inserted about only doing such things as are lawful for a charity, and a catch-all sentence, which allows it to do things that are lawful and incidental to its five related objectives.

Organization

An opening clause states that the 'Association shall be composed of individual members, affiliated local organisations, and affiliated national organisations; it shall function through Groups, Areas and a Central Office'. Then follows a description of areas and local groups, setting out how they are formed and what they can and cannot do, a requirement to follow the appropriate model constitution as provided by the Association, and a requirement for areas and local groups to provide audited accounts and to hold an annual general meeting (AGM). (With something over 400 groups and around 50 areas this means many annual general meetings have to be held each year.) There is a procedure for the closure of a group or area.

Various types of membership are described, together with ways of expelling members (part of the flexibility we referred to earlier). The privileges of membership are described, which include the right to be a member of an area and group.

Trustees

The word 'trustee' only appears in one specific sense in the constitution, the appointment of people to hold property on behalf of the Association: it is unincorporated, and therefore cannot do so in its own name. Instead, property is invested in the name of between two and four trustees appointed by the Executive Committee. (There is a significant section in the constitution about property.)

However, it does not matter what title is taken by the trustees of a charity; it is their role that is important. In this case the trustees are the members of the Executive Committee, and they are clearly designated as trustees in the annual report. The constitution has a lot to say about the Executive Committee, but things will be clearer if we first describe what the Association sees as its governing body, although by doing so we are not following the order in which things appear in the constitution.

General Council

The General Council 'is responsible for the general policy and control of the association'. It includes the 'retiring executive committee, and delegates representing Areas and affiliated national organisations'. The constitution defines a formula to calculate the number of delegates an area is able to send. Delegates hold office up to, but not including, the annual general meeting of the General Council in the year following that in which they were appointed.

At the AGM the General Council:

- considers the Executive Committee's annual report and audited statement of accounts;
- appoints officers for the following year;
- elects an Executive Committee to hold office until they are replaced (presumably to allow for variations in the date of the next AGM);
- appoints an auditor;
- considers and votes on motions put before it;
- may amend the constitution (in accordance with the provisions of the constitution);
- approves and amends the standing orders.

The number of motions that may be put at an AGM is limited to five from the Executive Committee and one from each area and each affiliated organization. The standing orders include the use of an agenda committee for each AGM, and a motion can be rejected under certain defined conditions without going to the AGM.

Although it functions and is constituted differently from the Coram Family's Court of Governors described in Chapter 1, there is at least one thing in common: the appointment of trustees.

Honorary officers and Executive Committee

The constitution lists the titles of the honorary officers who are appointed each year by the General Council. Many are automatically members of the Executive Committee. Nine other members are elected by the General Council, and may be area delegates or retiring members of the Executive Committee; three more can be co-opted by the Executive Committee (another move that gives flexibility if circumstances change). If not already elected, the chairpersons of the Welsh and Scottish Councils also become automatic members. The constitution covers the replacement of an elected representative who dies or resigns by the person who was the runner-up in the vote.

Welsh and Scottish Councils

The Executive Committee is directed in the constitution to form Councils for Wales and Scotland. There is a page in the constitution describing these, but their constitutions and composition are decided by the Executive Committee.

Standing orders

Six and a half of the 16 pages of the constitution are very detailed standing orders for the conduct of the General Council, the responsibilities and duties of the Executive Committee, and finance. They describe things like the frequency of meetings, periods of notice of meetings, the power to elect subcommittees, as well as detailed instructions on the split of income between the centre and areas, the provision of the privileges of membership, control procedures, membership procedures and the delegation to the Executive Committee of the power to hire and dismiss staff. In general terms the lists are comprehensive, but the amount of detailed instruction under each is variable. There is provision for delegates to the General Council and Executive Committee to claim repayment of expenses, under rules delegated to the Executive Committee. If the constitution had not made this provision, there may have been confusion over how trustees could claim.

Changing the constitution

The General Council has the power to change the constitution, and indeed the Charity Commission register shows that it has been changed 10 times since it was revised in 1967 (the year the Association registered as a charity). In fact the register is not completely up to date as it does not include a change listed in the annual report for the year ended September 2000 (nor were the figures from this report recorded in the register when we looked them up in February 2002).

It is worth mentioning here that the General Council's decision is subject to legal constraints. The constitution provides that any alteration must be passed by two-thirds of those present and voting at the AGM, and there is also a statement that any change to the objects must have the prior consent of the Charity Commission. These clauses are standard for an unincorporated charity.

If the Ramblers' Association had been a limited company, it could only have made changes to the memorandum and articles of association if three-quarters of people attending at an AGM or extraordinary general meeting (EGM) had voted for it. The Act specifies the period of notice that must be given, and requires that signed copies of the resolution are sent to Companies House within 15 days. The same requirement for prior permission of the Charity Commission to alter the objects also applies.

If a constitution does not give power to make alterations, a more complex route would have to be followed, whereby application would have to be made to the Charity Commission for a scheme of alteration, which the trustees would then approve. When drafting a constitution for a new charity it makes sense to accept that changes may have to be made in the future, and write in provisions to allow changes.

Conclusions from the example

It is not our task to critique the somewhat complex constitution in this example, and we hope that it has given some of the flavour of the two key parts of the constitution: the objects and the administrative rules for running the organization.

The only comments we would make is that it is the trustees who have the legal responsibility, and nothing in any constitution can remove this. Although in theory the General Council has the power to set rules for the financial control of the organization, in practice no responsible organization would make rules that meant that if the trustees observed the constitution they would fail in their legal obligations. We certainly do not wish to imply that this would happen with the Ramblers. However, it does provide an opportunity to remind trustees of the primacy of the law, and that they should not follow rules blindly.

The democratic system followed by the Ramblers also makes it harder to follow the advice on the selection of trustees that we give in Chapter 5. It could be followed for the selection of those officers who are also trustees, but it is difficult to see how this could be done with the area appointees, as there is no provision in the constitution for a vetting procedure. However, we believe that our advice is worth following for all trustee appointments.

Pause for reflection

The best way to stimulate thinking about the governing documents is to look at those of your own organizations. Are they readily accessible? Are they as comprehensive as they should be? Is there anything in them that surprises you? Are they in need of a change, to meet the current situation?

THE DUTIES OF TRUSTEES

Charity law is indifferent to what trustees are called, and in a limited company they are of course directors. But anyone who becomes a trustee takes on responsibilities that may not always be obvious.

Firstly, not every person may become a trustee. The Charity Commission now checks the validity of the trustees of any new charity to hold office, but does not have the resources to follow up on the 2 million trustees of existing charities. So the first line of defence should be the persons involved in recruiting trustees, who should check the eligibility of every new trustee. Provision for who may appoint trustees should be set out in the constitution, as was the case with the Ramblers' Association. If no explicit provision is made, it is assumed that the other trustees have this responsibility.

A person is disqualified from being a trustee if he or she is under the age of 18; has been convicted of an offence of dishonesty or theft (unless the conviction is spent); is an undischarged bankrupt; has previously been removed from being a trustee of a charity by the Charity Commission or a court; or is the subject of a disqualification order under the Company Directors Disqualification Act. The rules are similar in Scotland. It is possible to obtain a waiver for someone who is so disqualified from the Charity Commission, but waivers are not given lightly.

It may seem superfluous to suggest that every new trustee should be given an information pack as a matter of routine, but the findings of Scottish Executive Central Research Unit (1999) and the Charity

Commission (2002), which we reported in Chapter 1, suggest that for many charities it is essential advice. And there is no reason to expect that similar findings would not have emerged from a survey of voluntary organizations that are not charities.

As a minimum, the pack should include:

● a copy of the governing document;
● copies of any other documents that describe the roles of honorary officers and key paid staff;
● the latest annual report;
● minutes of meetings for the previous year;
● the current budget and the period results to date;
● a strategic plan, if there is one;
● a note on the responsibilities of trustees. (We recommend the document, 'Responsibilities of charity trustees', which can be obtained from the Charity Commission. A similar document is available from the authorities in Scotland.)

Before accepting an appointment as a trustee, the person should ensure that he or she has the time available to do the job properly. It is not just that the organization will be let down by someone who does not spare the right amount of time, but that the person will also be failing in his or her legal duty. The problem with all voluntary appointments is that there is a tendency, by those offering them, to underestimate the time requirements, and the written documents can also mislead.

The Ramblers' Association's constitution requires its trustees to hold a minimum of three meetings a year, and it would be easy for anyone reading this to think that becoming a trustee would not require much time to be devoted to the organization. In reality, if this is all the trustees were to do they would fail in their duty, and of course they actually do a great deal more. The annual report for the year ended September 2000 gives a better flavour of what is really involved. In that year there were five formal meetings. However, in between each principal meeting three of the trustees designated as officers met informally to review progress. In addition there were six subcommittees or working parties active during the year. There is the annual general meeting of the Association. On top of that various trustees attend some of the annual general meetings of areas and groups, and represent the RA in other ways. Documents have to be prepared, read and understood.

Although the amount of work will vary with the organization, it is always more than just turning up for a periodic meeting.

What must trustees actually do?

In Chapter 1 there was an indication of how Coram saw the role of trustees:

The main role of the trustees has been defined as:

● Establishing the long term strategy
● Agreeing the annual budget
● Agreeing the capital budget
● Monitoring progress, with particular attention to the three, six and twelve month accounts, set against the provision of the quality of service.

There are some legal rules about how trustees must act:

● Apart from the recovery of justly incurred expenses, trustees may not benefit financially from the charity, whether this is directly or indirectly. For example, however tempting and convenient it might seem for the charity, no trustee can do business with the charity.

There is an exception to this rule where the constitution makes express provision, but any personal benefit must be strictly confined and there must be procedures to justify it and ensure that it is transparent. Where there is no such provision, the Charity Commission may grant permission. A document is available from the Charity Commission called 'Remuneration of charity trustees', an extract from which appears in the box. In practice it is hard to see more than a few situations where payment can be justified.

The following checklist is abstracted from 'Remuneration of charity trustees', Charity Commission, Crown copyright 2001:

Factors to consider in any case where a trustee is being paid:

● What procedures will the remaining unpaid trustees put in place to manage the conflict of interest?

- Will the paid trustee have any conflicts with outside commitments (other trusteeships, business interests)? If so, are there sufficient arrangements in place to manage the conflict of interest?
- Have arrangements been made to disclose any payments to trustees in the charity's annual report?
- Have the trustees considered consulting the charity's stake-holders (ie major funders, members, beneficiaries, donors)? If they have consulted stakeholders, what was their response?
- Are the number of trustees to be paid in the minority on the trustee body?
- Are there appropriate independent ways of deciding the level of payment?
- Are there appropriate budget provisions and financial fore-cast systems in place?

Additional factors to consider when paying a trustee for services provided to the charity:

- Have the trustees obtained quotes for the work to be done and drawn up a shortlist of those people/companies which should be asked to tender for the work?
- Does the contract contain features to protect the charity's interests?
- How will the trustees be able to demonstrate that the contract is in the charity's interests as represented by value for money?
- Do the trustees have any arrangements for testing or challenging bills which might be disputed?
- Was the affected trustee protected from seeing any confidential information about the tender process?

Additional factors to consider when paying a trustee for being a trustee:

- What evidence do the trustees have to show a lack of willing volunteers with the required skills?
- Could the duties for which the trustee is to be paid be shared amongst the whole trustee body, or could the number of trustees be increased to spread the load of work required of the trustees?

- Are all the duties to be undertaken appropriate to a trustee or could they properly be delegated to an agent or employee?
- How will the charity ensure that the payment represents value for money?
- What arrangements are in place for reviewing performance and for assessing whether there is a continuing need for paid trusteeship?
- What arrangements are in place for bringing payment to an end, and how will this affect the trusteeship of the individual in question?
- Has the impact on the degree of personal liability been discussed with the trustee in question?

Additional factors to consider if an employee is also a trustee:

- Is the position of paid employment to be advertised on the basis of fair and open competition, and if not, why not?
- If the trustees are looking to fill a vacancy in the trustee body, what have the trustees done to demonstrate a lack of suitable unpaid candidates for the trusteeship with the necessary skills?
- How has the payment package been determined?
- Why is it necessary for employment to be combined with trusteeship and what special dimension will this bring to decision making?
- Does the situation apply to the individual or the post?
- Is there clear segregation between the duties performed as a trustee and as an employee of the charity?
- How will performance be measured?
- What arrangements are in place for bringing employment to an end, and how will this affect the trusteeship of the individual in question?

- Trustees have to apply the income and property of the charity solely to the approved charitable purposes.
- Although trustees have a duty to maintain endowments, if the charity has these the Charity Commission advice is that income should not be allowed to accumulate unless the trustees have in mind a specific future use for it.

- There is a duty to act reasonably and prudently. Decisions have to be made with the interests of the charity in mind, and personal views must not obstruct the duty as a trustee.
- Many of the duties involve proper accounting, systems of financial control and the making of statutory annual returns. Although the size of the organization influences the nature of the annual return, and the complexity of the accounts and controls, the duty is never removed. Further guidance is given in Chapters 6 and 7.

Tasks can be delegated, provided the trustees maintain overall control. Outside advisers can be used (and paid by the charity), as can the charity's own employees or volunteers. If the procedures and policies are not defined in the constitution, the board of trustees should fill the gap. Obviously it is easier to prove that there are proper procedures and controls, firstly, if they can be produced and shown to be actually used and, secondly, if there are adequate monitoring and control methods in use by the trustees. It is important for trustees to be able to prove that delegation has not been abdication.

Case study 4.1: Tracheotomy Patients' Aid Fund (Registered Charity No 327795 – removed from Register)

Introduction

1. This report sets out the findings of the Charity Commission Inquiry into the Tracheotomy Patients Aid Fund under Section 8 of the Charities Act 1993. The Inquiry considered a number of issues which are detailed below.
2. The charity was established in 1988, its objects being to help tracheotomy patients and to promote research into the prevention of the condition giving rise to tracheotomies.
3. Following a complaint from another charity and the Commission's own observation that there appeared to be little charitable activity, an Inquiry was opened in May 1993. An initial evaluation had also revealed that the founder trustee had secured his appointment as paid Chief Executive and that his wife remained a trustee notwithstanding the conflict of interest which had arisen as a result of the appointment.
4. Unfortunately, full co-operation was not received from the trustees and staff of the charity nor from some of their legal advisors and this prolonged the course of the Inquiry considerably.
5. The main issues considered by the Inquiry were as follows:
   - The appointment of the Chairman of the trustees to the post of paid chief executive

- The conflict of interest faced by the founder's wife in respect of her husband's position as chief executive
- The degree of management and control exercised by the trustee body
- The level of charitable activity undertaken
- The level of fund-raising costs and expenses.

6. During the course of the Inquiry officers sought to interview the trustees and obtain detailed explanations from them. However, for the reasons explained below, it was not possible to speak to all of them, and it was only the founder and his wife who were able to provide us with any useful information in response to inquiries made. Inquiry officers also analysed financial and administrative documents and spoke to members of the medical profession involved in tracheotomy work.

Findings

7. Of the four trustees reported as acting at the time the Inquiry began:
   - One had died.
   - One could not be contacted or traced. The Commission had been provided with an address in Czechoslovakia, but one which the Czech authorities advised did not exist. The local authority had no record of his occupancy at the address given for him in this country and letters addressed to him there were returned by the Post Office.
   - Another trustee advised the Commission that he had not attended any meetings but had been asked to (and did) sign minutes which recorded him as attending. This cast doubt upon the validity of the minutes of trustee meetings which had been supplied to the Commission.
   - The remaining trustee was the wife of the founder trustee who had been appointed as chief executive.

8. The original Chairman of the trustees and founder had been appointed chief executive in April 1990. He was awarded a ten-year contract with a remuneration of £6,000 per annum plus 15% of all charity income over £15,000. There was no apparent recruitment process and the key roles and responsibilities were not set. Whether any independent trustees were involved in the appointment is not clear for reasons outlined at 2.1 above.

9. The founder and subsequent chief executive had received remuneration of £17,648 during 1993 and 1994. Since his appointment, he had received a total of £36,332. In addition, indirect costs including his expenses, entertainment, fund-raising costs, stationery and telephone costs over the same two years came to £26,716.

10. The charity had been charged for use of part of the property belonging to the founder and his wife.

11. As stated in 1.3 above the founder's wife remained a trustee and continued to act despite being subject to a conflict of interest.

12. The Commission could not establish that an independent trustee body had ever taken part in the management and administration of the charity. It appeared that an effective trustee body had never existed.
13. Little charitable expenditure had taken place, charitable expenditure from the formation of the charity being just under £2,000. There was no charitable expenditure during the two years mentioned above, 1993 and 1994. The reason given to us for this situation was that it was intended to raise sufficient funds to provide equipment for the whole country before making any substantial charitable expenditure.

Conclusions

14. There was no effective independent trustee body and the running of the charity had been left to the founder who became chief executive.
15. The founder had resigned his position as trustee in order to take on the paid post of chief executive. He was accountable therefore for the remuneration received and the contract was potentially voidable.
16. The founder's wife had acted where she had been subject to a conflict of interest.
17. The terms of the contract were in the Commission's view inappropriate and might be viewed as excessive. Both the length of the term, 10 years, and the level of remuneration, a percentage fixed fee without condition or cap, did not appear to be in the best interests of the charity.
18. The level of fund-raising costs and the level of expenses was high. There was no effective trustee body to monitor and control these expenses.
19. The Commission's view was that insufficient steps had been taken to apply the income of the charity. It appeared unreasonable for a charity of this size to await funds to cover the whole country before applying any of the funds. While we could see some merit in the publicity value of a nationwide launch, there would have been a lengthy wait during which many beneficiaries would not have been served. (At least fifteen ventilators would have been required to provide one per health area.) In addition there was some doubt amongst the medical profession as to whether the type of equipment being considered by the charity was efficacious.

Outcomes

20. In the absence of an effective and independent trustee body, the accounts of the charity were frozen and the chief executive suspended from his employment. The assets of the charity were vested in the Official Custodian.
21. A receiver and manager (Mr A M H King of Messrs Stone King) was appointed to deal with the assets of the charity and consider any claim which the charity might have against the founder and his wife for the recovery of unauthorised remuneration and benefits.

22. After determining the assets and liabilities of the charity, the receiver and manager concluded that in the absence of a sound administrative base and a long-standing name and reputation for its charitable work, the charity's assets should be distributed to established charities with similar aims.

23. Before the receiver and manager was able to wind up the charity he had to deal with both the charity's claim against the chief executive and a claim made by the chief executive against the charity for loss of earnings in respect of the unexpired term of his contract and outstanding expenses. The receiver and manager reached a full and final settlement in respect of those claims which avoided costly court procedure.

24. The net assets of the charity (£102,479) were distributed amongst three other charitable institutions involved with the needs of tracheotomy patients.

Wider lessons

25. Charity trustees need to avoid and be sensitive to conflicts of interest. Where such occur, the trustee concerned should take no part in the decision at issue, whether it be a direct conflict or a strategic decision which may affect the future operation and staffing of the charity.

26. The duty to account for remuneration as a trustee is not avoided by resigning to take up employment. The individual in question would have obtained employment by virtue of his or her position of trust and resignation would not affect liability.

27. Every charity needs an effective trustee body which has control over the administration of the charity and its staff and acts as a whole, especially because all trustees are equal in responsibility.

28. In formulating plans, charities must pay heed to what is feasible given their size.

(Charity Commissioners for England and Wales, Crown copyright 2001)

Pause for reflection

If you are a trustee you should make sure that you fully understand all the responsibilities that you are accountable for. Whether or not you are a trustee, think about the role in relation to your organization. Do new trustees receive the sort of welcome pack we have described? Is there any induction training for new trustees? Are there mechanisms for reviewing the performance of trustees?

FORMAL MEETINGS

There are meetings of all types in the management of any organization. Some may be informal, so that various people can share information or explore a problem; others may be more formal, in that they are scheduled and work to a formal agenda: staff meetings are an example. These are a matter of management style and preference, as is the way they are conducted and the nature of the records kept.

There are three types of meeting that are formally required, the minutes of which form part of the records of the organization. Trustees' meetings are required in all voluntary organizations: generally the requirement is spelt out in the governing documents. Annual general meetings are not required by all charities, whether or not they are incorporated: it depends on the governing documents. Extraordinary general meetings (sometimes called special general meetings) are called for special purposes, such as amending the constitution, when the matter cannot wait until the next AGM.

Some general points

For these three types of meeting it is important that the correct period of notice is given, and that it is delivered in an appropriate way. Fax and e-mail addresses can be used if the details have been provided by a person who has a right to receive notice, and there has been prior agreement with that person over the method. Otherwise it is the normal post or hand delivery. For trustee meetings it is worth using e-mail as far as it is possible, because this is also a convenient way of supplying copies of all necessary documents, provided of course that all have the ability to open the particular types of electronic files. There can be a considerable saving in postage costs. The actual copying cost is transferred to the receiver, but it spreads across all the trustees the time spent collating documents.

The notice of meeting should specify the date, time and place, and the type of meeting. It may be helpful in some circumstances to include directions of how to get to the venue, and where cars may be parked. The agenda normally accompanies the notice, and should be written with care. 'Any other business permitted by the chairperson' is a useful way of gaining some flexibility, but should not be used to spring major items on the meeting for which no one has had a chance to prepare. Meetings are generally more effective if the agenda is clearly set out, and items can be divided in such a way that they do not overlap; where an issue spreads over two or more agenda items the meeting may end up wandering to these other items without fully discussing any of them.

No meetings can be conducted unless there is a quorum, usually set in the governing document. This prevents important decisions from being taken when too many people who are entitled to vote do not attend the meeting. Annual general meetings are not always seen as exciting by those entitled to come, and there must be many people who share with us the experience of sitting in a meeting that the chairperson could not open because the requisite number of people have not yet arrived, and of the collective sigh of relief when another person arrives and the society no longer faces the prospect of having to call the meeting for another date (with all the costs this involves).

The chairperson makes a considerable difference to the quality of the meeting, and has to exercise a mix of firmness and tact. If things get out of control, the meeting can spend its time going round in circles never reaching the decision point. The tact is how to stop this happening without upsetting those at the meeting. Care in planning the agenda can help, although it can also be unhelpful if badly thought out. The agenda may specify a timetable for each item, which is helpful if the right amount of time is calculated for each item and there is enough overall time to do the job properly. It is not a helpful practice if inadequate time is allowed for each item or for the meeting as a whole.

Board of trustee meetings

These meetings may have a variety of names. It may be the board meeting, the executive committee or any other name the organization chooses. The critical point is not what it is called, but what it does. The frequency of the meetings may be specified in the governing document, although it would make no sense to do more than set a minimum number of meetings. The real issue for the board is how often it needs to meet in order to manage the organization, what board subcommittees should be set up and how progress may be managed between meetings.

Employees, advisers and particular volunteers may be invited to attend all or part of a board meeting, some on an as-required basis and some as a regular routine. It would clearly make sense for a chief executive or general manager, if there is one, to attend, as this person has up-to-date information that is of interest to the trustees and may have views on an issue that they should hear. The number of people who can make a useful, regular contribution is of course limited, and the decision has to be made on the merits of each situation. It is useful to have someone other than a trustee who will be the board secretary, as it is difficult to participate fully in a meeting and take the minutes. Other people may be brought in for just one agenda item.

Making meetings more successful: guidance for the leader of a meeting

In addition to the planning and system aspects of meetings, whether they are board or management meetings, there are process and behavioural issues. The meeting is more likely to be effective if attention is given to the people issues:

- *Preparation.* This is the essential starting point. What outcome do the trustees need from the meeting? Which individuals are likely to delay or block an issue? Who is likely to support it? What internal political or faction issues are likely to arise, and what might be done about them? What information should people have in advance so that they can contribute to the discussion and decisions?
- *Focus.* It is too easy for a meeting to drift. The chairperson's role is to keep the discussion on course, without inhibiting participation. Allowing no laxness at all will appear draconian, but too much will lead to feelings of frustration among the participants and prevent the meeting from achieving its purpose.
- *Active listening.* It is important that all participants, as well as the chairperson, listen carefully to what others are saying. This may involve asking supportive questions to draw out the idea fully. There should always be respect shown for the opinions of others. Many people will stop participating if their ideas are ignored or treated with contempt.
- *The personality mix.* People are not all the same, and for a management meeting it is often worth while selecting people to achieve a mix of personalities, although this is rarely possible for board meetings, because of how trustees are selected. This means that the task is to understand and

---

manage the different types of personality. Hamlin (1988) suggests four basic types: movers, opposers, followers and bystanders (Belbin, 1996 gives a different and more detailed classification). Movers are the people who propose the new ideas and have the energy to drive them forward. Opposers tend to react negatively to ideas put forward by others. Followers go with the herd, and may not contribute much beyond supporting what seem to be the popular ideas. Bystanders absorb and watch the proceedings, without letting themselves be drawn in. All these types can be valuable. The movers may be the engine that helps drive the meeting, but they are not always right. If those who have a natural role in opposing can be managed so that they provide constructive criticism, it may be possible to end up with better solutions. Bystanders often have creative ideas; the chairperson's task is to draw them into the discussion.

- *Participation.* The chairperson should encourage everyone to participate. This is most easily done when the chairperson knows the people well, and knows whether asking a direct question to a person is likely to increase participation. It certainly will with the movers and opposers. It is often more effective if a direct question can be related to something that the person has specific knowledge of.

- *Preventing one or two people from dominating the meeting.* This can be more difficult than it seems, because the motivations may be mixed. Sometimes it is one or two enthusiasts who have the ideas and drive to progress them; in other situations it may be that one or two people like to feel they are leading the pack, even though their contributions are no better than anyone else's. The chairperson has to ensure that people are cut off, preferably diplomatically, if they are taking too much airtime, and other people encouraged to participate. If the issue on the table is not important, the right decision might be to cut the discussion and move on to another agenda item.

- *Insisting that there is a rational basis behind discussions.* This does not mean that the opinions and values held by participants are unimportant, even if sometimes it is difficult for them to be articulated. However, it is important for people to be pressed to justify the statements that they make, so that some rationality can prevail. A statement like, 'I could not support this because it is contrary to my religious beliefs' at least lets the others know where that person is coming from. However, debate is generally better when people can support their views with a rational argument. Often the decision that comes from a meeting builds on to suggestions made by individuals, and this building process should both lead to a better decision and develop commitment to it.

- *Decisions should be unambiguous.* We have all come out of meetings not quite knowing what has been decided. We would go a stage further and argue that it is not just what has been decided but how the decision will be progressed that is important. This means reaching clear agreement on both the decision and the next steps, and an unambiguous commitment from the person who is to take it to the next stage. It is no help if there is lack of clarity about the decision, or if the person charged with implementing it fails to deliver. An important element in getting things done is to set completion dates at the meeting.

- *There should be disagreements.* It is always worrying when there are never differences of opinion in a meeting, as this implies that there is only one mover, and the other members are followers or bystanders. Disagreement is an important mechanism for developing good decisions. The chairperson has to establish a climate where people can disagree, without letting the meeting descend into emotional chaos.

- *Encouragement.* The chairperson should also encourage and support the participants at the meeting. This may be thanks for a detailed report that someone has presented, statements like, 'That's a very good point', or even a few private words after the meeting saying how much a particular contribution was appreciated. Trustees are sometimes people who have been involved in meetings for much of their lives. However, they may also include people who have never before attended any form of business meeting and who have had no experience of putting over a point of view in a formal meeting. Emotional support at the beginning may make all the difference to the contribution they can make in the future.

The minutes and board papers are important documents, but they are not normally open to public scrutiny. However, they may be demanded by the regulatory authorities, the auditors and other professional advisers. They are important in providing proof that the board has acted in a prudent and careful way, and with integrity, as well as being evidence of what decisions were taken, very useful if there is ever confusion in the future.

Boards can only work properly if people do their homework, and both read and consider the various papers and reports that support the meeting. It is advisable for weighty documents to be sent out as early as possible, even before the notice of the meeting, something that can be done fairly cheaply for a board meeting, but which would be expensive for an AGM. If the document is not to be discussed in detail at the AGM, and is just a courtesy (like a copy of a new brochure) there is no need to send it out in advance. If it is something that people are supposed to act on in some way at the meeting, it is unrealistic to think that good decisions can result when there has been no time to study the issue, and the material must go out in good time.

In any organization there are a number of standard items that appear in every meeting, and the agenda should reflect this. Apart for the obvious approval of the minutes of the previous meeting, and matters arising (more of this in a moment), standard items might be to receive the report of each subcommittee, and to consider the financial results of the year to date against the budget. There may of course be others. Each item should be numbered. The second item is usually matters arising from the minutes, and each should be listed on the agenda, but in many cases there will be a more appropriate place to discuss them under another agenda item, so they should be cross-referenced to these. A lot of time can be wasted at meetings by people wanting to discuss matters arising under this heading, without noting that there is a better place on the agenda.

Each member of the board is entitled to ask for items to be raised at the meeting, and should be encouraged to do this in time to include it on the agenda. Although there is the ubiquitous 'any other business' item, as far as possible this should be kept for late news and pieces of minor information; otherwise the meeting may end up discussing important items for which no one has prepared.

There are three types of item discussed at board meetings:

● The first is the formal motion, which if passed will become a resolution. An example is the approval of the annual returns, which will have already gone through several levels of scrutiny and are now ready in final draft form. The issue is quite clear before the meeting is called. Voting is required on this issue.

- Some items are for information, and no action has to be taken on them at this stage. One example might be the results of a survey of users, which at this stage is being tabled to ensure that all trustees have a chance to understand it. There might well be a presentation on the survey by an informed person to help the board absorb the contents. Also in this category is a progress report from a working party or subcommittee. Trustees might well have useful ideas to contribute, but at this stage the item is to share information and there are no decisions to be made.

- The third category consists of items where decisions may have to be made, although what they are may not be completely obvious until the board has discussed the matter. Sometimes the decisions may be simple, like appointing someone to investigate further. Others may be more complex, for example a review of progress against the budget, where it has to be determined whether additional actions are required. Such decisions may sometimes be very definite, like postponing the recruitment of a staff member to fill a vacancy, if funds are lagging seriously behind target. They may be to identify a number of options, as for example if the organization has been successful and is generating more funds than it expected and has to begin to think about additional projects on which to use them. Votes may be required for many of these actions.

Minutes should record the number of people voting for and against each item where a vote is needed, but names should only be listed if the individual concerned specifically requests this. It sometimes happens that an individual is so strongly against a resolution that he/she wants this to be recorded. The aim of minutes is to record the main points about what happened at the meeting; it is not to produce a verbatim report of everything said. So the main arguments for and against an issue should be recorded, but in a compressed way.

All minutes should have an action column showing who is responsible for progressing the decision. Where it is someone who was not present at the meeting, a note should be included of who was delegated the task of informing that person.

For a board meeting the names of those present should be recorded at the top of the first page, followed by a heading that states something like 'Minutes of a meeting of the Board of Trustees of the XYZ charity held at 3 pm on 5 January 2002 at the premises of the charity'. It is useful to have people sign in on a sheet of appropriately headed paper when they arrive, and to attach this to the back of the official copy of the minutes. It is important that, if someone leaves the meeting early, this is recorded in the minutes so that it is clear that that person played no part in subsequent discussions and voting.

Minutes should be completed quickly after a meeting, before memories fade. Although they can be kept electronically, there is much to be said for old-fashioned files that hold the signed copies of the minutes, as well as most of the supporting documents prepared for each meeting.

Pause for reflection

Almost every manager in an organization gets involved in meetings, although not all of these are board meetings. Think of how meetings you attend are run. Are they an effective means of furthering the business of the organization, or time wasters? Check through the points we have made, to check that they are followed in your organization. Remember that problems in meetings may be issues of people rather than procedures. This goes further than our text, but do check that the meeting has the right balance of skills and personalities.

Annual general meetings

The governing document determines whether or not an AGM has to be held, and who is entitled to attend. In the Ramblers' Association the AGM is attended by the past year's officers and trustees, and delegates from the membership, appointed by a semi-democratic method. The agenda and the conduct of business are highly formalized, and as we have seen the AGM has several critical tasks to perform without which the Association could not function.

The articles of another membership organization, the Strategic Planning Society, entitle any paid-up member to attend. Normally there is only one formal purpose to the meeting, which is to approve the year-end audited accounts, but of course it is also an opportunity for the board to give an account of its stewardship.

While it is relatively easy to see the need for an AGM for an organization with a membership, it is less apparent for other types of charity, which is one reason why, regardless of legal form, many do not have AGMs. Some governing documents require an AGM so that the charity can report back to its main suppliers of funds or to its clients, in which case both the entitlement to attend and the business that may be conducted are as defined in those documents.

Agendas for AGMs are more likely to be highly formalized and consist mainly of the motions that will be considered. In the Ramblers' Association the number of motions that can be submitted by each area is limited, and the proposed motions go through a formal agenda committee, so that things recently rejected are not raised again. Although some of the motions might concern the internal management of the charity, many may be about other actions that the proposers want the Association to take. Motions that are essential to the internal management of the Association are generated by the board of trustees (the Executive Committee).

Extraordinary general meetings are called to deal with extraordinary business and, as with the AGM, have to follow the procedures of the governing documents. These set who can call an EGM, which would usually be the board of trustees, or a certain percentage of those entitled to attend the AGM. They are an additional expense, and the circumstances in which they may be called should also be carefully controlled. The requirement will be directed by the governing documents.

ETHICS AND SOCIAL RESPONSIBILITY

Increasingly in the business world the emphasis on governance is more concerned with social responsibility than legal structures. It is about how the organization behaves and the nature of its internal procedures. The same concern applies to the governance of voluntary organizations, and should begin with the board of trustees, and pervade the whole organization.

Voluntary organizations exist to do some form of good to humanity, an aspect that is reinforced when they are registered charities. In certain types of organization there is a danger that the cause may be seen as so important that the end justifies the means, and for some of the essential elements of modern governance to be seen as unnecessary impediments.

It is not an issue of whether the individual trustees are ethical and socially responsible but of how the organization operates, so that ethical behaviour becomes part of the culture and is reflected in its procedures.

Among the basic requirements are transparency and openness. There are still many charities that see their annual results as no one's business but their own, and ignore the legal requirement to make copies available to anyone. It is also surprising that comparatively few organizations make their annual reports available on their Web sites. We know of at least one charity whose annual report, although accurate in what it reports, currently conceals the real underlying problems it is facing, by not referring to them in the report. This may be expedient, but is certainly not ethical.

In any organization problems can emerge because of the behaviour of individuals and it would be foolish to suggest that this will never happen. We are all familiar with the proven cases of abuse in orphanages and homes for the elderly, or of those who are mentally infirm. There have been cases of abuse by priests, covered up by the church authorities. Good governance means that the opportunities for abuse are reduced by care in selection of staff and volunteers, the establishment of procedures to prevent it and processes of inspection that make it harder for such actions to be concealed. Above all, although it may seem expedient to try to conceal such things, it is never in the long-term interests of the organization to do so, and is hardly ethical behaviour.

Not all problems are so vile. The values at the top that do not reach through the whole organization are more likely to be matters of fairness in dealings with clients, volunteers and staff, sometimes because of personal prejudices and sometimes through carelessness. One charity we know has regularly made mistakes in its literature and membership application forms, because the assumptions it makes about what happens in its local branches are not universally true (and no funding is provided to make them true). This is wishful thinking or sloppiness rather than any intention to mislead, but it should not happen.

Some charities have a charter for staff and volunteers, which sets out the responsibilities of the charity to its workers, and the workers to the charity. The Prince's Trust has ethical provisions for its business mentors including a prohibition from buying products or services from their particular clients unless a particular procedure is followed. It might be argued that those interested in helping young people to set up businesses are unlikely to exploit them, but a defined policy makes the position of the charity clear.

The British Red Cross has an equal opportunities policy (which at the time of writing could be downloaded from its Web site). Of course such a policy is in part driven by the law, but also expounds the ethical values of the organization.

All this starts from the top, and is driven as much by the perceived behaviour of the trustees as the policies and procedures that are developed. To be successful a charity needs a good name and reputation, and it all starts with governance.

REFERENCES

Belbin, RM (1996) *The Coming Shape of Organisation*, Butterworth-Heinemann, London

Charity Commission (2002) *Trustee Recruitment, Selection and Induction*, Charity Commission for England and Wales, London

Hamlin, S (1988) *How To Talk So People Listen*, Harper & Row, New York

National Audit Office (NAO) (2001) *Giving Confidently: The role of the Charity Commission in regulating charities*, October, NAO, London

Scottish Executive Central Research Unit (1999) *Scottish Charity Legislation: An evaluation*, Scottish Executive Central Research Unit, Edinburgh

FURTHER READING

McGregor, L (2000) *The Human Face of Corporate Governance*, Palgrave, Basingstoke

Wheeler, D and Sillianpää, M (1997) *The Stakeholder Corporation*, Pitman, London

5

Management of people

There are many major differences between managing other organizations and running a charity, and among these is the overriding importance of leadership. Of course this is important for all organizations but, where businesses and the public sector can often get away with weak leadership, charities cannot.

Before explaining this view we should explain the difference between 'headship' and leadership. Managers may command obedience because of their position in the hierarchy and because they can provide rewards and sanctions to individuals who work for them. A new senior manager appointed to an organization will receive a measure of respect and attention even before he or she has done anything.

In an 'ordinary' organization in either the public or private sector of the economy, people are paid to do things. The organization depends on goods or services for which it is paid (if only through taxes). Both the pay and the origin of the income to the organization have a fundamental psychological impact on the human behaviour and how the organization responds to situations.

Staff, for example, are paid at a 'market rate' in the capitalist economy. Though this is often imperfect it does affect the quality of the staff who are hired. It also means that because many staff seek to maximize their income, if pay levels become uncompetitive they will move on. This is the market economy working, and we all take this for granted. So people may stay in organizations because it is worth their while to do so, even if the top management show no leadership qualities at all. The pay and conditions may be good; they may enjoy the actual work and have a feeling of belonging. Headship leads to some sort of order, even if its motive power is to push people rather than encouraging them to follow. Much of the civil service could continue to operate efficiently even in periods of a leadership vacuum, by following established procedures. Of course the really great organizations in the private and public sectors are great because of good leadership, but there are many more that survive, even if they never achieve greatness. We could also argue that all organizations really need leadership, but in voluntary organizations the need is fundamental.

The voluntary sector has at least three important aspects that bring about this greater need:

- *Idealism*. Charities, for example, exist to do something worth while that is in some way for the benefit of humanity. This is a great motivating force, to the point where for some causes people may risk their lives for an ideal, as with Médecins Sans Frontières. But commitment to a cause can also make it harder for a charity to succeed, because different people interpret the cause differently. Animal rights charities attract many law-abiding people, but there are also people with similar ideals who are not content to stay within the law and who believe that their cause is so powerful that it justifies arson, breaking and entering, theft, vandalism and criminal assault. Leadership is needed so that the vision of the charity is clear and so that it is people who share this vision who are attracted to it.
- *Volunteers*. All voluntary organizations depend on volunteers, if only at trustee level. A few are run entirely by volunteers. Many have a nucleus of paid staff, and could not function without an army of volunteers, whose jobs can encompass the whole spectrum of the charity's activities. The volunteers can leave just as quickly as they joined. Leadership skills are needed to get the best from volunteers, but also to avoid the tensions that can arise between paid staff and volunteers. It is all too easy for volunteers to feel that they are not appreciated, and are bombarded with too many irrelevant requests from the staff. Staff may feel frustrated because they cannot complete tasks quickly, because volunteers cannot respond quickly enough or because volunteers have a lack of interest in a particular request.

● *Staff.* Except in the largest organizations, rates of pay and benefits at all levels may be much lower than for equivalent jobs in the other sectors. This is often particularly true at senior levels. There may be few opportunities for personal development, for promotion and for the prospects of future salary increases. Although the ideals of the organization may be the critical motivators of people, and many high-calibre individuals work in this sector, there is also a danger that a low-pay profile can affect the expectations held of staff and lead to a willingness to accept lower levels of performance. It is important that this is not allowed to happen.

This is where the subject of Chapter 2, the vision, values and strategies of the organization, is all-important. But, particularly in charities, this idealism, this sense of mission, the whole reason for the very existence of the organization, often has to take much of the place of normal economic incentives. This is where leadership is so important. Although every manager needs to display leadership qualities, it all begins at the top. The old saying, 'There are no bad soldiers, only bad officers', is particularly evident in the charity world.

What is leadership? How do you recognize it, recruit for it and develop it? The vision process in Chapter 2 gave a view of one aspect of leadership, to which we invite you to refer. There we were discussing transformational, or visionary, leadership (the 'easier' method), and provided a model and some of the actions that relate to it. Here we were discussing the process of developing a vision, creating enthusiasm for it throughout the organization and giving the necessary psychological support to those helping the leader to implement the vision. In addition to these behavioural elements, we stressed a number of system and process issues that had to be undertaken in parallel.

Numerous books have been written on leadership, and there are differences of opinion over what various authorities consider to be important. Initially there was considerable focus on the personality traits of a good leader, resulting in long lists of virtues, any possessor of which must be well on the way to canonization. The 'easier' model follows more modern thinking, which instead of looking at personal traits is based on what good leaders actually do. Although personal traits like charisma can help someone be a good leader, all charismatic people are not necessarily even capable leaders: many are salespeople. The advantage of the approaches based on what people do is that it is possible to derive from these a series of competencies, which can be used to measure how a leader is operating and which can also be used to help people develop leadership skills.

For a summary of a number of significant contributions to thought about leadership we recommend Georgiades and Macdonell (1998), the bibliography of which will lead to the works of many of the most useful contributors to thinking about leadership.

There is now a general acceptance that different types of organization, mission or situation call for different aspects of leadership. In business a small, very profitable, fast-moving, high-tech, high-growth start-up company will require a different leadership style to that needed by an old, well-respected, but rather moribund company that has run into hard times. Equally a small start-up charity needs a different leadership style to that of an older charity whose mission has been rather overtaken by events.

Although there is a popular belief that a democratic style of leadership is better than an autocratic style, the reality is not as clear as this. There are occasions when the autocratic style is best.

Stace and Dunphy (1996) postulate the need for different styles for leading change, which depend on the nature of the change (incremental or transformational), the urgency of the change and the degree of internal resistance. Four different styles were identified, each fitting a different set of circumstances ('fit' means the appropriateness of the organization for the situation in which it finds itself:

1. *Participative evolution.* Use when the organization is in fit, but needs minor adjustment, or is out of fit but time is available and key interest groups favour change.
2. *Charismatic change strategies.* Use when the organization is out of fit, there is little time for extensive participation but there is support for radical change within the organization.
3. *Forced evolution.* Use when the organization is in fit but needs minor adjustment, or is out of fit but time is available, but key interest groups oppose change.
4. *Dictatorial transformation.* Use when the organization is out of fit, there is no time for extensive participation and no support within the organization for radical change, but change is vital to organizational survival and fulfilment of the basic mission.

Hersey and Blanchard (1977) gave us a way of looking at leadership style that is closely related to day-to-day management. It has great practical value. We make no excuse for the age of the reference as the tools and questionnaires developed to support their concepts are still used today. The two components of leadership behaviour that they use are task and relationship. Task in their context measures the extent to which the leader engages in one-way communication, explaining precisely what has to be done, when, where and how to do it: in other words directive behaviour. Relationship is the extent to which the leader uses two-way communication, providing facilitating behaviour, and socio-emotional and psychological support: in other words supportive behaviour. Supportive and directive behaviour form the two sides of a matrix, measured on a scale of low to high.

From this matrix are derived four leadership styles:

- S1: high task, low relationship – 'tell' style, with high direction and close monitoring;
- S2: high task, high relationship – 'sell' style, where decisions are explained and the leader allows questioning for clarification;
- S3: high relationship, low task – 'participate' style, where ideas may be shared and there is opportunity for joint decisions;
- S4: low relationship, low task – 'delegate' style, where people are fully trusted and allowed to take full responsibility for the decision and its implementation.

It is not that one style is better than another, but that one is more appropriate than another for a particular situation. Leaders have to have followers. Hersey and Blanchard developed an accompanying matrix, which had the job readiness of the follower on one axis and the psychological readiness on the other. Job readiness was knowledge, experience and the skills to undertake the task alone: able to do the job. Psychological readiness was the confidence, commitment and motivation to undertake the task: willing to do the job.

This gave rise to four follower profiles:

- R1: unable and unwilling (eg someone who has been put into a job for which he or she is unsuited and does not want to do);
- R2: unable but willing (eg a new graduate recruit who wants to work in the charity field, but has not yet developed all the competencies needed);

- R3: able but unwilling (eg an employee who has been with a charity for a long time, but has become disillusioned, or a person with many skills who joined a voluntary organization after an early retirement from a large company and for whom the job is the least bad option);
- R4: able and willing (eg a competent person who is dedicated to the organization).

Now we come to the practical part. It is matching the leadership style to the state of readiness of each person. It is fairly easy to see that an S4 style would be a disaster if applied to an R1 person, and that an S1 style would not get the best out of an R4 person. The numbers match the style to the state of readiness, and tell us that to get the most out of people the leader will not exercise only one style of management, but will adapt the style to the person. However, it also tells us that the style should change when the readiness of a particular person changes. S4 may no longer be appropriate to use with someone who has lost motivation, and an R2 person may improve job readiness and then require a change of style.

Although flexing style can help get the best out of people with varying abilities and motivation, the fact is that leadership requires delegation and the empowerment of others. It is a way of increasing the organization's capacity and effectiveness. This means ensuring that there are enough people, whether staff or volunteers, who are either already at the R4 level or who, through good management, can progress to this level.

What factors are critical for developing a committed organization? Martin and Nicholls (1987) found three common pillars in their study of a number of industrial companies that had been re-energized:

- a sense of belonging to the organization, achieved by ensuring people are informed about the organization, that they are involved and that they are allowed to share in its success;
- a sense of excitement about the job, by enabling people to take pride in their work, demonstrating trust and making people accountable for results;
- confidence in management's leadership, by exercising authority, demonstrating dedication and displaying competence.

Pause for reflection

Think about the Martin and Nicholls findings in relation to your organization. Are the three pillars valid? How effective is the organization in building these pillars? Would employees and volunteers see the organization in the same way? If you rate your organization as effective in building the pillars, what has been done that creates this feeling? If you have not rated it very highly, what actions do you think are desirable to build the pillars?

Everything we have discussed is relevant for successful leadership in charities, but we should like to emphasize three points, which are derived from the discussion so far and which we see as particularly important for charities.

The first is to demonstrate enthusiasm, and to engender similar feelings among others. It is this aspect of leadership that can make staff feel it is all worth while, and that they want to strive to achieve the vision, values and objectives of the organization. It is helping people to make effective the motivation that drew them to the voluntary world in the first place.

The second, which flows from enthusiasm, is energy and drive. This is important for leading all types of organization, but is particularly so when people have chosen to sacrifice some economic benefit because of the drive they feel to do something that benefits society. It is essential that the tempo of the organization is driven by a sense of enthusiasm and commitment, which must emanate from the top. Founding a charity, or revitalizing one that has lost its way, requires a lot of hard work. A relaxed, easy-going, happy-go-lucky boss, however attractive as an individual, is unlikely to lead the staff into a new successful history. So a high-energy output and drive are often critically important. Some will say the corollary of drive is impatience. This in business is often a useful attribute, but in the charity world this may be less desirable, as it can lead to frustration and a destructive intolerance.

The third key feature of the leader of a voluntary organization is skill at human relations. To motivate, encourage, enthuse and develop others, and to stimulate them to work in a similar way with the people they manage or are involved with is a critical part of the management process. It will be said that this is true of all leadership.

The point is that in the business world high pay or rosy prospects for promotion can lead people to tolerate a difficult and discouraging boss. In the voluntary sector this will not happen: staff just leave.

> ### Pause for reflection
>
> Before reading the next section jot down what you feel are the 10 things that characterize the effective management of other people. After reading the section compare our findings with your list, and see if you are still of the same opinion.

10 UNIVERSAL QUALITIES OF EFFECTIVE MANAGEMENT

Management and leadership are not identical, although they are not entirely separate. The 10 universal qualities apply to all managers at all levels, although some adaptation may be needed to suit particular circumstances. There are big differences between managing a group of highly qualified professionals and managing a factory. So we would not present these 10 aspects as an immutable truth; judgement is also required. So perhaps the word 'universal' is a slight exaggeration, but they are certainly widely applicable.

Once something is refined to 10 points, there is the fair question, 'Why as many as 10?' followed by, 'Why are there only 10?' Of course there are more, but these 10 arose from a particular and unusual piece of research. A firm of management consultants, Harbridge House Inc (the firm was acquired by what was then Coopers & Lybrand in 1993), had for some 20 years made extensive use of 360-degree feedback instruments across numerous organizations in various countries. Sometimes this was to collect information about how managers were actually managing, and sometimes it was linked to validated measures to assess leadership and organizational climate. In addition to the feedback on how their bosses actually managed, those completing questionnaires were asked to rate the importance to them of each practice on the questionnaire. One result of this was a vast data bank of information, covering many thousands of managers, which could be analysed in various ways. The 10 qualities were derived from this data bank. The list was published by Harbridge

House Inc (1990), but the descriptions, although derived from this work, are our own:

1. *Giving clear direction.* This includes:
   - Establishing clear goals and standards for subordinates. The word 'establishing' is used because it does not mean that this has to be a one-way process.
   - Ensuring that the overall goals for the unit are set in the context of the organization, and are properly communicated. Teamwork is important, and is more likely to thrive when everyone knows the overall goals, as well as what they themselves are expected to do.
   - Involving people in setting their own goals, and where practicable the goals for the overall unit. This requires open, two-way communication, the aim being for both parties to discuss the implications of goals and targets. It is not about letting people get away with easy targets, and from what we have already discussed it is clear that the depth of involvement will be affected by the ability and motivation of each person.
   - Delegate responsibility to others. Be clear about what is delegated and what your expectations are. If practical, move from delegation to empowerment to allow members of your team to take personal responsibility for their work.
   Delegation is the transfer of part of the authority of a manager to a subordinate. Effective delegation requires careful definition of what portion of the authority has been surrendered. The manager remains responsible for actions taken by those to whom authority has been delegated. *Empowerment* is: 'The process as a result of which individual employees have the autonomy, motivation and skills necessary to perform their jobs in a way which provides them with a genuine sense of ownership and fulfilment while achieving shared organisational goals' (Lowe, 1994).

2. *Encouraging two-way communication.* Effective two-way communication between managers and their subordinates should create a good work climate. It creates a climate where people feel that they can approach their manager with problems and suggestions. The risk of confusion is reduced, and a feeling of involvement created. Two-way communication is very different from giving orders without any opportunity for questioning or obtaining feedback. It requires:

- active listening, to ensure that the manager understands both what is said and the underlying current of what is meant;
- soliciting feedback in an active way, both to check understanding of what has been said and to make it easier for people to provide input about problems and issues;
- double-checking important points, so that both parties share the same understanding of them;
- ensuring that both parties to the communication are aware of the context behind the discussion: it is a mistake for a manager to assume that people know this without checking;
- modifying the communication style to suit the situation, if necessary, as the motivation and capability of individuals may vary.

3. *Coaching and supporting people.* Three aspects of coaching and support identified in the Harbridge House study were:
   - Having a helpful attitude. People will only let a manager know that they need help if they feel that this will not lay them open to criticism. This does not mean encouraging people to evade responsibility by referring all their decisions upwards.
   - Without lowering the expected standards, to work with people to find ways of improving their performance.
   - Sticking up for subordinates with senior managers. This is a difficult path, as there are some things that should not be condoned, but at the same time never supporting people when their actions are justified can lead them to an unhealthy belief that they are exploited, and it is everyone for him- or herself. Team building needs people to feel that they have the support of the team and are not left isolated every time there is a dispute or criticism.

4. *Recognition of the work of others.* Recognition should be objective and sincere. It involves:
   - Making sure that good work is praised. The need is for fairness and balance between giving credit when this is due and pointing out things that need attention. Of course the need for recognition of good work may occur on one occasion and the need to criticize on another. The balance is over a period; the fairness should be ever present.
   - Basing rewards on job performance, rather than cronyism or length of service.
   - Giving thanks in a sincere way for particular efforts, which

can do much to make people feel that their efforts are genuinely appreciated. Insincerity, or repeated thanks for things that do not justify it, can of course have the opposite effect.

5. *Establishing ongoing controls.* The emphasis here is appropriate controls over job performance. Often it means appropriate information so the person can assess his or her own performance. When people are highly motivated and capable, control may be exercised with a very light touch:

   - The manager should follow up on important issues and actions to find out how things went, and this follow-up is likely to be based on talking to subordinates rather than information that comes out of a formal information system. The trick is to remain involved in important aspects of the work, but without giving the impression that you are always checking up on people because you do not trust them.

   - Give regular feedback to subordinates on their performance against your expectations. This should be a regular, generally informal activity, although it should for the most part be done out of the hearing of other people.

6. *Selecting the right people to work with you.* Getting the right people is essential for success. This is both about selection and about enabling people to develop so that they have the competencies required. Motivation, as we have seen, affects performance, and although it comes from within a person the manager can do much to create a situation where people are both willing and able. It is much easier to cause people to become demotivated than to inspire them! A poor manager can turn the 'right' people into a shambles, while a good manager may build a team out of apparently unpromising material.

7. *Understanding the financial implications of decisions.* Increasingly managers at all levels need to have some understanding of the consequences of their decisions, and one of the causes of problems in voluntary organizations is when this knowledge is absent. The need is much greater for managing directors and senior managers, whether they are full-time staff or volunteers:

   - Effective managers understand the economic underpinning of the organization.

   - Managers are not expected to be accountants, but they should be able to interpret the figures they discuss, and have enough knowledge to enter into a sensible debate about them.

- The financial implications cannot always be read off the accounts. Many HR decisions can have far-reaching financial consequences. For example, it can be expensive if employees are dismissed without going through proper procedures, or if there is unfair discrimination on grounds of sex or ethnic origin (age is likely to be added to this list). Similarly contracts entered into cannot be unilaterally cancelled without due cause, without laying the organization open to financial consequences.

8. *Encouraging creativity and innovation.* What prevents creativity and innovation in organizations is rarely that employees lack creativity, although there are of course differences between individuals. To become innovations, ideas have to fight their way through the organization, and if this is difficult many employees will no longer try:

- The Harbridge House research found that most employees believed that they could contribute new ideas.
- A manager who acts to reinforce this belief, for example by asking subordinates for opinions and suggestions even if he or she could reach a decision without this, may find that the different insight that a subordinate holds does indeed lead to more innovation and better decisions.
- Give new ideas a fair hearing. This does not mean that every idea is good for the organization. Often, it is not the rejection of an idea that demotivates as much as the way it is rejected.

9. *Making clear-cut decisions when they are needed.* Participation and involvement are good things when appropriate for the situation, and many employees welcome them, but:

- In the end it is the manager's job to make decisions (subject to limitations of authority and a frequent need to coordinate with other areas of the organization). The fact that people have been involved does not always mean that a consensus will emerge, and the manager has to make the ultimate decision.
- Generally subordinates want things to progress, and it makes it harder for them to do their jobs if there is dithering or a refusal to make a decision.
- Be sure to make it clear that people's involvement is valued, and that it has helped to give insight and clarity so that a decision could be made.

10. *Personal integrity.* The Harbridge House research confirmed what most of us probably feel. We prefer to work for someone we respect, whose word means something. Respect cannot be demanded. It always has to be earned, but when it is earned it can help greatly to take the organization through the bad as well as the good times.

RECRUITING THE RIGHT PEOPLE

One does not need much imagination to visualize the chaos that can result when any organization is directed, managed and staffed by the wrong people. One of the 10 universal qualities of management from the Harbridge House research is selecting the right people. The reason this occurred in this type of survey is that it can be just as devastating for people to have to work with colleagues who for reasons of capability, personality or motivation are not up to the job as it can for the manager to have such people working for him or her. Helping to shape personal capabilities of a highly motivated new recruit can be one of the most worthwhile experiences a manager can have, and ranks alongside having subordinates and colleagues whom one respects. But being staffed with inappropriate people can be stressful for the manager and damaging for the organization. Our discussion deals with several different categories of people, beginning with trustees.

TRUSTEES

Every charity has a legal need for a board of trustees. These trustees will have to act like a board of directors, while working within the legal framework of charities as laid down by the Charity Commission (see the Charity Commission publication CC3 and CC3a). Very often there will also be the need for a board of management who will seek to lead and guide the operational management of the charity. The need for clear definition of these two respective bodies and their relationship cannot be too highly stressed. All too often the trustees are weak and ineffective, or they meddle with the detail, get in the way and frustrate the true management role of the executives. The legal roles of the trustees, and the oversight and direction of management need two very separate skills and are therefore addressed separately.

The Charity Commission 1998 gives positive advice on the recruitment of trustees:

> We recommend that trustees be selected for what they can contribute to the charity. They ought not be appointed for their status or position in the community alone: this is the function of patrons. Trustees need to be able – and willing – to give time to the efficient administration of the charity and the fulfilment of its trusts. We recommend that they be selected on the basis of their relevant experience and skills and need to be prepared to take an active part in the running of the charity.

Getting the right board of trustees is always of critical importance, and especially so in the launch phase of a charity. They should be recruited with a specific role in mind. This may include:

● Credibility in the eyes of specific interested parties. This may be prospective donors, as well as politicians at a local or national level. Professional, trade, industry or ethical/social background may also be essential. However, as noted above, they should not be recruited solely for their status in the community.

● Knowledge of the actual topic in which the charity is engaged. This is important. It is surprising the way trustees can be assembled and new names added without anyone asking the question, 'Well, what do they actually know about the issue the charity is formed to help?'

● Experience of the administration of an organization of the same scale of size as the charity.

● Full understanding of their legal responsibilities, and the competencies to fulfil these.

It is also helpful if trustees have fund-raising ability, or personal control of potential funds, or 'door-opening' ability to introduce the chief executive and senior managers into the right places. However, it would be an error to recruit trustees who could do this but who did not possess the other requirements of the task. 'To be a charity trustee is not a position of honour without responsibility: it requires time, understanding and effort' (Charity Commission, 1998).

Often recruiting good trustees is difficult. Those people who are most wanted are, not surprisingly, the busiest. The opposite is also true. Trustees, like everyone else, grow old, and some become stale or lose their vitality. They may also no longer be in a position to 'open doors' or give advice if they have retired from the position that made them uniquely valuable. A charity can also grow beyond the capability and time availability of some of the original trustees, or may require additional skills and experience because of the way its activities have developed.

It is wise to write into the governing documents a way of removing trustees without their loss of face or goodwill. It is suggested that trustees should always be appointed/elected for a specific period of time. Beyond that period there should be a need formally to reappoint them. Reappointment should involve an assessment of the value of the trustee to the charity.

Finding the chairperson for the board of trustees is even more important and more difficult. It is he or she who should play the major role in finding fellow trustees. One danger is a natural inclination to go for some obvious well-known public figure, often known nationally or locally as one of the 'good and great'; while it may be appropriate to recruit such people as patrons, they are not automatically a good choice as trustees. Another typical danger is just to play safe and find someone already known to the other trustees. It is easy for this to become the 'old pals club' and in a sense for trustees to be too similar to each other: cosy, but lacking the variety that sparks creative thinking and innovation.

Often a better course is to try to find someone who is up and coming – the next generation of the good and the great. Such a person may have more time and commitment while bringing a fresher and less-tiered troupe of colleagues around him or her. This can and should be invigorating.

PATRONS AND OCCASIONAL USE OF CELEBRITIES

In Britain we are still overly impressed by titles. There is a role for titles in the letter-heading of a charity, but it should not be overdone, as people become highly sceptical when they see names of people who appear to have no relevance to the aims of the charity. Again the more appropriate role may be as patron rather than trustee.

There is sometimes the temptation to bring in a professional entertainer or someone from the stage, screen or sports field. Here again one needs to be clear as to why an individual would make a contribution. A nine-day wonder of the pop scene or the football field may have a very short shelf-life. An ageing actor may appeal to aged trustees but not to anyone younger. In many cases it would be inappropriate to invite such people to become trustees, unless they have a personal interest in the charitable purpose and possess the other qualities required of a trustee, not least of which is having time available to fulfil these duties. Celebrities do not have to be offered a permanent role in order to gain their help. When it comes to a special event, such as bringing the opening or launching of some special activity to the notice of the general public, there is no doubt that someone in the news produces the draw and media attention that may be impossible to generate any other way. Similarly the presence of a celebrity or two at a public fund-raising activity can draw in the public: a modern version of the lady of the manor presiding over the annual church fete. Men in particular are prepared to pay heavily, for example, to have a round of golf with a celebrity, particularly one known to have golfing ability.

There is therefore scope for the high-profile individual to play an important occasional role in charity promotion. Members of the royal family, even in the 21st century, certainly still do generate an immense amount of interest. Any event that involves them generates attendance and media interest.

The young may be attracted to events opened by the latest pop star, although there is a danger that such a person can fall off the charts by the time the event takes place. The celebrity's aims may not be entirely altruistic, in that such events can generate useful publicity for the entertainer, but if handled with tact and cooperation by both parties there is no reason why both cannot benefit.

BOARD OF MANAGEMENT (OR MANAGEMENT COMMITTEE)

Recruiting volunteers for the board of management is no less impor-tant, and just as difficult. Much will depend on the extent to which the charity is run by paid officials, volunteers or a combination of the two. There may be a mix of volunteers and paid staff.

Every board needs at least one person with accounting skills. When recruiting a paid or unpaid member to fill this role it is important to distinguish between the expertise of a professional auditor, a bank manager and a company accountant. Additionally there are some accountants who have specific experience in charity accounting.

Professional auditors may ensure the accuracy of figures and help ensure that the charity meets the legal requirements. The danger is if a lifetime of auditing experience makes them negative in attitude, good at cost cutting but tending to be risk averse. This is not inevitable, but it is true of many auditors. How good will they be at making positive suggestions on what can be done to further the objectives of the charity?

The term 'bank manager' covers a multitude of different experiences, and the role has changed as the traditional high street bank manager has largely disappeared. Bankers dealing with routine corporate or personal finance will certainly have an understanding of accounting data, but again may have been conditioned to be ultra-cautious. Those from merchant banks may be more used to finding creative, entrepreneurial solutions but may find it hard to drop their scale of thinking from multi-million-pound transactions to situations where £100 may be very important.

Company accountants may be invaluable because of a past experience involving spending money and taking risks, where their analytical approaches will seek to find a policy that maximizes cost effectiveness. Persons with experience as accountants within companies may be expected to know more about management accounting than the average auditor or banker. These skills may be much needed on the management board.

Accountants experienced in charity accounting may have similarities with the company accountant, plus a specific awareness of charity accounting. Their experience could include management accounting within charities. However, it may be harder to find such people except as paid staff, unless a volunteer can be 'borrowed' from another charity.

These differences in experience and the way they may affect the usefulness to the charity are, of course, very wide generalizations. The requirement should be related to the size and issues faced by the charity. However, it is certainly true that many small charities often face problems involving expenditure and risk. Indeed the founder of one charity asked another who had launched a very successful charity many years before what special tips he would pass on. The advice may surprise those who are faint-hearted. It was to take risks, steering very close to financial problems and regularly making it appear that the charity would fold unless another heroic effort was made to help it survive. This of course is not a blanket suggestion to act irresponsibly, and the right type of accounting input can help the charity steer a course somewhere between imprudence and overcautiousness.

The next expertise that is needed by the board is likely to be legal. Of course legal advice can always be purchased, but the other board members have to know that they have a need for it. In reality problems often arise because no one on the board has an understanding of law, and therefore the board can get into situations that cause problems later. Expertise on tap can make a big difference. Problems we have observed in our careers that were caused by a complete ignorance of the law include: unilaterally cancelling a contract and then being surprised at being sued for the damages suffered by the other party; unfairly sacking an employee; unthinkingly discriminating against an employee; failing to protect intellectual property, and being surprised at an invoice because contract terms had not been read properly.

Some voluntary organizations have ongoing specific needs for legal knowledge, not only on the board of management but deeper in the organization. The Ramblers' Association is involved in planning legislation and other laws concerning national parks and rights of way. It has itself brought a private prosecution against a landowner who has blocked a public footpath and where the county council has refused to take action. Age Concern deals regularly with the numerous laws that affect elderly people, and frequently finds councils that are not applying these correctly.

Three other skills that are critical are public relations, marketing and fund-raising. These three will vary in importance between organizations, but should be perceived as essential expertise that cannot be left to the amateur. Later in the book there are chapters devoted to these topics. One problem for charities that cannot afford paid staff to head these functions is that, although public relations and marketing skills are widely available and volunteer staff can be found, most of the fund-raising expertise lies in the voluntary sector. It may be very difficult for a small charity to find people with these skills.

The core component of the board of management should be made up of people who actually know something professionally about the work of the organization. This is obvious when there are a large number of paid employees. It is much harder when the organization is mostly run by volunteer effort, and here the membership of the board of management will inevitably consist of a large number of volunteers. In Britain we have a historic love of the intelligent amateur who turns his or her hand and opinion to anything. If an organization is to be run well, this should not be seen as good enough, as there is no substitute for people with a great depth of appropriate experience and knowledge.

In the business world, one often finds that in a professional practice such as a firm of civil engineers, accountants, lawyers or management consultants, the whole ethos of the firm is that the dominant profession is all that matters and that everyone else is a second-class citizen. The same can happen in a voluntary organization. Guard against it, and respect the expertise of others.

PAID STAFF

We have referred to paid staff several times, and of course getting the right people begins with the managing director and the employees who are on the board of management, and continues to every employee in the organization. We have looked at some of the issues of leadership and the management of people, and to some degree discussed the need for a charity to obtain people with the appropriate skills and experience.

Getting the right people obviously begins with recruitment and selection, but it does not stop there. To retain them there is a need for performance management, a rewards policy, and development and continuous learning to meet the changing needs of the charity and to enable the individual to progress. Selection occurs again as people are promoted or chosen for different jobs within the organization.

The key things to think about are those policies and procedures that facilitate recruitment and that provide employees with reasons for staying with the charity. So quite early on there needs to be a clear policy for reward, including periodic salary reviews and the other contractual terms of employment, such as holidays, sick pay and periods of notice (many of the basic elements are driven by law).

Part of retention is about how people are managed, something discussed earlier, but part is about whether the organization can meet people's personal needs for development. Some people love routine repetitive jobs, and others get bored after doing them for a while. So although it is not sensible for a manager to make value judgements about whether a job is boring or not, it is important to find out how the incumbent sees it. Life can often be spiced up by a change of duties or adding different responsibilities.

Some people, particularly those at the start of their careers, have ambitions and want to develop and attain higher levels of responsibility. Careful thought should be given to how far it is possible to help all employees strive towards their personal objectives. A small charity with only a few employees cannot offer the same career opportunities as one of the giants. But what every organization can do is to feel responsible for the development and personal growth of those people, within the constraints of what they themselves are seeking and the money available, so that, even if people leave after a few years because they cannot achieve promotion, they are better equipped to fulfil those ambitions than before they joined. Personal development is not all about expensive training programmes, although these can play an effective part. It is also about deliberate policies for coaching staff, giving them the opportunity to gain experience and learn through projects and changes of responsibility, and encouraging personal learning.

There should be a degree of integration between the various human resource management (HRM) policies and procedures, so that they become part of a coherent whole and so as to incorporate all legal requirements. Although initially these may be fairly basic, a voluntary organization does not have to employ many people before it needs something comprehensive. The British Red Cross, for example, has a clear charter for volunteers, which sets out the expectations they may have of the charity and what the charity expects from them. This is supported by careful policies, one example of which, dealing with discrimination, could at the time of writing be downloaded from its Web site (www.redcross.org.uk).

The small charity with few paid staff may feel that all this is a luxury, but small charities can get bigger, and an organization does not have to be very large before it needs to move from one employee who does everything, supported of course by volunteers, to a situation where there is a need for more people with specialized competencies. So even if there is a full-time staff of only three or four people the issue has relevance, and as the numbers increase so does the importance of a comprehensive approach to HRM.

Burnell (2001) gives reasonably detailed guidance on policies and the law. Croner, a specialized publisher, offers a loose-leaf guide to employment law, which is kept up to date through an annual subscription. It offers a similar method to help organizations keep up to date on sound HRM practice and procedures. The second service has a particular value for a small voluntary organization where it is not possible to employ a personnel manager.

Case study 5.1: A multi-area charity

This particular charity decentralizes much of its activity to areas, each of which has an area board (volunteers). These area boards vary greatly in their composition and competence.

In addition to a small paid staff, most of the operational work is undertaken by skilled and experienced volunteers, who typically are retired executives with experience in large companies. There is therefore a need to have in the area board those who can match and expand the skills of the operational volunteers.

Inherent in any charity which employs people is the potential conflict between the paid and the unpaid. Though hopefully the paid staff will believe in the cause, or mission, and objectives of the charity, it is inevitable that the underlying motivations of these two groups and their priorities may differ to a marked degree.

A charity should therefore seek to recruit paid staff who are able to understand and adjust their attitude and style to accommodate the differences. This aspect of their work should be explored in their induction training, and they should be sensitized to the issues.

One area manager in this charity, who had been seconded by a large company with an expectation that the appointment would be made permanent, was a classic case of this problem. He was soon in trouble. On the second day he announced that the trouble with the charity was that it had to use volunteers, and proceeded to treat them as second-class citizens. He made it plain he was a natural leader who knew everything about the charity's activities

Unfortunately neither premise was correct. The volunteers he so despised were in most cases very experienced executives, many years his senior, who had themselves successfully built their own companies. Soon after his arrival he took his year's entitlement of leave, and announced that he never took work home or worked in the evening or at the weekend, and indeed never took business calls at home. This in some jobs might be quite acceptable and reasonable. However, in this particular situation he was depending on volunteers to do 95 per cent of the work, and they only worked from home on the charity's business, normally saw their clients in the evening and always in their spare time. His home number was not known beyond the personnel department, which made him unreachable in a crisis.

The area organization was soon in disarray and inefficient, and mistakes abounded. His cry was that he was overworked, yet at the same time he refused to delegate. This was just the start. Having little sense of his real role, he moved in to do jobs that were already being well done by a volunteer. If there was media publicity in the offing, it was his name and face that were put to the fore. Office mail was intercepted and unilaterally handled, while a focus on peripheral issues seemed preferred.

It is fortunate that he did eventually make good. However, time was wasted, and many excellent volunteers just walked away. The moral of the story is that the manager's supervisor should have recognized the cause of the problem, weighed up what the volunteers were saying and taken prompt action.

Pause for reflection

In Case study 5.1 the area board members were volunteers. If you were an area board member what action do you think would have been appropriate in the case study situation? Do you believe that the board should exercise authority over a paid staff member? Would you have made any concern a formal matter, or would you have handled it by coaching the manager? What circumstances might affect which is the most appropriate course of action?

It was stated earlier that the essence of voluntary sector management is leadership. This extends down to every level. This manager should have realized that leadership at area level meant delegation and motivation of volunteers. It was the volunteers who were willing and able to do the work more competently than he could, and his key role should have been the coordination of their work, which he could have done much to facilitate.

In any induction process for paid staff it is important to raise and discuss the whole topic of relationships. Paid staff need to be sensitized to these issues, and those who cannot or will not respond may prove to be a burden to senior management.

SECONDED STAFF

The practice of organizations seconding a member of their staff to a voluntary organization has grown in recent years. Sometimes it is genuinely to broaden the interests and perception of a person. This is when it is perceived as part of management development, where widening the experience of a narrow specialist can bring real benefits to both parties. In these cases the staff member returns to the seconding company after an agreed spell – frequently six months but sometimes for as long as three years. The longer periods of secondment are often a difficult policy for a company to follow, because of difficulties in handling the re-entry of the person at the right level.

Unfortunately, all too often secondment is a device of large companies to 'park' unwanted staff who are too young to retire or too expensive to make redundant immediately. In these situations the voluntary organization is wise to be wary. For charities these secondments may be a mixed blessing. They may be free, but those seconded may not have the experience or knowledge to fill the charity's vacancy. For example, an accountant may not necessarily make a good fund-raiser, or someone whose whole experience has been in a single function may not cope well in a broader role.

Equally such staff are not always well-motivated, high-performing high-flyers. All too often they may be disenchanted and demoralized and, perhaps quite wrongly, feel failures. They may resent being put in such a role, and only accept because it leads ultimately to a better financial package. The secondment may be for a set period of time, which the newcomer sees as a penance to be undertaken before the company's pension can be collected. When this is the case, such staff will not be motivated to provide the much-needed leadership and drive.

This must be taken as a challenge to revitalize the individual. Ideally there should be a trial induction period. The candidate has a chance to prove his or her worth, respond to the new challenge and become excited about the role of the organization. Perhaps he or she can put down the foundations of a second career instead of taking an early retirement. It can be an opportunity for the organization to test out potential senior staff, select the best and be confident of suitability when the person is moved on to the payroll at the end of the allotted period.

It would be wrong to underemphasize the management qualities needed in voluntary sector managers if an inappropriate secondment is to be turned into a success. Think back to the discussion on situational leadership. The challenge may be to inspire someone who is capable but unwilling, or to turn someone who is willing but not yet capable into a success. Hardest of all is to turn around someone who is neither motivated nor capable, and it sometimes has to be accepted that the game is not worth the candle. But you can also gain someone who is both capable and motivated, in which case the business experience brought into the organization can be of considerable value.

VOLUNTEERS

According to the Institute for Volunteering Research, some 22 million adults are involved in formal volunteering at least one a year, providing an economic value of £40 billion per year. One has only to look at the Web sites of some of the medium to large charities to gain an impression of both the number and the economic value provided. The British Red Cross has some 45,000 contributing £30 million value in the effort they put in. The Samaritans, if it paid its volunteers at the national minimum wage, would have to find £11 million: it has nearly 19,000 volunteers. The charity REACH, which places volunteers with other charities, states that it delivers some £16 million of expertise each year. It is no exaggeration to suggest that without volunteers many voluntary organizations would be unable to function.

Different organizations use volunteers in different ways. For many charities the main use is as collection agents on flag days, plus of course trustees. Many others are dependent on volunteers to fulfil the charitable purpose, whether as mentors for the Prince's Trust, staffing the Samaritans' telephone support service, transcribing and indexing records in the various family history and other societies associated with archives, and numerous other types of activity. Volunteers help many organizations with various jobs in the office, enable cafés and tearooms to operate, and are the enablers of many charity shops.

Several summary survey reports about volunteering and the management of volunteers can be consulted on the Web site of the Institute for Volunteering Research (www.ivr.org.uk). Among other things these include information on the reasons why people volunteer, and the benefits they get out of it. While this is helpful information, it is of more value for charities and other voluntary organizations to explore the motivation of their own volunteers, as it may vary from the general picture. It is also useful to be aware of the criticisms that are frequently voiced by volunteers. For example, some 70 per cent felt that volunteering was not well organized by the organization they worked with, and there were issues of boredom with what they were asked to do, overload in relation to the time they wanted to spend, and lack of appreciation. What is the position in your organization?

The thing to remember is that people do expect to gain something from volunteering. They are, by definition, not seeking a monetary reward, but they do want things like a feeling of doing something worthwhile, meeting people, developing new friends and numerous other possible motivations. There needs to be a positive strategy and policies for working with volunteers, just as there needs to be for employees.

The hospital case study (below), by showing things that were mismanaged, helps identify some positive management actions that would have delivered a better result.

> ### Pause for reflection
>
> As you read this case study jot down the good and bad points you see in the way this situation was handled. Could it have been improved? What would you have done if you had been the coordinator? Do you recognize any similar problems in the way your organization manages volunteers? Our summing-up appears after the case study.

Case study 5.2: A volunteer (name disguised) at Horsham Hospital

Expectations

A short time after she retired as a teacher, Mary saw an advertisement in the local paper for voluntary help at her local hospital. She responded because she had the time and wanted to use it to help the community. She knew that most of the patients at the hospital were elderly, and that many became lonely, friendless and bored. Here was a real need she could meet.

Her expectations from her initial contact were that she would be able to help these patients, perhaps play board games with them, listen and talk. In addition, as nurses were overworked, she hoped that she could save them some time by doing various bits of unskilled work.

Horsham Hospital was under the hospital trust 10 miles away at Crawley, and volunteers were recruited and coordinated from this headquarters. There were 25 volunteers, committing to various periods. Mary agreed to work one afternoon a week. The coordinator organized the roster into morning and afternoon shifts, every day, always having two people on duty at any one time. Mary by chance was paired with an older experienced worker, who had been doing voluntary work with the Friends of Horsham Hospital for many years before she volunteered for this new initiative.

The new volunteers were given a two-hour induction programme, and were shown the ward where they would work, given ideas about the jobs that could be done and told what to do if they had to be absent for any length of time.

What actually happened

Mary found that the reality was different from her expectations. When she arrived for her afternoon shift all the suggested jobs (like helping patients with personal care, seeing to flowers and helping with menu choices) had already been done by the morning people. Many of the patients were, as expected, elderly and those who were confused or infirm were unable to play games. Those who were alert usually had their own visitors in the afternoon. Without specific tasks to fulfil, it was harder to open conversations with patients. Progressively there were fewer long-stay patients, which gave no time to build relationships.

'On the whole I did not feel that the role the volunteers were intended to play had the support of the paid staff,' Mary explained. 'Although there were one or two exceptions, most of the nurses and auxiliary staff seemed to be suspicious and sometimes resentful of our presence. Most of the time I was just tolerated. Instead of feeling I was being useful, I felt that I was wasting my time and was not wanted.'

The new volunteers very quickly began to leave, and within a few months Mary and her team-mate were the only survivors of the original 25. Although there were some occasional replacements during the two to three years Mary remained, none stayed. No support was given by the coordinator. 'I met her once or twice in the corridors, when she seemed to be trying hard to remember who I was.'

There was no follow-up by the coordinator to find out how well the new volunteer scheme was working. Annually there was a meeting at the main Crawley hospital, where an update on the state of the trust and the volunteer services was given. However, the part about volunteer services applied only to the Crawley hospital. One session Mary found useful was about fire and other safety precautions. On the last meeting Mary attended, one of the speakers did not turn up, and the space was filled by the coordinator who spoke at length about the proposed merger with another trust, the impact of the merger on the paid staff and herself in particular, and her own job insecurity.

Over Mary's whole period as a volunteer there was only one afternoon meeting at Horsham Hospital, to give the volunteers an opportunity to present problems and be given advice and support. However, by that time there was only one volunteer in addition to Mary and her colleague, so the meeting was these three plus the coordinator, in a small room around a table with tea and biscuits. Straight away the coordinator started telling the others about her personal domestic situation and her concerns over her future with the trust. Mary said, 'I was so astounded that I wondered if I had got it wrong and this was meant to be a social occasion. By that time my opinion of the coordinator was such that I saw no useful purpose in trying to bring the conversation round to what I had thought was the purpose of the meeting.'

Why Mary stayed so long

As the other volunteers quit, there were a few more things to be done. Arranging the flowers gave an opportunity to talk to some of the patients. However, the main reason was loyalty to her colleague who was dedicated to the task and inspired in ways of fulfilling it.

Eventually, her colleague became too old to continue. This coincided with the fact that Mary's own elderly mother was taking up more of her time. Mary saw no purpose in continuing and left shortly after.

It is hard to find anything right about the way this project was managed:

- The hospital should have made a realistic assessment of the work and the number of volunteers needed to do it. If this had been done, the volunteers could have received a much clearer briefing about what the tasks were and the reason for them.
- The local paid staff should have been consulted and their concerns identified and allayed. In a situation like a hospital, it is patently impossible to gain much value from the volunteers, unless there is support from the nurses and other professionals. When those with the prime responsibility for the day-to-day work have little idea of where volunteers can be useful, the whole scheme becomes unworkable.
- Both the HQ and the local paid staff needed to be committed to the project. Commitment is rarely achieved when solutions like this are imposed by a remote head office, and without it volunteers can be made to feel most unwelcome.
- More care should have been exercised in the choice of coordinator, who herself should have been effectively managed. One of the Institute for Volunteering Research surveys found that 80 per cent of charities that used volunteers had a designated volunteer coordinator or manager. Yet, as we have seen, 70 per cent of volunteers felt that volunteering could have been much better organized. There is a gap. In the hospital case study there were issues around the coordinator, but problems can emerge if whoever has this role is overburdened with other duties.
- Volunteers often need more initial support than paid staff, because they are unfamiliar with the organization and their roles. This is not a long-term need, but depending on the role the volunteers are required to play it is an issue that should receive some attention.

- The organization has to show by actions that the role of the volunteers is important. This comes back to the need volunteers have (and employees too) to feel that their efforts are being appreciated. This is not only what managers say; it is how the whole organization behaves towards them. We have already looked at a case study where a new manager was hostile to volunteers. If volunteers do not feel that their personal needs from volunteering are being met, why should they continue?

- Communication should be regular, and can be formal or informal. One of the secrets of managing anybody is regular communication. If no one ever keeps volunteers involved, by telling them what is going on and making sure that they share in the successes of the organization, as well as regular discussion about how they are coping, why should they continue to be interested?

- Meetings to examine the role of the volunteers and their issues should include some of the local paid staff. The first of these should be early in the relationship. In the hospital case study it was noticeable that the few meetings that were held did not include any of the local full-time staff. Of course nurses and other hospital staff are rushed off their feet, but there must have been some opportunities to make the volunteers feel that they were part of a team with the paid staff.

- When a volunteer is to work alongside paid staff, someone should be delegated to act as sponsor on the first day to introduce him or her to the staff with whom he or she will work. Failure to do this sets everything off on the wrong foot. The volunteer does not know whom to speak to, and the paid staff wonder why this stranger is wandering around. And where is the feeling of being needed?

When thinking of the motivation of volunteers, it is sensible to be aware that not only do volunteers work for nothing but it often costs them money to do so. The evidence about the number of charities that reimburse expenses is confused. One Institute for Volunteering Research survey found that 93 per cent of charities in their survey made some sort of reimbursement of some expenses, but another survey found that less than half of volunteers were able to claim reimbursement. The difference could be because of a bias in the sample of charities, or it could be because the ones that do reimburse are not as large a user of volunteers as the ones that do not.

There are more and more laws and regulations, and volunteers, particularly if they are trustees, can find themselves personally at risk. Adequate insurance by the charity to cover such risks may be important in encouraging volunteers to come forward, whether as trustees or in other roles, as can the willingness of the organization to spend money on taking expert advice when it is needed.

There are issues on the other side of the relationship, when volunteers for whatever reason do not perform effectively. Many organizations that are large users of volunteers have policies to deal with performance and discipline of volunteers as they do for paid staff, but there can be a hesitancy in applying them. A problem ignored does not disappear and, as some problems of attitude or performance can infect other people, in addition to impairing the work of the charity, management must face up to such issues.

Case study 5.3: Taking positive action to deal with a volunteer problem

In one area of the Prince's Trust – Business over half the volunteer mentors were found to be ineffective. Management was scared to do anything to rectify the situation. A new volunteer mentor coordinator came in and tactfully set about culling the underperforming half. He also let it be known that only keen, competent applicants would be recruited. The outcome was instant.

The remaining volunteers realized they could not assume their standards were praiseworthy and acceptable. Standards, enthusiasm and, above all, pride rocketed. The trickle of volunteers became a flood. Very politely turning a volunteer down was a stimulant for many others who now strove to be selected. The loss of mentors was quickly made up, and the spirit of common aims and standards was exhilarating.

Some charities struggle to recruit volunteers, and this can lead to an attitude that all are welcome and need to be fitted in. At the same time other charities have an appeal and image so that more people come forward than are really needed. This is the ideal situation. Part of the policy towards volunteers should be about ways of making the charity and its volunteer work appeal. And part of that is the value of word-of-mouth recommendations from volunteers that the charity behaves well to volunteers and is worth supporting. And if there is a selection procedure and a feeling that the charity has standards, this can make it even more attractive.

The key to the management of volunteers is to generate a spirit of enthusiasm, a belief that the effort given is worthwhile, and sense of recognition of the role they are playing. We know that the reasons people volunteer vary enormously. Only by exploring the main reasons in the particular situation does it become possible to find ways of ensuring that volunteers receive satisfaction from what they do.

Do not overlook the extent social interaction may play. People want to meet other people. Often people find it difficult to meet other like-minded souls, and voluntary work may be one such route. Most voluntary organizations are not meant to be social forums. But all work tends to serve a major social purpose for people, and a feeling of belonging can be a major reason for continuing to be a volunteer.

The effective volunteer must be prepared to leave behind his or her social or business position when working with a voluntary organization. Outside the organization the person may be a supervisor, a managing director or the world authority on a particular subject. Any natural inclination to take charge and give instructions must be sublimated, as must any feeling that more respect is due to such a person than to any other volunteer. Some will enjoy the absence of responsibility; others will find it irksome. Those with such managerial experience should try to use their knowledge to understand the difficulties that exist in running a voluntary organization, and use their good will to alleviate the difficulties.

Nowhere is leadership more important than dealing with volunteers. Remote head offices or desk-bound directors can spread a very negative message. The benefit of senior management spending time meeting the 'troops in the field' cannot be overstated. The lady of mature years who arranges flowers in a hospital ward or serves tea around the office must be made to feel as valued as the person who as a volunteer has a management role. The skills and talents each has to offer may be different, but what is common is that both are doing what they can to further the aims of the organization.

Some managers never forget a name. This can be a very valuable attribute in such situations. In the hospital case study, one of the negative feelings experienced by the volunteer is that her coordinator never recognized her when they passed in the corridor. Using names can personalize interaction and, if used sincerely, can make people feel valued. Volunteers who feel standards are slack, that anything goes and their contribution is not noticed or valued, are not going to give of their best. Volunteers who feel noticed, feel they are doing something worthwhile and are valued will be motivated to give more and raise their performance.

REFERENCES

Burnell, J (2001) *Managing People in Charities*, 2nd edn, ICSA, London

Charity Commission (1998) *Responsibilities of Charity Trustees*, Charity Commission, London

Georgiades, N and Macdonell, R (1998) *Leadership for Competitive Advantage*, Wiley, Chichester

Harbridge House Inc (1990) Ten universal qualities of effective managers, in *Key Issues in Management Training*, ed D Hussey and P Lowe, Kogan Page, London

Hersey, P and Blanchard, KH (1977) *Management of organisational behaviour: utilising human resources*, 3rd edn, Prentice-Hall, Englewood Cliffs, NJ

Lowe, P (1994) *Empowerment: What organisations really do*, Harbridge Consulting Group Ltd, London

Martin, P and Nicholls, J (1987) *Creating a Committed Workforce*, Institute of Personnel Management, London

Stace, DA and Dunphy, DC (1996) Translating business strategies into action: managing strategic change, in *The Implementation Challenge*, ed D Hussey, Wiley, Chichester

6

Financial accounting and record keeping

Although this chapter is written in the context of charities, almost the whole of it applies to all voluntary organizations. An understanding of accounting and the ability to understand financial reports are essential for every trustee and manager. Our experience is that many trustees do not have this knowledge; one solution to save embarrassment might be to offer private briefing and counselling.

About a third of charities do not submit their annual reports in good time or in some cases at all (NAO, 2001). Although the larger charities fully understand the value of accounts for management as well as the legal requirement to keep them, some of the smaller charities may not share this understanding. And even for the larger charities there is sometimes difficulty when authority is decentralized to volunteers, who may see record keeping as unnecessary red tape.

The legal requirements vary by country. Our comments are in a British context, and for charities legislation refer particularly to England and Wales; the term 'Charity Commission' refers particularly to the Charity Commission for England and Wales. Scotland has different legislation, although the principles are similar. Northern Ireland does not have regulations governing the form and content of accounts. In all four countries, there is a further variation if the charity is incorporated. If so, it also falls under certain requirements of the Companies Act.

Pause for reflection

Before continuing, spend a few moments thinking why the legislation has a requirement for charities to keep proper accounts. What are the various purposes of accounting?

There are many good reasons why proper accounts are essential, quite apart from wishing to avoid infringing the law. In fact, the accounting and reporting requirements of the law exist in part because of some of these reasons. We have grouped them under three main headings, of equal importance:

1. *Custodian.* Trustees and directors of charities have a legal duty to safeguard the assets of the charity, and anyone with a management responsibility also has this duty. This requires something more than a passive bean counting.
   - *Maintaining solvency.* We can offer a very selfish reason why trustees should be concerned about ensuring the continued solvency of the charity. If the charity is not also a limited company, the trustees become personally liable for any debts that the charity is unable to pay. Where the decision is properly made, all the trustees are jointly and severally liable, which means that, if one of them has no assets, the others have to pick up his or her share of the debt. When a charity is incorporated, that is registered as a company, it becomes a legal persona, and the directors cannot normally be pursued for its unpaid debts. There is a legal responsibility for the directors to maintain solvency, and it is an offence for them to allow the charity to continue to operate once it is insolvent. Obviously they are also personally liable if they have acted outside of their powers or have infringed the various laws in any way.

     Insolvency can take one of two forms. The first is when the liabilities of the charity exceed its assets. The second, and perhaps the most likely, event is when the charity cannot pay its debts. Any creditor can apply for the charity to be put into liquidation if the charity continually fails to respond to requests for payment on overdue accounts.

     The danger of insolvency is probably higher now than in the past, because more charities receive grants from various sources. It is not hard to see how a failure of the source to renew an expected grant, or even a delay in renewal, could make a charity insolvent almost immediately.

Accurate accounts, and a management control system that includes continuous reforecasting of cash flows on a month-by-month basis are essential tools for good financial management. They reduce the risk of taking decisions that lead to insolvency and increase the likelihood that actions can be taken if the forecasts suggest that a problem is developing. It goes without saying that accounts have to be produced monthly and on a timely basis.

– *Prevention of fraud or inappropriate use of assets.* Accounts are an essential tool for detecting internal fraud, although they have to be supported by clear policies and various checks and control procedures. Obviously the trustees and senior managers not only have to see and discuss the figures, but they have to understand them.

There have been charities established for fraudulent purposes, and the Charity Commission has various measures to try to detect this. More frequent is mishandling of money through inadequate accounting and the financial ignorance of trustees. Case study 6.1 is a Charity Commission report that shows that things can and do go wrong if the management and accounting controls are inadequate.

– *Care of assets.* Accounting can only help to a degree. Assets may be lost because somehow they have disappeared or because the people who operate them have abused them. In the latter case this may show up in abnormally high repair and replacement costs flowing through the accounts.

Accountants divide assets into two groups: current and fixed. The former are those items that are cash or will be turned into cash in the normal course of activities: inventories (stocks), trade debtors and marketable securities. Fixed assets are the items that are expected to last for several trading periods, such as buildings, computers, machinery and vehicles, and are in effect the things the charity uses to enable it to operate. The statement of recommended practice (SORP) issued by the Charity Commission suggests that property and other investments intended to be held for the long term should be treated as a separate category in the accounts under fixed assets.

Organizations should keep a register of fixed assets, which usually is maintained by the accountants. This details each significant asset, with date of acquisition, purchase price and accumulated depreciation. This may not seem very useful for a small charity, with very few fixed assets, but is critical for an organization like the National Trust, which has fixed assets spread across the whole country.

2. *Management direction and control.*
   - *Management control.* Looking after the organization's assets is one thing; looking after the business is quite another. We believe that it is impossible to manage a charity effectively unless it has a good budgetary control system, which reports variances against budget regularly, in a timely way and with careful explanations of the serious deviations. This should not be merely a method of being wise after the event, but should be forward-looking to anticipate and deal with problems.
   - *Decision making.* Management accounts are an essential aid to good decision making. Without access to real numbers, and the ability to assess the costs of a changed situation, much decision making would be guesswork.
3. *Communication with stakeholders.* Annual reports are public documents, which can be consulted by anyone. However, the report and accounts do something more than satisfy a legal requirement. They are one means of communicating to the stakeholders what the charity has done in the past year. This is so important that a number of charities put these documents on their Web sites so that anyone can read them. It is not only current supporters who may be interested; sometimes a person making a will and considering leaving a bequest to a charity may want to see these accounts. We would not argue that this should be the only way a charity should communicate to its stakeholders, but it is certainly one aspect of openness that is important.

Case study 6.1: Foundation for Nephrology Ltd (Registered Charity No 800194)

Introduction

1. This is a statement of the results of an Inquiry under section 8 of the Charities Act 1993.
2. The Foundation for Nephrology Ltd was established to relieve people

suffering from kidney disease. It did this by way of supporting hospitals treating kidney patients and by the funding of research.

3. The Commission's Inquiry, which commenced in July 1997, resulted from the Commission's active monitoring of the charity following concerns about the administration and management of the fund-raising operation which had been identified in an earlier inquiry into the charity.

Findings

Fund-raising operation – amounts raised for charity

1. The fund-raisers generated an income of **£4,754,842** from the public in the four years from 1 February 1996. However, only **£262,650** of this total was paid over to the charity, representing only 5.5% of total fund-raising income. In one accounting year no money whatsoever was passed over to the charity.

2. The remaining 94.5% of funds raised from the public went in supporting the fund-raising operation.

3. Included in the income for the fund-raising operation was a significant amount of charitable donations collected in cash from the public. These should have been applied in their entirety to the activities of the charity. Despite this, the fund-raising companies kept these funds as part of their income to use to defray their expenses.

4. In the period from 1 February 1999 to 31 December 1999, the Commission found that £244,000 of donations had been collected and improperly retained by Medical Aid (UK) Ltd, the company conducting the fund-raising during the relevant period.

5. The Commission considered that the cost structure of the fund-raising was excessive in proportion to the amounts passed to the Charity. Furthermore, charitable funds, which were the property of the charity and as such should have been handed over directly to the charity without any deductions, were not appropriately treated. We found therefore that the fund-raising operation retained charitable funds to which it had no legal entitlement. In the Commission's view, this was a clear abuse of the public's trust.

Relationship between the charity and the fund-raising operation

6. The charity conducted its fund-raising primarily through a fund-raising operation controlled by the Executive Chairman and the financial controller of the charity. The charity and the main fund-raising company Medical Aid (UK) Ltd shared office premises, staff, equipment and other resources and overheads. The division between the activities of the charity and the fund-raising operation were not kept separate and distinct, as they should have been.

7. The Commission was not satisfied that the allocation of costs and recharging of overheads were entirely accurate.

of control exercised over the charity and fund-raising operation by the trustees [*sic*]

8. The trustees are respected medical professionals, who determined how the income of the charity could best be applied for the relief of kidney patients and were responsible for administering the grants made by the charity. However, they relied upon their 'management team' of the Executive Chairman, who was not a member of the board or a trustee, and Financial Controller to supervise, monitor and control the relationship between the charity and the fund-raising operation.

9. The trustees had never met with the Auditors of the charity and exercised limited controls over the expenditure of the charity. The management team took on responsibility for these processes and decisions, including instructing the Auditors over the allocation of costs relating to fund-raising in the accounts.

10. The Commission found that both the Executive Chairman and the Financial Controller had personal financial interests in the fund-raising operations. As well as their salary from the charity, they had received payments from the fund-raising operation. Given that personal interest they were placed in a position of conflict which made it entirely inappropriate for them to act on behalf of the charity in the monitoring and supervision of the fund-raising activity.

Adherence to fund-raising legislation

11. When the inquiry commenced, the fund-raising was being conducted by companies which were professional fund-raisers as defined by the Charities Act 1992. The Commission found that the trustees and management team had failed to ensure that agreements were in place which would satisfy the requirements of that Act and the Charitable Institutions Fund Regulations 1994.

12. The Commission also found that Medical Aid (UK) Ltd, the name latterly given to the fund-raising operation, had failed to make solicitation statements to the public about their remuneration and the sums received by the charity as required by s 60 of the Charities Act 1992.

Charitable activity

13. Of **£7,121,491** raised from the public by the charity in four years (including the amounts detailed in para 3 for the fund-raising operation) charitable activity amounted to only **£725,439**. This amounts to only 10% of total income. Furthermore, included in this charitable activity are grants to a connected charity of £470,922. Therefore, charitable grants to independent organisations and charities amounted to only £254,517, or 3.5% of total income.

14. The cost structure of the charity and fund-raising operation included payments and benefits to the management team and their family that were regularly in excess of charitable expenditure.

15. The Commission found the total management and administration costs of the charity to be excessive.

Conclusions

19. The Commission reached the following conclusions from the Inquiry:
    - The level of return from the fund-raising company was unjustifiably low.
    - The activities of the charity and the fund-raising company were not sufficiently separated. This led to charitable resources being applied in support of non-charitable purposes.
    - The trustees had not exercised a sufficient degree of control of the management of the charity and its relationship with the fund-raising operations.

Outcomes

20. The Commission's detailed concerns were put to the trustees. They made a number of proposals aimed at addressing the concerns over the relationship with the trading company, including a proposal that Medical Aid (UK) Ltd become a wholly owned trading subsidiary of the charity. However, the underlying concern of the extremely low level of return from the fund-raising operation was not addressed by the trustees and management.

21. The Commission, therefore, met the trustees to discuss alternative proposals. The Trustees agreed that they did not have the financial expertise that the charity required and were unable to assess the financial viability of the fund-raising operation. They therefore welcomed the Commission's decision to appoint a Receiver and Manager.

22. On 29 March 2000, the Commission appointed Peter Engel of Solomon Hare Chartered Accountants as Receiver and Manager to the charity. His duties included managing the charity, conducting a review of fund-raising and deciding either to implement changes to reduce fund-raising overheads, or to wind up the charity.

23. Mr Engel came to the conclusion that:
    - it was impossible to reduce the high level of fund-raising costs to justify the charity continuing the fund-raising operation;
    - in the absence of alternative sources of funding the charity should wind up.

24. Upon the completion of the liquidation of this charity and the discharge of the Receiver and Manager, it is estimated that £150,000 will be distributed to other charities in this field.

Wider lessons

25. Trustees must be able to devote sufficient time to their duties to effectively monitor the actions of their senior employees.
26. Trustees also need to take an active interest in major fund-raising initiatives conducted by their charities, and to ensure that they are provided with sufficient data to make informed decisions about whether the net return is acceptable. If it is not, they should be prepared to take timely action to stop the fund-raising. The viability of the charity may also need to be considered in these circumstances.
27. Decisions such as whether a fund-raising initiative should continue should not be delegated to anyone who has a financial interest in its continuation.

(Charity Commission for England and Wales, Crown copyright 2001)

We will look at some of the above issues later in this chapter, but first we should spend some time on revealing the mysteries of the accountant's trade. Obviously accountants and many managers will already have this basic knowledge, but for everyone who does not it is essential for the interpretation of accounts.

CONCEPTS OF ACCOUNTING

We follow the list of 11 standard, long-established, universally recognized concepts in the order used by Anthony and Reece (1983). In the UK the list is usually compressed to fewer headings, but the overall content is basically the same:

● *Money measurement.* Accounts include only information that can be expressed in terms of money, which means that, although the accounts convey a great deal of information, there may be even more important facts that are not included. Extra information can be provided in the notes to the annual financial accounts, but these are usually about matters that directly affect the figures, such as the explosion of a summarized heading to provide extra information, or any other information needed to understand the accounts properly. This is partly why charities are asked to make an annual report, which is expected to show other information to help explain the charity and its effectiveness, such as the extent to which its activities depend on a continuation of significant volunteer support or the renewal of a large grant. The organizational structure may be creaking, one of the key managers may be incompetent and there may be a boardroom battle over specific policies, but none of this will appear in the accounts.

- *The entity concept.* The accounts relate to an entity and not the people who are associated with the organization. We know from practical experience how difficult it is to make a self-employed person see that his or her business accounts, and the assets reflected therein, have to be kept quite separately from the personal accounts. Bill Smith may be legally liable for the debts of Bill Smith Plumbers, but this does not mean that he can mix his personal bank account up with that of the business. The same concept applies to a charity. There is a temptation for a small charity not to be clearly separated in every aspect from the affairs of its founding trustees, and this includes not just the accounts but also the bank accounts, cash receipts and payments, and all transactions. Apart from the personal danger in which this places trustees, it may make it impossible to prepare accurate accounts for the charity.

- *Going concern.* In most circumstances the accounts are prepared on the basis that the charity is a going concern and will continue to operate in the future. The exception would be if a charity were set up with a finite life for a particular purpose, or if a charity were to become insolvent. The main impact of the going concern principle is that things are valued on the basis of what they cost, not what they would be worth if you had to sell them. With a few exceptions, there is no need continuously to revalue assets to reflect their current market price.

- *The cost concept.* The cost an accountant records in the books is what was paid or received for an item. For fixed assets, which are expected to last a number of years, the value in the books is depreciated under the matching principle (see later). Other exceptions are land, buildings and shares held purely as investments, where the value is periodically adjusted to reflect market value.

- *Double-entry accounting.* The great invention of accountants around 1300 was double-entry bookkeeping. This was not a job creation scheme for accountants intended to double their work opportunities. It is a principle that makes life much easier, even if it is difficult to remember whether the debit side is on the right- or the left-hand side (the convention is that it is the left). At the root of the concept is the fundamental accounting equation

ASSETS (debits) = EQUITIES (credits). Equities are made up of two different things, liabilities and owners' equity (or in charity terms 'funds'). In the simplest of terms the process can be illustrated with the purchase of a computer for cash at a cost of £1,700. There is a liability to pay for the computer so our current cash balance, which is an asset, is reduced by this liability (an entry of the credit side). However, we now own the computer, which is an asset, so we set up an account for this, entering the amount on the debit side. This one transaction has caused two entries.

If all the debits in the books are added up, they should equal all the credits. This trial balance, as it is called, gives a quick check for errors. If the two sides do not balance, there has clearly been an error, and this gives an opportunity to find it. Of course if they do balance, there can still be an error, which could be unrelated amounts of equal value or a transaction may have a debit and credit entry but the accounts they have been entered in are wrong. An example is if we had entered out computer as a trade debt instead of a fixed asset. The two columns would balance, but there would still be an error.

- *Time period.* A going concern hopes to be operating if not for ever at least for several years. This means that accounts have to be looked at in time periods, so that the results of activity can be established. The normal accounting period for reporting is 12 months from the start date selected by the entity. This year is divided into smaller accounting periods. Typically these are either the 12 calendar months, which have the disadvantage that they are not all the same length, or sometimes 13 accounting 'months', which gives a more standardized length of time. The intermediate periods should be chosen to suit the control needs of the organization, because clearly waiting a year before the charity knows what is going on would mean that the trustees and managers could not perform their duties in managing and administering the entity. At the end of the year a line is drawn under the results of the activities of the charity, and the net effects transferred to the year-end balance sheet.

- *Prudence.* The principle is that a conservative view is always taken in the accounts, which gives rise to many arguments between managers and accountants. Accountants will not recognize an income figure until it has happened. For example, a trading company like that owned by the Woodland Trust may have secured a contract to manage a woodland, starting in the next year. Although the books may record the order for management control purposes, they will not recognize the value as an income at this point. Even if the contract provided for a sum to be paid on signing the contract this would not be recognized as an income for the current year. It would appear as a liability in the balance sheet for this year, because an obligation was owed that had not yet been settled.

But if there is some bad news around, like an expected large bill for electricity that relates to the year but has not yet arrived, this should go into the accounts even though the exact amount of the cost is not known. And the accountant is likely to take a much more conservative view of what the cost impact will be than most managers.

● *Realization concept.* This is about when the accounts should recognize an item. If we continue our example of the management contract, and are now on the first day of the new year, can we now recognize the revenue? After all we have the money. The accounting answer is still no. Revenue can only be recognized in the period when goods are delivered to the customer or a service delivered. So what would happen in practice is that the revenue would be recognized at intervals during the year, as the contract is fulfilled. Obviously there are issues to be decided, like how to determine how much of the contract has been completed each year, and there are accounting standards for dealing with long-running contracts, but the basic principle holds good.

● *Matching concept.* Realization is related to the matching concept, which in part is about ensuring that revenue for a period is matched to the costs associated with achieving that revenue. The idea behind this is to ensure that funds are not unduly deflated or inflated because income and expenditure are not matched. There is another manifestation of this concept. When a fixed asset is purchased its value goes into the books as described earlier. However, this would cause enormous distortions if every fixed asset was treated as an expense and immediately charged against income. It could, particularly if there was an especially large capital expenditure in any one year, make it look as if the charity was spending far too much on its management and administration.

The matching concept solves this problem. Instead of charging the whole capital expenditure as an expense, only a proportion is charged. For example, if the fixed asset was expected to last 10 years, only 10 per cent of its costs might be taken as an expense. There are in fact several different ways of calculating this proportion, the technical name for which is depreciation. In the books there is a credit entry to enable the current depreciated value of the asset to be calculated, and a debit entry to increase an expense account called depreciation.

There are two points to make about depreciation. The first is to dispel the myth that it is to provide a fund to replace an asset when it is worn out: the concept is not about replacement but about matching costs to the right period. The second is that there is no cash outlay associated with a depreciation charge, because the money was spent when the asset was purchased. So we have here an expense that does not reduce liquid assets, which helps to explain why commercial organizations that own high-value assets like oil refineries, ships and aeroplanes may not see their liquid assets reduced even if they make a loss. Obviously it depends on the size of the loss, and what has happened to other items that affect cash flow, but depreciation itself causes no further outflow of cash.

- *Consistency.* Accounts are intended to provide accurate information, and to enable period-to-period comparisons to be made. Consistency is very important. For example, if there are two expense accounts, one called computer supplies and the other stationery, it is important that clear rules are established about what each means. Under which would ink-jet cartridges be charged? Whatever decision is made should be followed consistently thereafter, so that like can be compared with like, and if the information is important to management for the trends to be tracked. There are numerous accounting policies, such as depreciation, the valuation of stocks and the calculation of bad debt provisions, where the calculation method used lies within the discretion of the entity. However, the method has to be used consistently year after year. If there comes a point when it really has to change (for example, if two charities with different policies merge), the notes to the year-end accounts are expected to mention the change and illustrate what effect it has had.

- *Materiality.* The final concept is that the accounting policies adopted should concentrate on what is significant. For example, it is undoubtedly true that an office stapler costing around £5 is an asset of the company and will last longer than most much more expensive assets. Does this mean that we should put it in a special account as a fixed asset, and charge a few pence depreciation each year? The answer is that the issue is so trivial that treating it as an expense item when first purchased does not distort the final results by any significant amount and makes them easier to relate to because the reports have not wasted time on something that does not matter. However, in this example the fact that the amount is small does not mean that we should leave it out of the books altogether. An amount of £5 has gone out of the entity and £5 has been added to one account or another, and there may be thousands of small items like this in the course of a year. We would just lump it in with our other stationery and not waste any more time on it. What is material varies with the size of the transaction and the size of the entity.

Pause for reflection

Think of these principles in relation to your organization. Try to find examples of how they are applied. Do they change your own previous views about accounting?

ACCRUAL OR CASH ACCOUNTING?

The foregoing concepts describe the accrual method of accounting, which is enshrined in the Companies Act and in tax law. It means 'that all income and charges relating to a financial year shall be taken into account, without regard to date of receipt or payment' (Parker, 1984). The accounts thus reflect a true and fair view of the state of the entity at the time they are drawn up. Although the quotation refers to a year, in practice it means all the time, and the same principles apply during the year.

All charities with an annual gross income of £100,000 and above are required to keep their accounts on an accrual basis. There are concessions for charities below this figure, which may keep their accounts on a cash basis, and this also applies under the Companies Act if they are incorporated. In Scotland, the limit of discretion is reduced to £25,000 under the Charities Accounts (Scotland) Regulations.

Cash-based accounting ignores the realization and matching concepts, and the accounts take note of income and expenses only at the time they are paid for, which means that some of the items in any year's accounts may refer to a prior or future year. If a charity's only role is to receive donations and then pass them on to a particular cause at the end of each month, there is probably little difference in what the two methods reveal. For any charity that does more than this the deviation can be significant. What this means in terms of the annual reports will be returned to later.

RECORD KEEPING

The basis of accounting is record keeping. Firstly this means transactions should be supported by written evidence, such as invoices, bank statements and expense claims, and internal authorizations (copies of board minutes, requisitions and the like) both for purchases and for the disbursement of funds. These documents become the foundation for the figures that go into the accounts, and provide evidence for auditors and charity inspectors. It is good practice to put a transaction number on each document and to record this against the entry in the accounts. This helps to establish an audit trail, and to keep an orderly system.

When the first known book on accounting appeared in the 15th century, quill pens and parchment were the norm, which was an improvement over tally sticks and wax tablets. Through most of the 20th century organizations kept their accounts in ledgers, large books into which the information was recorded. Some still use this system. Then computers came in and accounts were held in electronic form, with printouts as needed. The personal computer has put electronic accounting into the hands of even the smallest organization.

Our laws require accounting records to be retained for a number of years, and records in this sense are all the supporting documentation plus the ledgers into which the books are written (in paper or electronic form). Where records are kept in electronic form, it is essential that they are backed up, and the back-up should ideally be stored in a safe place on different premises.

The heart of the accounting system is the chart of accounts. This is a list of all the accounts in the entity's ledgers, and shows the scheme of classification used by the entity. For charities some of the headings are constrained by the statement of recommended accounting practice: obviously it has to be possible to produce financial accounts that match these headings. However, these are mainly summary accounts, and the chart of accounts should also show the detailed accounts that go into each. For example, the annual return has a recommended one-line entry for cash at bank and in hand: this could be an addition of cash held in various offices, and a number of bank accounts. Control would be next to impossible unless there were also separate accounts for each.

A final division is into different types of ledger, such as the personal ledger for the accounts for debtors and creditors, and a nominal ledger for accounts that deal with income and expenses.

In effect the chart of accounts is both an outline description of the accounting system and an index to all the accounts. Setting it up calls for considerable thought, so that it reflects the legal, financial control and management information needs of the entity.

SOME LEGAL REQUIREMENTS

Reference has been made to the legal aspects, and some of these have been mentioned in more detail. All charities have to keep accounts. In England and Wales, charities with an income of under £1,000 and no permanent endowment do not have to register with the Commission. Those with an income of under £10,000 need only submit annual reports and accounts to the Charity Commission if requested to do so, but their accounts have to be able to provide the appropriate information. Once this limit is reached all charities have to lodge accounts with the Commission.

The Charities Commission has detailed guidance notes for the statement of recommended accounting practice for both cash and accrual accounting, and has specimen forms for the various year-end accounts and reports. These can be downloaded from its Web site (http://www.charity-commission.gov.uk). Randall (2001) provides a concise guide to the legal requirements for charity accounting.

SUPPORTING PROCEDURES

Charity Commission (2001) has prepared an excellent summary of the importance and nature of the internal controls needed. Part of the control is exercised not only through the records themselves, including the substantiating documentation, but also through how the tasks are divided up inside the charity, and the system of approvals for purchases, payments to creditors and the disbursements of funds. The document discusses the argument that charities can operate on the basis of trust, and do not need control procedures:

> While this may be the ideal situation, it is not realistic. Charities are unusual organisations in that they are management for the beneficiaries of that charity, rather than for the benefit of shareholder/members. It is advisable therefore that trustees be able to show to both donors and beneficiaries that the property is safe. Without the ability to show that checks and controls have been implemented it would not be possible to offer that security.

Case study 6.2: No one would steal from a hospice

Petworth Drive in Horsham has achieved a level of publicity over the years, as the whole street puts up lights and decorations over the Christmas period. These attract several thousands of visitors, many of whom make donations to the local hospice, St Catherine's, through a collecting box that is placed within a nativity scene as part of the street's decorations. In 2000 this box raised nearly £2,000.

The *West Sussex County Times* on 4 January 2002 reported that on the Friday before Christmas 2001 the box was raided by thieves, who used bolt cutters to open the box. Fortunately the box had been emptied regularly, and was believed to contain very little cash. However, the residents of the street have since installed a surveillance camera as an additional security measure.

There is a message here for anyone who believes that no one would steal from a charity or a church. Unfortunately there are too many people who would.

In reality sound control procedures offer some personal security to staff and volunteers. If they are followed correctly, and if fraud does take place or there is theft, it makes it easier for individuals to clear themselves of suspicion. Where procedures are lax, the innocent may have little ability to clear themselves, and the atmosphere can be poisoned if everyone feels they are under threat of being falsely accused.

The trustees have a responsibility to oversee the record keeping and control system, but can delegate, provided this is done in a responsible way. However, they remain responsible for ensuring that control is exercised. The delegated powers should be clearly set out in a written document, and it should be totally clear which decisions with financial consequences can be taken by management and which by the board or a subcommittee of the board.

When designing a control procedure it is wise to think in terms of the tasks that have to be undertaken and not in terms of the current people who undertake those tasks. In this way it is possible to think out the areas of vulnerability, where procedures are needed to protect the assets, without obscuring the issue by the fact that the individuals are known and fully trusted. Think where the risks are, and for the time being forget the fact that you have complete faith in the integrity of the people. Obviously one aspect of control is in selecting people who are expected to have the competence to do the job expected, and to be trustworthy, but this should be in addition to making every-thing as secure as it is humanly possible to do.

The areas of risk should be considered in relation to the nature of the charity and its organization and reporting structure. Common sense should be enough to think through the vulnerable areas and to grade the dangers. Here are a few principles to consider when setting up or reviewing internal control procedures:

● Try to split responsibilities so that more than one person is responsible for handling the various aspects of a single transac-tion. An example is payments for purchases, where the person who has authorized the purchase should not also write and sign the cheques, and enter the transactions in the books. In practice, the purchase would be authorized by a manager (assuming it is within his or her delegated powers), the bookkeeping would be undertaken by someone in accounts and accounts would draw up the cheque. The cheque itself should be signed by two autho-rized people, whose role is not just to sign but to check that the amounts paid are valid. In this way the opportunity for fraud is reduced and, possibly as important, there is double checking at various stages to reduce the chance of error.

● When mail is likely to include cash and cheques, ensure that it is opened promptly and in the presence of two people. Ensure that any cash and cheques received are immediately recorded by one person and checked by another, that both sign they have done this and, if the money is given to a third person to bank, it is signed for by that person.

● Bank all cash and cheques as soon as possible. To preserve the audit trail the whole amount received should be banked, even if cash has to be withdrawn at the same time for petty cash or other valid purposes. Secure storage facilities should be provided for any money that has to remain on the premises overnight.

- Those charities operating shops, cafés and the like should ensure that the takings are checked and banked daily, and that little or no money remains on the premises overnight. Security measures against shoplifting should be operated as justified. Security measures are also essential when the charity owns valuable antiques and paintings in buildings that are open to the public (for example, the National Trust).
- Particular care is needed over the procedures for collection boxes and fund-raising events. Charity Commission (2001) offers extensive guidance on both.
- Check the petty cash regularly, particularly in any decentralized operations.
- Ensure that proper procedures are written so that there is total clarity about who should authorize purchases and disbursements, including expense claims by staff and (if permitted) volunteers.
- Ensure that all the internal control policies and procedures are not only available in writing but explicitly made known to all staff and relevant volunteers.
- Rotate staff and volunteers where possible so that the same people are not always exercising the same internal control tasks. Ensure that all staff and volunteers who handle money, record keeping or accounting take regular periods of leave from the office.
- Remember that regular reporting of results against budgets (see the next chapter) can sometimes show if problems are occurring.
- Be willing to obtain specific professional advice to set up or audit existing procedures. This is likely to be a qualified accountant for the internal control processes, and a security adviser for the security of shops and premises.
- Trustees should ensure that there are periodic checks to confirm that the laid-down procedures are being followed.

Big, decentralized charities have particular problems because of the wide dispersion of people who receive money for and spend on behalf of the charity. The numerous areas and groups of the Ramblers' Association mean that there are at least 500 different centres in addition to the main head office.

Small charities have a different sort of problem, in that they may have insufficient volunteers and staff to provide all the double checks listed above. Here it may be even more necessary to assess the areas of high vulnerability and ensure that these are covered, and for the trustees to exercise extra vigilance over what is going on. There is a temptation in very small charities for a trustee to use his or her own bank account for charity income and expenditure, or to 'live out of the till', using incoming cash to meet immediate outgoing needs, because this appears to save time and effort. Either of these actions will confuse the audit trail and make control close to impossible, and may make it impossible for the trustees to prove that they have properly exercised their responsibilities.

Not all theft and fraud are premeditated and deliberate. Sometimes it is a spur-of-the-moment action, driven by an individual's need to pay an unexpected bill. It often sucks the individual in further as additional frauds are carried out to conceal the first one.

Case study 6.3: A failure of a control system

One charity investigated by the Charity Commission in 2000 was established by Royal Charter, with one of its main activities the giving of support and advice to a number of independent charities across the UK, all with a related sphere of activity. The charity has two non-charitable trading companies and a significant number of paid staff.

On 21 February 2000, the attention of the honorary secretary was drawn to a number of suspected abuses by the managing director. The trustees suspended the managing director, informed the Charity Commission and instructed the auditors to undertake an investigation. As a result of the auditors' report, the managing director was interviewed by a disciplinary board, and left the charity at the end of March. The Charity Commission inquiry was opened as a result of the auditors' report.

The issues included:

- The organization's credit card was used for personal expenditure on non-business transactions, including withdrawals of cash that were not subsequently accounted for.
- A second car was purchased for the managing director's personal use, without justification, the car issued to him as part of his employment package being then used by his wife.
- In 1998 the previous auditors had queried cash withdrawals of £4,000, and costs of nearly £12,000, which were said to have been expended by the managing director on behalf of one of the client charities and for which no supporting evidence had been produced.

- A number of senior managers had cars as part of their package, but this had not been reported to the Inland Revenue. When the Inland Revenue caught up with the personal tax liability for these managers, which included the managing director, the obligation for all was settled with an unauthorized payment from charity funds.
- The managing director had approved loans without going through the loans committee.
- He had also authorized repayment of a security bond to a private company involved with the charity, without having the authority to do so. He had been giving considerable time to this company, and it was found that he was on its payroll while still working for the charity.
- It was found impossible to judge the quality of much of the work he had undertaken, although there were some improvements that he had made to the charity.

The trustees took legal action against the managing director for the recovery of misapplied funds, and judgement was given in favour of the charity in July.

The Charity Commission does not expect trustees to check every transaction, and it is important that there is trust between the trustees and senior managers who are properly empowered to do their jobs. In this case, the trustees had veered too much the other way, and had not ensured that there were adequate internal controls; nor had they ensured that those that were there were followed. There was laxness in not taking action earlier, when irregularities were brought to their attention by the previous auditors. It was not enough to rely on the annual audit to detect fraud. No spot checks had been made to ensure that procedures were followed.

As a result of the enquiry, the charity took seven major steps, establishing a risk management strategy, financial standing orders, an investment policy and an internal audit committee, setting up anti-fraud procedures, and publishing a staff handbook that included staff appraisal processes, and a policy document on such things as the use of mobile phones, travel and subsistence, and working from home.

Pause for reflection

Hindsight is useful in seeing what went wrong, but effective internal control requires foresight. Could the problems revealed in the case study occur in your organization? How effective are the internal control procedures? Could they be improved?

SETTING UP AN ACCOUNTING SYSTEM

Record keeping is a fairly simple task once a system has been set up. However, designing and establishing a system is a daunting task for anyone not familiar with accounting, even with all the valuable documentation available from the Charity Commission. And if the system is not set up properly, chaos can result. Similarly, professional help may be desirable in establishing internal control procedures.

Anyone establishing a new charity, or any existing charity that has problems with accounting, should obtain help from a qualified person. If it is not possible to afford a paid employee to perform this important function, volunteer help should be obtained. Fortunately there are a lot of qualified accountants around. The charity REACH (www.volwork.org.uk) is one possible source, through its register, which includes retired accountants and non-retired people with time to spare. Another is to seek help from one of the local businesses, which may be willing to second someone to undertake this initial task. Many charities find volunteers from personal contacts in the local community.

Entering the records in the accounts is a clerical job, but requires an understanding of accounting and an empathy with numbers. It has to be done regularly; otherwise control is impossible. This basic book-keeping could be undertaken if necessary by a less-well-qualified volunteer. However, the need for higher skills again appears for completing the year-end accounts and returns, and for tasks such as budgetary control systems, so if it is possible to obtain ongoing help from the volunteer who sets up the systems this would be the best option.

For larger charities, accounting becomes so much a part of day-to-day management that full-time help is needed, which is likely to mean at least one paid employee.

Accounting may seem a chore, but it is an essential part of running an effective charity. In the next chapter we explore some of the aspects of management accounting that go beyond the legally based requirements but are equally important for success.

REFERENCES

Anthony, RN and Reece, JS (1983) *Accounting Text and Cases*, 7th edn, Irwin, Homewood, IL

Charity Commission (2001) *Internal Financial Controls for Charities*, Charity Commission for England and Wales, London

National Audit Office (NAO) (2001) *Giving Confidently: The role of the Charity Commission in regulating charities*, October, NAO, London

Parker, RH (ed) (1984) *Macmillan Dictionary of Accounting*, Macmillan, London

Randall, AJL (2001) *The ICSA Guide to Charity Accounting*, ICSA, London

7

Management accounting

In this chapter management control and the use of accounting data in decision making are discussed. The umbrella term for this is management accounting, which is defined by Parker (1984) as: 'That part of accounting which is concerned mainly with internal reporting to the managers of an enterprise. It emphasizes the control and decision-making rather than the stewardship aspects of accounting.'

There are few legal constraints, and accounts can be prepared in any way that management finds useful. Estimates can be included, and the accounting system becomes a source of information from which various calculations can be made to assess the financial implications of certain types of decision. Both managers and accountants can use the information in this way.

Part of the skill is to produce management reports that are meaningful: it is possible to offer totally accurate figures that are meaningless. They can be made more useful if the current figures are compared to those of a past period, and to a budget or plan, and include an analysis of past trends. Ratios, such as costs per unit or time per unit, can bring more meaning to a table of figures, and again trends can be helpful. Comparisons between operations in different areas of an organization may show up issues that should be addressed, and useful comparisons can sometimes be made with other organizations that do similar things. Successes and failures should be analysed and studied.

BUDGETARY CONTROL

Introduction

The annual budget is one of the oldest tools of management control. It is a form of plan for the forthcoming year, and for this reason should have a close relationship with the strategy the charity is following. A weakness of some budgetary control systems is that budgets are set without regard to the strategy, and instead each successive budget is based on what happened the previous year adjusted for inflation. We need to do better than this.

Budgets should be based on what realistically can be achieved. There are two faults to avoid. The first is when a boss insists on a budget that is totally unattainable: all this does is cause the organization to run into crisis after crisis. It may be politically expedient for the boss, but it does harm to the organization and destroys motivation. The second fault is to veer too much the other way, and set budgets that will be exceeded by a wide margin. A budget should stretch managers somewhat, but must still be seen as attainable.

Although the budget may begin with a view of the whole year, it has to be broken down to a period basis. We will assume this to be 12 periods that match the calendar months (in some very small charities four periods of three months each may be adequate). A monthly budget gives the ability to compare progress with what has actually happened, and helps to direct the attention of the board and senior managers to areas where there is under- or overperformance. This immediately brings us face to face with another problem. If all we do to produce figures for each month is to divide the total by 12, it is likely that we will always be above or below budget, and until we get to month 12 we will have little control. So each monthly budget should be an attempt to show what we actually expect will happen during each and every month, so the action can be taken much earlier if things are not working out as planned.

At board level, the initial focus is of course on the budget for the whole charity. In a small charity this may be all that is needed. However, once the organization gets a little complex and the size of the figures increases, there is a need for subsidiary budgets to stand behind the main budget. This is partly so that various managers can be held accountable for controlling their part of the budget, and partly so that there is detailed information to help the management of the charity see and deal with issues. We will look at this in more detail later, but a simple example may be of help here. The National

Trust owns numerous properties, which incur expense and produce income. If these were always added together and presented as one figure, the board would not know where to start looking if total costs were up and revenue down. The appearance would be of a universal problem, whereas in actual fact all the problem properties might lie in one region and those in the rest of the country may have been doing better than budget. A remedial action that applied to the whole country could cause problems in the well-performing properties, and could well be inadequate to deal with the issues in the badly performing ones.

Outline of a budget process

Figure 7.1 suggests a generalized view of how to develop and use a budget. The detail of this will vary with the nature of the activities undertaken, the number of branches and the size of the charity. Although we are not able to encompass all these differences, Figure 7.1 does provide the bare bones of what is involved. The model builds from the strategic planning models described earlier, and indeed the strategy provides our starting point.

Strategic guidelines

The annual budget should be one of the tools that helps the charity achieve its longer-term strategies by breaking them down into what is effectively a short-term plan. It follows that this can only be done if there is clarity over what these strategies are and if management has determined which elements will be implemented during the forthcoming year. The guidelines to those involved in the budgeting process are partly about this, but they are also about keeping other actions and initiatives within the framework of the strategy. In small charities, thinking through the guidelines in relation to the new budget is likely to be an informal process, as only a few people are involved. As the charity increases in size, so does the need to ensure that every person who has some involvement in preparing the budget is thinking and planning in a way that is compatible with what management wishes to do.

Assumptions

Quite separate from the strategy are the assumptions that need to be drawn up so that budgets that may be prepared in various units of the strategy have the same underlying base of logic. One such

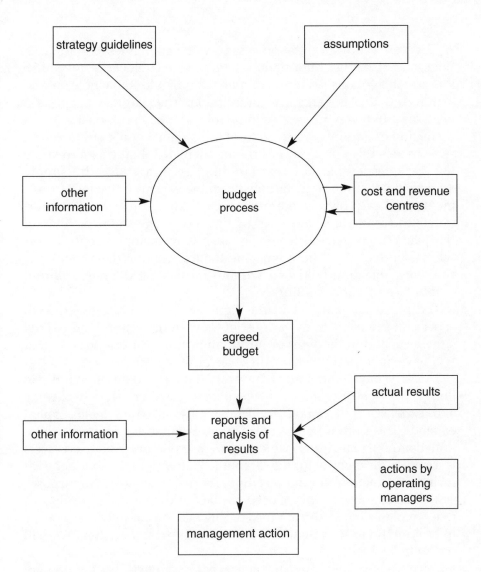

Figure 7.1   *Outline budgetary process*

assumption might be about the rate of staff salary increases that
should be used in the budget. Another might be for any rent
increases that are currently under negotiation. There may be a central
assumption to be used in the budget about the renewal of a grant
during the forthcoming year (or it may be prudent to prepare two
sets of budgets, with management actions, one assuming renewal
and the other assuming the opposite).

Budget process

As Figure 7.1 indicates, the process uses the guidelines and assumptions, and also other information that may have relevance. Of course it is possible for one person to prepare a budget for the whole organization, but this is generally undesirable. The diagram suggests a need for a two-way process with people who have responsibility for managing or administering a part of the organization's activities. We will discuss this box later. For the moment we should like to stress the dynamic tension between building up to a budget by simply adding together the contributions from the various units and departments, and carrying out the process by finding a way for the direction of the centre to be leavened by the knowledge and experience of the whole management team. The task is to maintain control over what is budgeted, without ignoring the information that other parts of the organization hold and without preventing the delegation of authority and responsibility.

The process illustrated in the figure is the melding together of aspects of the plans from various levels with the visions and overall strategies, and in the light of information from various sources that will have an impact on either the costs or the revenues.

This is a convenient time to draw attention to two different types of budgets. Much of what has been discussed so far refers to income and expenses, but organizations may also need to make capital expenditures from time to time. These of course are part of an integrated annual plan, but as we saw earlier, expenditure on fixed assets is treated differently in the accounts. Although the budget will include calculations for depreciation, for cash management purposes as well as overall control we need to plan for the capital expenditures that we plan to meet during the coming year. Separately there needs to be a method for evaluating such expenditures, something we will return to later.

Once we have these two different types of budgets, we can prepare a projected balance sheet for the year end. This leads to another budget document, a projected cash flow statement, so that there is less chance of things going wrong because we have been unable to manage our liquid resources.

As mentioned earlier, all this information has to be broken down into operating periods. Although we may not have much direct use for a monthly balance sheet, all the other different components of the total budget are needed on a period basis, so that the process can be used to control the affairs of the charity.

Other information

An example is a known fact that will change a cost or revenue compared to the previous year, such as a switch to a new energy provider, which will mean that the rate per unit of energy will fall. This information is different from the assumptions, in that it is already a known factor.

Cost and revenue centre managers

All except the smallest of charities will have an organizational structure, even if no one has ever written it out as a chart. The budget should follow this structure to a degree, and seek some involvement from those people who have responsibility either for managing significant costs or for managing significant revenue streams. (This does not imply that managers of revenue streams are not also responsible for costs.) In larger organizations there may be several levels of management responsibility, and the first point to decide is how to cut up the organization for budget purposes, including how many levels of budget are needed for effective control.

Examples will make this clearer. Take the shops of the trading company of a charity such as Oxfam. There would certainly be a need for a budget for the whole of the retailing activity, and there is no doubt there should be a manager who is responsible for all this activity and who should be involved in the preparation of its budgets. In addition we should want to be able to look at what is going on in each shop, so there is also a need to prepare a budget for every shop. Although there is a need to be able to assess the economic contribution of each shop, the key to whether we should involve shop managers in the budgetary process depends on their responsibilities. What is it that they can be held responsible for managing? It may be every aspect of the shop, but it may be much less. So, although for motivational reasons the shop managers should see the budget and reports for their shops, the role they are responsible for may be much less than the whole. Typically in a network like this, certain expenses may be outside their sphere of responsibility. For example, the lease of the shop may be arranged centrally, and the rent may never be under the control of the shop manager. The number and salaries of paid staff may also be determined centrally. In these situations a manager may be able to influence sales levels and gross margins, and prevent pilfering, but may only be able marginally to affect most of the costs. So the manager can affect results, but cannot control many of the costs that enable the final profit to be struck. In this case shop managers can only fairly be asked to help set the budget for the things for which they do have full responsibility, and the rest should be a given (for them). However, if the individual shop managers had the freedom to change premises, or increase or decrease the level of paid staff, they could fairly be held responsible for every aspect of their budget, and their level of involvement would be greater.

What also has to be considered is responsibility centres within a head office unit. Let us imagine that the charity is large enough to have a human resources department, and that this is structured into an overall responsibility centre, which reserves specific strategic tasks to itself, and two subsidiary departments, one dealing with training and the other with HR administration. If this were a small unit we would have only one budget for the whole department. However, if it were large, there might be one budget for the whole, and two subsidiary budgets, one for each department. In the former case we might expect the HR manager to play a role in preparing the budget, but in consultation with the two under-managers. In the latter case, the under-managers might be responsible for preparing an initial budget for their departments and then agreeing this with the overall manager who has responsibility for the entire department. What finally goes through may be modified from what the under-managers wanted, but the difference should be discussed and the reasons fully understood.

The managers of the various responsibility centres would receive the strategic guidelines and assumptions, plus a schedule that shows the revenue and cost account headings under which the budget is to be organized, plus an extra schedule for listing capital expenditure needs. By its nature the next year's budget has to be prepared before the year starts, so the schedule should also provide information to help in the budget preparation, such as a column showing the current year's budget, year-to-date results and the forecast to the year end.

However, although the budget comes together as figures, it only makes sense if thought about in terms of projects and actions. A second part of the budget should list the main actions to be taken during the forthcoming year to support the strategy. It is also useful to use a matrix approach that, besides including the total budget for each account heading, adds a number of columns to show what is budgeted for particular key projects. An example might be if three specific fund-raising initiatives are planned for the next year. This would give rise to four columns, one showing the costs and revenues budgeted to arise from ongoing activities and the other showing a similar picture for each of the new initiatives.

We would advise budgeting the projects or initiatives on an incremental basis, that is showing only the additional costs that would be incurred and the revenue that would result. If all the costs are apportioned across the projects, it becomes unclear what the economic effect might be if one is abandoned, because some costs will be in the business whether or not the initiative goes ahead. We will return to issues of decision evaluation later.

All the responsibility centre managers send in their budgets to the central budget manager. This frequently results in discussion and almost invariably some revision as an attempt is made to balance revenues and costs and at the same time to keep the whole budget in line with the strategy.

From this description it is possible to see that for a small charity the task is much simpler than for a large one. But why should anyone bother to complicate the issue by involving other managers? We could do all the calculations centrally and then tell them what their budgets are.

There are good reasons:

● In all except the smallest of organizations other managers and key people have information about things that will affect the budget that are not known elsewhere in the organization. This is a way of tapping into this knowledge.
● Successful management requires effective delegation. It is not easy to get this unless the manager has reasonable responsibility to determine how his or her role is carried out. To have no role in setting the budget would mean that there is no role in deciding how to carry out the delegated responsibility.
● The above point means that motivation is impaired if managers have no role in setting budgets, and improved when they do, even if as so often happens the final figures are arrived at through a negotiation between what they want and what top management feels can be done.
● As organizations get larger, the control process also has to be delegated, although those at the top never lose their overall responsibility. Of course, it is possible to hand managers their budget, and still hold them accountable for achieving it. However, this provides lots of reasons, many of which are valid, that can be used to justify a failure to keep to the budget. Everything that goes wrong can be blamed on the person who set the budget for not taking facts that 'everyone knew about' into account. When managers are involved, they are forced to accept

responsibility and accountability, and are much more likely to manage their units so that they keep to budget.

The agreed budget

Simply adding up all the budgets from the rest of the organization may not produce a valid budget, and as mentioned above there is usually a process of negotiation where top management tries to contain the budget. These meetings should be robust. It is unwise for top management simply to cross out items without a discussion, for both practical and motivational reasons. Unless the discussion takes place, serious mistakes can arise. Those we have seen include accepting a revenue figure but crossing out an expense figure essential to secure part of that revenue. An example is accepting a planned increase in donations from companies but refusing to accept the cost of an additional fund-raiser, without which the revenue cannot be achieved. A variation of this type of problem is agreeing the revenue and cost budget, but refusing to allow the capital expenditure essential if the budget is to be achieved. This negotiation may involve looking at alternative ways of achieving if not the same thing then at least something better than simply removing an item.

When the management has agreed the budget, it still has to be agreed by the board. If the job has been done well, the board should be able to agree it but should be given the opportunity of fully understanding it. Just dumping schedules of figures in front of trustees, some of whom may not be used to examining figures, is not helpful. They should be taken through the budget and its supporting actions to ensure that approval also means that it is understood.

Reports and analysis of results

We have already mentioned that the budget should be broken down into accounting periods. Let us assume that the budget has been approved, and we have now completed the first month's activities. The first thing we need is a format for reporting our progress against the budget. The revenue and expense headings will have been determined when the budget was set up. Imagine them running down the left-hand side of the form. What columns of figures should we put on this form? There are of course various ways in which it can be done, but we would suggest a minimum of eight headings:

1. Budget for the period. This comes from the work we have already done.

2. Actual results for the period. Here we record what has actually happened.
3. Deviation from the budget. For each item on the budget this shows the amount we are above or below expectations.
4. Budget year to date. This is the cumulative budget for the periods that have passed. In month 1 it will be the same as the period budget, and in month 12 the same as the full year's budget. For the rest of the year it is a useful tool.
5. Actual results year to date. This begins to allow for errors of timing in our period budget and helps us to gauge our progress.
6. Deviation year to date. This gives us a measurement that helps us see how serious an issue is becoming. An overspend on a particular budget might have been rationalized away in month 1, but if it has been widened by month 3 it may indicate that there is a serious problem.
7. Budget for the full year. Through this we are able to keep an eye on what we expected to achieve.
8. Forecast year to date. This column regularly revises how the year is expected to turn out. If we are over or under budget in month 1, we may not feel justified in changing the forecast from the budget. However, if we suddenly lost an expected grant, even if this had not been expected to come in until month 5, we would want to change the forecast to highlight an impending problem. This column gains in its value as the year moves on, but also is affected by actions taken to redress the situation. Thus initially we may just show the effect on revenue of not having the grant. Actions are decided to trim costs or obtain funds from elsewhere, and in the next period we can reflect these actions in the forecast.

So far we have discussed the budget as if it were all in money terms. In reality we should wish to include key ratios in both the budgets and the reported results. We may also find it helpful to include some non-accounting information that helps management assess performance, such as number of employees, volunteer hours provided, number of calls received by a help line or whatever makes sense to the particular charity.

These reports can be in round figures. Whatever the size of the charity, it should not bother with the pence. Large charities may find it adequate to complete the overall report in thousands of pounds, while those of medium size may find that thousands of pounds to one decimal place is adequate. The accounts should be kept accurately to the last penny, but this level of detail does not improve ability to exercise management control, and can clutter the reports and make them harder to understand.

We will return to this part of the overall budget process in a moment, but before we resume we should look at the other boxes of Figure 7.1 that feed into it.

Actual results

This part of the figure needs little explanation. What is important is timeliness. Even with sophisticated computer-based accounting it is not possible to produce last month's figures by the first working day of the current month. Key information such as bank statements may not even be available until a few days into the new month. Time is needed for whoever handles the accounts to pull the whole thing together, so the earliest realistic day by which figures can become available must be around the middle of the month. In some organizations it will be later than this. However, if it is too late, it may also be too late for management to make good use of the reports. One thing to remember is that the budgets are management accounts, and it is possible to sacrifice a little precision for a faster report. Management can usually take appropriate action on something that is 99 per cent right, while waiting another week to make it 100 per cent right would prevent some actions from being effective. With financial accounts, precision is important, because they have to give a fair and accurate view of the state of the organization.

Reports that are similar in format to those prepared for the whole organization should be passed to every budget holder.

Actions by managers

The budget holders have two tasks. The first is properly to understand the reasons for any deviations from budget, and the second is to initiate any actions they consider necessary to remedy the situation. Those senior managers who have budget holders reporting to them should review the budgets with those people, so that they are in a position to speak for the whole of their department. Managers should also consider which of the actions they should have taken to support the strategy have been successfully completed. At this stage managers are concerned only with their own budgets, and the level of detail in their reports may be greater than the corporate report that was discussed earlier. Figures may also be reported in greater detail in these reports. The results of these activities become an important part of the corporate-level consideration of results.

Other information

For simplicity Figure 7.1 shows this feeding into the main delibera-
tions. In reality it may also feed into the reviews by managers of their
own budgets, and it may be the individual managers who bring relevant information to the notice of corporate management. What sort
of information is likely to be relevant? We have already seen one
example that would affect future results, the rejection of a grant
application, which although it had not affected the results so far
would do so in forthcoming periods. There may be many other pieces
of information that could affect future performance, and others that
mean that the various tasks planned to implement the strategy
should be changed. Information may come from inside or outside the
organization.

An example of external information is an economic change or
political change, which might affect trading operations. The
Ramblers' Association draws a large part of its annual income from
Ramblers Holidays. An event such as the terrorist attack on the
World Trade Center in New York on 11 September 2001 can seriously
affect the prospects for the holiday business, and therefore have a
fairly quick impact on the results of Ramblers Holidays. If unemployment begins to rise in the UK, the Prince's Trust for Youth –
Business may need to begin considering whether it could deal
with an expansion of the number of young people who are seeking
to become self-employed because they have been unable to find
jobs.

Internal information might be: the resignation of several key staff;
the fact that a project in one department has been completed sooner
or later than planned, with a knock-on effect on other departments; a
policy decision that affects costs.

Reports and analysis revisited

It is now possible to appreciate the amount of information, thought
and analysis that enable the corporate review of the budget to take
place. Part of the analysis is of course the preparation of the revised
forecast, but more might be undertaken perhaps to highlight the
reason for a major deviation from budget or possibly to draw attention to the fact that, although the figures are in line with the budget,
the organization has not been taking the steps needed if it is to implement its strategy.

Management actions

Just shuffling paper and issuing directives can bring results, but is not the best way of building a budgetary system into a powerful management tool. The results should be formally reviewed at two levels. Firstly the senior management team should go through the report together in a meeting, with the various heads of department explaining the causes of deviations, and the actions already taken to put things right. This meeting should ensure that there is a full understanding of performance. Additional actions should be taken where necessary. After this the board should review results and the actions already taken, to determine whether other actions are desirable.

When everything is going well, these meetings ensure that the senior management team and the board gain a greater understanding of the complexities of the charity. They also bring reassurance that everything is on track and that there is unlikely to be a sudden cash flow problem. In addition, continually looking at factors that may affect future performance means that adverse factors can be anticipated and in many cases avoided. The sharing of information also helps to build a team spirit.

When things are going wrong, the process brings the opportunity of looking at the extent of the problem, not just for the current period but for the whole year. The whole process is action-oriented, but tries to avoid panic actions that are not thought through.

> ### Pause for reflection
>
> What is your opinion of the value of a budgetary process? What are the pitfalls in such a process? How does the process we have described compare with how your organization prepares and uses budgets?

Of course there are variations in the process described. Although the process looks complex, it is in fact self-adjusting to the organizational structure and operations of the charity. Smaller charities tend to have simpler structures and less complexity in their operations, so the whole process may be relatively easy to set up and administer, without adding considerably to costs. Large, complex charities may find that there is significant cost in running their budgetary process, but these usually have the critical mass to support it.

The alternative of trying to manage even a modest-sized organization without the basic tools to control progress and cash flow is too frightening to contemplate. There may be an argument for not bothering when the charity is very small, with little expense and where its operations are simple. Any charity of even modest size that does not have a budgetary process is making itself more difficult to manage and increasing its risks of failure.

FINANCIAL RATIOS

Give an accountant some schedules of figures, and he or she will probably start to calculate various ratios. Sometimes a ratio is based purely on accounting data, and sometimes it is an accounting figure in relation to another piece of information, such as corporate donations obtained divided by the number of full-time people engaged on raising such funds. Answers are usually expressed as a percentage, a figure such as £ per person or an expression of coverage like 1.2 times.

Many of the ratios commonly used in business have limited value for charities, except for any business owned and operated by a charity. Return on investment after interest and tax (which is net profit divided by total net assets expressed as a percentage) is useful in conventional business, but has no relevance to the final accounts of a charity whose reason for existence has nothing to do with profit. But there are ratios that are useful, and it is these that we will touch on.

One ratio we could calculate is the relation of what was spent on performing the charitable purpose to the total revenue obtained. There are two ways this could be expressed. The Woodland Trust states that investing in and caring for the UK's woodland heritage costs 81p per £1 earned. This could have been expressed as 81 per cent. Is this a good or bad result?

This question immediately shows up one thing about all ratios. Although ratios make it easier to make comparisons between charities, or between performance at one time and another, they only make sense when we have something to compare them to. This may be a general standard of knowledge. For example, if the ratio had been only 50 per cent we might from general knowledge think that this was not very good. We can make more sense of the ratio if we can use it to compare performance with:

- other similar charities;
- the expectations of the Charity Commission;
- the charity's own target (the Woodland Trust's target is 80 per cent);
- the previous year.

We also have to ensure that the ratio is relating two things that have meaning when looked at in this way. One complication in the Woodland Trust accounts is that, in addition to expenditure on managing and preserving woods and educating people about them, it also makes capital purchases from restricted funds to buy woodland. This mix of capital and revenue expenditure can make it difficult to calculate one ratio to reflect the whole activity of this particular charity.

In its 2000 accounts the Suffolk Family History Society had incoming revenues of £53,110 and expended £43,146 for its charitable purposes. The following year the equivalent figures were £55,343 and £41,936. Simple inspection would have told us that the ratio has changed. In fact 2001 had a ratio of 76 per cent, compared with 81 per cent in 2000. Although the ratio has changed, the ratio cannot explain the underlying reasons. The treasurer's report shows a possible partial explanation, in that the charity had passed the VAT exemption limit and had to register. It made sense to delay certain expenditures for the charitable purpose because by waiting until after registration it was possible to recover VAT. Ratios are therefore a trigger for questions, rather than an answer to them.

The measure we have been discussing is a performance ratio. It is possible to think of a number of others that might be useful, although whether they are will depend on the activities of the charity. One particular charity uses a ratio relating to its fund-raising from corporate organizations. Its target is that the costs of raising these particular funds should not be more than 28.6 per cent of the funds raised.

What the charity does will change what is an important performance ratio. The Prince's Trust for Youth – Business makes loans to help adults who are under 30 to establish small businesses. It only lends to those who cannot obtain support from commercial lenders. One performance measure might be the ratio of bad debts to loans. Although a higher level might be acceptable for the charity than for a high street bank, because the risks are higher, nevertheless there is a level that is clearly good and another that is clearly bad. One use of this type of ratio could be to make comparisons between the various regions of the Trust. Here the differences can be used to trigger exploration of the differences, to identify best practice, which can then be applied in all regions.

There is another family of ratios that examines the financial condition of the organization. Although many of the standard ratios used by accountants are appropriate only for trading operations, there are a few that should be understood.

Liquidity is important, because as was discussed in the last chapter an organization can go insolvent if it runs out of liquid funds to pay its debts, even if it has other assets. Two ratios are commonly used.

Current ratio is calculated by dividing the current assets by the current liabilities. Obviously if the current liabilities exceed the current assets the answer will be less than 1, but the ratio will not help decision making as the problem would have already been uncomfortably visible. What is a 'good' figure will depend on the nature of the charity. If funds flow in at a regular rate, it is possible to operate safely on a ratio that is not much over 1. A charity that has to react quickly to international disasters may need to maintain a higher ratio, so that it has the liquid funds to react to the emergency in advance of any special campaign for funds that it might launch. Although this ratio is commonly used, it has the disadvantage that not all the items included in the current assets can easily be turned into cash. This is particularly true for those charities that for various reasons hold stocks which, although they are valued in the books on the basis of the going concern principle, may not be able to realize their full worth if there is a forced sale. For this reason another ratio is commonly used.

The *quick ratio* (*acid test*) strips out of the current assets those items that cannot be converted quickly and reliably to cash. Typically it is described as current assets minus stocks divided by current liabilities, although there may be other items that prudent financial management would also strip out to leave only the monetary assets. This is a more stringent test, although for those numerous charities that do not have stocks the two ratios will give similar answers.

Charities that have debtors need to control the amount of credit they are giving. Many charities, of course, have no debtors, but there are a number that do. The Woodland Trust shows debtors in its accounts, as would any other organization that has trading operations with business customers. Management colleges like Roffey Park Management Institute deal extensively with the employers of the people to whom management education and training is provided.

For day-to-day management control an aged debt analysis, which shows the length of credit being given, is probably the most useful tool. Debtors should be rigorously managed, initially in the payment terms allowed and then in the efforts made to secure payment of overdue accounts. At board level there are two ratios that can be helpful.

The *debtors to sales ratio* is total debtors divided by total sales, expressed as a percentage. The ratio can only be sensibly interpreted when looked at against a trend or in comparison against a target. The lower the figure, the better the collection rate. If only a small proportion of sales are on account, a more accurate figure will be to use total credit sales as the denominator. It is the collection period as well as the percentage that is of interest. If we want to look at the collection period in months, we use the *average months' debtors* formula: total debtors divided by average monthly sales. Average monthly sales are obtained by dividing total sales by 12. The answer is expressed in months. If days are wanted we use 365 as the divisor. A similar calculation can be made to see how much credit is being taken.

Numerous ratios can be calculated to suit a particular charity, but the skill is not in simply dividing one number by another but in choosing ratios that have meaning and are useful to trustees and managers.

It should also be remembered that financial ratios measure money. The important and commonly used ratio that shows the proportion of funds spent on charitable purposes does not show whether the money was spent wisely or in a way that is compatible with the vision and strategy of the charity. So although such ratios are important, they are by no means all that is needed to manage a charity.

Pause for reflection

Which of these ratios are appropriate for your organization? Which are not appropriate? What else is needed in order to help trustees and managers?

DECISION MAKING

A good accounting system, and knowledge of management accounting methodology, can help managers to make better decisions. This does not apply to every type of decision, and should not be taken as a recommendation for not including other considerations when a decision is made. So it is not that decisions should be made by the accounting view but that this view should be used to help management reach balanced decisions.

The accounting system as an information source

Many decisions do not need complicated analysis, but they are better made if there is information. For example, if various fund-raising schemes are being considered, any prudent person would want to think about the costs of each and the likely returns. Even if some of the schemes are new, information from the accounts about previous experiences can help define more accurate assumptions about likely income. Where the options being considered are the same as in previous years, a good accounting system can give information to help reassess the costs and should be able to show the historic success rate. Costs sometimes have to be estimated from a blank sheet of paper but, even when the actual figures all need to change, historic information can ensure that no cost headings are omitted. Of course, to serve this purpose, the accounts have to be set up in the right way in the first place.

There are numerous occasions when there is a need to look at the effect of a cost increase. It may be that phone charges are going up, or electricity, or postage. What will this do to costs for the rest of this financial year and for next year? The calculation is not difficult, if there is a history of information, and if the budget has been well prepared and has already considered the usage patterns for the rest of the year. Without accounting information someone just has to guess, or more likely will just wait until the bills come in. It is not just a question of being prepared to meet these extra costs; a significant increase may also trigger thinking about ways to reduce consumption, such as changing a supplier for electricity or making greater use of e-mail to reduce postage costs.

Accounting concepts as a way of understanding situations

So far our illustration has been of quite simple situations. But charities sometimes have to make significant decisions about expanding or contracting the scope of operations, making a significant 'investment' in a new department of full-time people, or relocating an office.

Any of these decisions could have implications on costs, revenues and cash flow. Although economic evaluation does not make the decision, it does allow the best possible calculation of the financial effects on the charity, and enables various options to be considered. There may be various non-economic factors to be considered in the decision, which may mean going against the evidence of the figures, but there is still value in being aware of the likely impact on results.

Examples can make things clearer than words. The figures in Table 7.1 are imaginary, but the activities are very loosely based on those of The Centre, a case study given in Chapter 2. We hasten to add that these are not the figures or the problems faced by The Centre, but what is described here could occur in a number of charities. Later we will expand the example to cover another type of situation that is common to all charities.

The table shows the year's results for a charity that runs a religious bookshop and coffee shop. The activities share the same premises, and the entrance to the bookshop is through the coffee shop. They each have the same floor area, which is why the space costs (eg rent, heating, lighting, insurance, cleaning) are divided equally between them. Management and administration are mainly the manager's employment costs and accounting costs. The manager of the charity spends about two-thirds of his time on the coffee shop. The coffee shop has a mix of paid staff and volunteers, and the bookshop is run by volunteers with some hands-on support from the manager.

Table 7.1 *Results for a year*

	Coffee Shop £	Bookshop £
Sales	100,000	40,000
Cost of Goods Sold	35,000	20,000
Gross Profit	65,000	20,000
Space Costs	15,000	15,000
Paid Staff	15,000	
Management and Admin	20,000	10,000
Net Profit	15,000	(5,000)

The manager argued that the bookshop was depressing the overall profits, which of course amounted to £10,000. If he closed down the bookshop, he argued, profits would rise to £15,000, so if there were no other options to improve the level of business in the bookshop this is what he proposed. Is he right?

The table presents the figures on a *full cost* basis, which is useful for day-to-day management control. When thinking of looking at what are effectively change situations, there is a need to think about costs and revenue in a somewhat different way. The fundamental principle is to look at these decisions on an incremental, or differential, basis. Our interest should be on the costs, revenues and cash flow that will change as a result of the decision. This takes us into a realm of costs that is claimed as their own by both accountants and economists.

Types of costs

Hitherto when we have discussed costs we have talked about them in account headings, like rent or postage. Now we need to think of them in terms of how they behave. The first concept, of fixed and variable costs, may seem strange to some charities that are not engaged in trading activities, or delivering a service like a hospice or management college. But stick with them because they will lead to other concepts that are applicable to all charities.

Variable costs

These are costs that vary directly with the rate of output. Typically variable costs include materials and components, energy and labour used in creating the output. If the output falls, the theory is that the variable costs will be reduced in total. If output rises the total variable costs will increase. There is of course a delay before some variable costs can be adjusted to the new output, and in some charities some labour may be fulfilled by volunteers so there is no cost to consider if labour changes.

The word 'output' is used broadly, and should not be seen as limited to manufacturing. For example, there is a variable cost in using a private car: the amount of petrol and oil consumed vary directly with the distance covered (and the average speed). A hospice's variable costs would include the obvious consumables like food and medication but, when we come to professional care staff, cleaning, and heating and lighting, the costs may not vary much if there is one less inmate, and we may have to think in terms of groups

191

of inmates. It is these variable costs that in the past various NHS hospitals have claimed to save by shutting down a ward. In our example, the variable costs are the cost of goods sold. In the coffee shop all variable labour costs for food preparation and table waiting are free services provided by volunteers; there is no further preparation to do in the bookshop. There could be some variable fuel costs in the coffee shop, but the example does not give us enough information to explore these, probably because there is no way of measuring them.

Fixed costs

As the name implies, fixed costs do not change with the amount of output. We should add that this is in the short term, because in the long term everything can be changed. In the car example, the fixed costs might include the rent of a garage, insurance and car tax. These would continue even if the car was never driven. In an organization, fixed costs include premises and all the other overheads. The NHS hospital would not save the management and administrative costs, and might not be able to reduce the number of doctors and specialist nurses by shutting a ward, unless the reduction of workload made it possible to reduce these staffing levels too. The Millennium Dome continued to cost several millions of pounds in 2001 after it had closed and there were no longer any variable costs. In our coffee shop/bookshop example we can assume that all the remaining costs are fixed.

The next two types of cost are relevant to every type of organization.

Direct costs

The name gives a clue. These are costs that are directly caused by the activity. Variable costs are clearly direct costs, but this is only part of the story. There may be some fixed costs that are direct. We have to be somewhat schizophrenic when thinking about this because the object we are looking at will affect the answer. If we are looking at a department, it will be correct to argue that the direct costs of that department include overheads such as departmental management and administration, the rent of any dedicated premises and, if it is responsible for its own marketing, these costs as well. However, if the department has a number of activities, and we want to look at one of them, these costs will not be direct costs because they are common to all the activities.

In a change situation, we have to be sure that costs that we have called 'direct' will disappear if the activity ceases. So if a department is in a separate building, rent will be a direct cost. However, if it is in the same building as the rest of the organization and any space it gives up could not be sold or sublet, we will not save these costs by closing the department. In our example, the paid staff in the coffee shop, which we have classed as fixed costs, are a direct cost. If we closed the coffee shop we would not employ these people. However, there are no similar direct fixed costs in the bookshop because the whole operation is staffed by volunteers.

Indirect costs

There are no prizes for guessing that any costs that are not direct are indirect. Indirect costs would not change with the removal of an activity, unless we took further specific action. In our example, they are common costs, which will still be there even if we close the bookshop. One of the complications of life is that many organizations apportion or allocate costs to the various activities. The assumptions are often arbitrary, and another organization in a similar situation might choose a different method. In any case the assumptions are also related to forecasts of the volume of each activity. So although the spreading of all costs across all activities to reach *full costs* is useful for some purposes, it can cause distortions in a change situation, where the volumes and relationships are distorted.

Contribution

This is another notion that is applicable only to the trading activities of a charity. It is the difference between the variable costs and the realization, and it gets its name because it is what the activity is contributing to the fixed costs and profit. In Table 7.2 it is used slightly differently, as the contribution to common costs and overheads.

Table 7.2 reworks the example using the concept of direct and indirect costs. We can see now what the effect would be if we simply closed down the bookshop. We would lose the £20,000 contribution to common costs, which would reduce the overall profit to a loss of £10,000. Of course, different situations would change how we viewed the figures. If we could sublet the space occupied by the bookshop, we would have a positive figure, which would reduce the loss, but in our example we would have to let it for more than £20,000 to improve our overall figure.

Table 7.2 *The results analysed by direct costs*

	Total Operation £	Coffee Shop £	Bookshop £
Sales	140,000	100,000	40,000
Cost of Goods Sold	55,000	35,000	20,000
Gross Profit	85,000	65,000	20,000
Direct Costs: Staff	15,000	15,000	
Contribution Level	70,000	50,000	20,000
Space Costs	30,000		
Management and Admin	30,000		
Profit	10,000		

If the bookshop were the main charitable purpose, and the coffee shop was set up as a means of supporting it, the trustees might feel that they had done well by both operating the bookshop and adding £10,000 to charity funds. However, our assumption is that we might want to improve the situation. What we have done so far has given us a better understanding of the situation, and a basis for thinking about other options.

One option might be to advertise the bookshop. The first step would be to explore the various ways we could do this, and cost them out. The objective might be to eliminate the bookshop loss on the full cost analysis (Table 7.1). If we know the amount we are planning to spend on advertising, and the financial objective to be achieved, we can use our figures to help understand whether what we want to do looks practicable. If our advertising calculation works out at £2,000, and we want to bring the operation to break-even on a full cost basis, we need to generate gross profits of £7,000.

This means that our sales would have to go up to £14,000. It also tells us that if our extra sales did not even reach £4,000 we would not recover the advertising cost. Put another way, we must as a minimum increase sales by 10 per cent, and would have to increase sales by 35 per cent to meet the target. The figures do not tell us what the results of advertising will be, but they give us some help in understanding whether the advertising option looks feasible. Advertising can often be piloted, so that we might be able to get some data on its impact on sales by spending a fraction of the advertising budget and assessing results, before committing to the whole campaign. That way we would have an objective basis for calculating both costs and benefits.

For a moment step away from the bookshop and think of fund-raising. Here the task may be to determine which of several options to take. There is a similar cost/benefit equation to work through, and the methods used to determine which to take roughly follow the advertising example. We need to know the costs and targets of each option. Piloting and/or analysis of past success rates from the accounts may give some guidance to help quantify the benefits, and the level of costs enables us to assess the risks with some objectivity.

Another option for the bookshop might be to reduce the space allowed the bookshop, and use this to extend the coffee shop. If there were times when customers did not come in because there were no available tables, this might indicate that this would be a sensible thing to do. How would we evaluate this change?

Again it is using a differential approach to determine which figures will change. To begin with we need to assess the sales income and variable costs. There are judgements to be made, but we have experience to help us. One judgement might be that we could reduce book-shop space by 50 per cent, with no effect on sales. Another might be that a 50 per cent increase in coffee shop space would ultimately yield the same percentage increase of sales, but it would take a year to get there. In year 1 we might expect a 25 per cent increase. All vari-able labour would be supplied by volunteers, and there would be no effect on the other fixed costs shown in Table 7.2. In the example, we can calculate most of the differences by looking at the gross profit line, because all our variable costs in this simple case are in the cost of goods sold. More complex situations require more effort to identify all the variable costs, but the principle is the same. Because the book-shop gross margin will not change, we can quite happily state that the increase in coffee shop revenue will bring in additional gross profit of £65,000 × 25 per cent = £16,250.

However, we would have to spend capital costs of £10,000 on refurbishment and additional furniture, crockery and cutlery. We will look more closely at capital expenditure decisions later, but this one is not difficult to take. Our differential increase will bring us a return of 162.5 per cent in the first year alone. Improvement projects looked at on a marginal basis often do bring in very high returns, but of course they represent a small fraction of the overall capital, and the impact is less marked when returns are calculated on the whole results of the activity. Of course, we have to be sure that we have done enough work on the assumptions behind the sales figures, and when the amounts of money are large it may be prudent to undertake some sensitivity analysis: that is calculate what the costs and benefits would be under various assumptions.

Simple, readily understandable examples make it easier to see the concepts, and only a limited number of charities are likely to face an exactly similar situation as that described. But every charity faces choices, and many of the decisions are easier to make if there is an analytical underpinning. The differential principle of analysis can bring clarity and a greater understanding of the implications of decisions.

Pause for reflection

What sort of decisions does your organization take that have financial consequences? What sort of analysis is undertaken to aid decision making? Which of the methods we have described so far, if not already used, might be beneficial to your organization?

EVALUATING CAPITAL EXPENDITURE PROJECTS

In the previous chapter it was noted that money spent on fixed assets was treated differently in the accounts from money spent on expenses. For cash flow purposes there is of course no difference: money spent is money spent regardless of what we have used it for.

In the exercise above we had to consider a capital expenditure as well as evaluating a change in operations, but this was so obviously a good investment that we did not have to do much analysis to justify it. This does happen in practice and, for many purchases of capital goods, evaluation is a choice between various products rather than a complex evaluation of the benefits of the expenditure. There may be a little more to it than just comparing prices.

For example, if a charity like the National Trust had to buy a replacement tractor lawnmower for one of its stately homes, the nature of the need is likely to be well established. The issue then becomes one of purchase price, fuel consumption, reliability and productivity. The most complex part would probably be producing the cost data to show that the old machine is now too costly or unreliable to do the job any more, and although all the approvals have to be gone through, the decision does not need much analysis.

But assume that all grass cutting had been contracted out across all properties, and the suggestion is that it would be cheaper to bring it back in-house. Here there would be a complex project to evaluate. We know the costs incurred at present, and should estimate these for a few years ahead. The next stage would be to calculate all the costs that would be incurred in bringing the job back in-house and estimate these forward for the same number of years. Then we must calculate the capital costs of buying all the lawnmowers we need. However, the benefits gained each year are the difference between what we are doing now and the cost of doing it in-house. In other words the capital expenditure has to be justified by the net saving. But there is another implication. We have to make the capital expenditure this year in order to obtain the stream of savings in the future.

Certain charities face a different type of capital expenditure. Their role is to acquire land, buildings or other assets in order to preserve them. Often there are no implications for future income streams, although there is a need to ensure that the charity can obtain the future resources in order to maintain the asset properly. Examples of this type of capital expenditure can be found historically in the National Trust's 'Operation Neptune' of many years ago, which resulted in the acquisition of a significant proportion of the British coastline. The Woodlands Trust and other conservation charities buy land in order to conserve it, and no doubt there are many other examples. As there is no or a negligible expected stream of revenue that will result, the only evaluation is to ensure that the purchase is appropriate for the charity, that the price is fair, that it can be properly funded and that the consequences of the purchase are fully understood.

Funds spent on acquiring one thing cannot also be spent acquiring another, which brings us to another concept, *opportunity cost*. This can be helpful in evaluating major capital expenditures that, while enabling the charity to fulfil its charitable purpose, are also intended to produce a revenue stream. Examples include charities like Roffey Park Management Institute (which was undergoing a major expansion of its buildings as this book was being written), charities serving the arts or sports, and those like the YMCA that provide accommodation.

Every choice made means that something has to be forgone, so the opportunity cost of the option we take is what we have to give up in order to be able to do it. If a management consultant has limited time and two projects to choose from, but can only take on one of them, the opportunity cost is what he or she has lost by not doing the one that was not chosen.

If a charity running homes for the elderly decides to build a new home in Birmingham, it cannot spend the same capital building a home in Oxford. This type of opportunity cost may appear a little abstract, but it has two practical implications.

Firstly, there is one type of opportunity cost that can be measured accurately. This is the loss of interest. If the money is spent on a building, it cannot be held as an investment yielding an income. So we know that there is a real loss of benefit every time capital expenditures are made, and therefore have a duty to ensure that the decision is made wisely.

Secondly, it makes sense to evaluate various options when major expenditures are contemplated. For example, in the case of the home for the elderly, the charity can make the investment itself, it may have several building schemes to compare, and there may be an option of having a developer build the home and rent it to the charity on a long lease. In any case there has to be an expenditure to furnish and equip the home. As each of these has different outflows of capital expenditure, running expenses and income, there is quite a lot to do to make an evaluation.

If this were a commercial proposition for a business (for example, the developer who is considering building the home to rent to the charity), profit would be an element in the equation. There may be very different objectives for the charity, and some of the capital may have been raised by a special appeal for the building and its furnishings. Nevertheless there needs to be some way of comparing the various possibilities. The project is of a significant size, and the cash flows it generates will cover many years. Even the capital expenditure may take more than a year to be spent. Some of the options that might be considered may reduce the capital spend, but may increase the running costs and/or decrease the revenue from the residents. If one scheme reduces the number of bedrooms, income, costs and capital expenditure may also be reduced. So how can we decide which is best?

Case study 7.1: Roffey Park Management Institute – building for the future

Val Hammond is the chief executive of Roffey Park, an institute originally founded in 1946. Over the years the Institute has several times refocused its activities to bring them in line with current conditions, and now has a fine reputation in management education, both as a provider of programmes and seminars, some of which have external academic accreditation, and in leading research into the human aspects of management.

It is situated in a woodland area just outside the town of Horsham in West Sussex, and has several times gone through building and refurbishment programmes to cope with its expansion and the changing needs that it meets. In early 2002 work was in progress to build another major extension to the facilities. During 2001 the current cycle of refurbishing the existing building was completed as part of the overall plan.

Val took up her role in 1993 and realized that, although there had been an extension of the buildings a few years before, there was still an imbalance in that there were insufficient bedrooms to optimize the use of the teaching facilities, and that many of these in any case could not be remodelled to meet the standards that people increasingly expected. The first thought was just to build additional bedrooms, but a consideration of the future needs and preliminary discussions with architects and other professional advisers showed that this would not be the best way forward. The final solution was for a substantial new facility, which would not only solve the bedroom problem but would also increase capacity to provide new sources of earnings.

The Institute earns its revenue from its activities and invests its surplus in its products, services, people, charitable works and site. Nevertheless, for major building projects, loans are necessary and these have to be repaid. Historically, although the first few years after a building programme were financially tight, the Institute was able to repay loans earlier than expected.

The trustees and senior management of any charity have a duty of prudence, and could not sanction a major expenditure, or the loans to enable it to happen, without very careful investigation and evaluation.

The foundation for the evaluation was a strategic business plan. Val said:

> It would have been immoral to ask the trustees to approve an expansion of bedrooms, and then return in a year or so for another major building project. What we wanted to do was to find the 21st-century way of interpreting our charitable mission, and expressing this to ensure that our successors would be in a position to guide the Institute so that it would be capable of meeting the challenges ahead.

The business plan covered a period of 20 years, looking at both the development of new activities and the shortfalls in the current facilities. It included an outline financial plan, which examined revenue and costs of existing and new activities. Capital and revenue expenditures for investments in technology and people were included as were the needs continually to develop new products and maintain the high standards of the facility. The plan was essential for the trustees to make an appropriate judgement, and a loan application. Although the strategy and the analysis of revenues and expenditures were critical elements, it was of course the forecasts of cash flow that enabled the viability of the project to be examined.

The first seven years of the financial plan were re-examined in greater detail, again with the emphasis on cash flows, as this was a critical period.

Such an evaluation exercise requires clear thinking and carefully defined assumptions that are rooted in reality. Although calculating cash flows into the future is difficult, it is an essential task. This example shows how a visionary view supported by clear, well-founded strategies can be the basis of a clear financial plan, which makes it possible for the trustees to take a reasoned decision on matters of great consequence.

Firstly any major capital expenditures should be rooted in the charitable purpose, vision and strategies of the charity. A capital expenditure plan should then be developed, with projections for several years. The financial implications of the investment should be thoroughly examined, and forecasts made of the revenue flows and the costs. This means considerable analysis, some of the information for which may come from the management accounting system but also will draw on external information. There is a need to be accurate in assessing the capital costs, and figures for revenues and costs should be the subject of careful thought, so that it is possible to justify them. The reasoning behind the figures, and particularly the assumptions, should be written up in the capital expenditure plan. Professional advice should be taken when needed.

The Roffey Park Management Institute example includes a statement about thinking through all possible requirements instead of continually returning to the trustees with unexpected requests for more capital expenditure. This is important advice, even if the ultimate decision is to take a phased approach to development. At least the shape of the whole is visible. The difference is like seeing a slice of salami, which is a flat circle, and then being shown other slices at various times, instead of understanding the true size and shape of the sausage.

The approach described in the case study was to calculate the cash flow for the whole organization for a lengthy period ahead, and of course this needs to be done. However, there is merit in looking at a major expenditure such as this on a marginal basis first, just examining in detail the resulting cash flows associated with the investment. This facilitates choice when there are a number of options that should be compared, as it throws the differences between them into sharper focus. In organizations that are considerably bigger than Roffey Park, the impact of a capital expenditure can be lost, as it is a much smaller proportion of the whole. Also there may be several projects being investigated in different parts of the organization from which a choice has to be made, even if it is only a question of deferring some of them. The marginal approach enables a choice to be made that cuts down the complexity of the calculations.

The principles behind the analysis should include:

- It is cash that is measured, so any expenditure or income of any type is included when the cash moves, not when the obligation is incurred. This is the opposite of normal accounting practice.
- Depreciation is not calculated, because the cash was spent when the resource was purchased, and no cash moves when depreciation is calculated.
- Sunk costs are ignored, although any cash that is received from the disposal of an obsolete asset caused by the project could be included.
- The projections should cover an appropriate period of time. Twenty years is not uncommon.
- This approach allows different options or different projects to be compared and can also be used to help assess risk and uncertainty.
- It is only as good as the care that goes into assessing the numerical facts.
- Qualitative matters should also be considered as they may be very important for a good decision.

Discounted cash flow (DCF)

There is an extension to this type of analysis that can make it easier to compare the cash flow profiles of two or more options. Discounted cash flow uses the concept of opportunity cost coupled with the time value of money. If someone has £1 today and is able to invest it at 10 per cent per annum compound, at the end of a year it will be worth £1.10, but if the person is owed £1 and does not receive it for a year he or she is deprived of the chance to earn interest, so what is received in value is £1 divided by 1.1, which is £0.909. If nothing is received until the fifth year it is equivalent to getting only £0.621 today.

For a more realistic investment opportunity of 5 per cent, using the same reasoning in year 5 the present value would be £0.784. If the rate were 15 per cent, the present value would be £0.497.

The information in Table 7.3 is published in books of tables, and is also built into spreadsheet programs on computers and in some pocket calculators. It has been shown in the particular way in the table so that the reader can 'prove' the figures if he or she wishes.

Table 7.3   *What is a pound worth?*

Year	Value of £1 at 5% Interest	
	Year-end Value	Present Value at 5%
0	1.00	1.000
1	1.05	0.952
2	1.10	0.907
3	1.16	0.864
4	1.22	0.823
5	1.28	0.784

The discounted cash flow method discounts the future cash flows relating to a capital expenditure project and expresses them as present values. Table 7.4 shows the values that would be entered for a project with a £1 million investment in year 0, followed by positive cash flows of £500,000 in years 1, 2 and 3, and a rate of discount chosen of 5 per cent. The process would continue for every year over which the project is evaluated.

Before we comment on Table 7.4 we should mention how the discount rate might have been chosen. In a business it is usually its estimate of its cost of capital, a weighted mix of its interest rates on loan capital, and dividends and other costs of equity. This calculation is not possible for a charity, so we recommend using the opportunity cost: the rate of interest that could be obtained if the funds were invested instead of being used for the capital expenditure. If the capital is borrowed, the interest rate paid might be used instead.

Table 7.4 *Discounting the cash flows (£000)*

Year	Cash Flow	Discount Factor	Discounted Cash Flow	Cumulative Discounted Cash Flow
0	(1,000)	1.000	(1,000)	(1,000)
1	500	0.952	476	(524)
2	500	0.907	453	(71)
3	500	0.864	432	361

DCF gives rise to a number of measures that are useful when comparing options, since it reduces the differing annual cash flow patterns to comparable measurements. The two most common measurements are net present value (NPV) and the internal rate of return (IRR).

Although we realize that Table 7.4 is not a realistic representation of most projects, and we have only worked out a few years, it does enable us to read off the NPV. At year 4 it is the final figure in the cumulative discounted cash flow column. If the NPV had been zero, this would have meant that the organization would have recovered all operating costs and the opportunity cost of its capital. In a charity a negative NPV is not always a problem, but it depends on the nature of the charity and the source of the capital funds. However, the measures still give one way of comparing different options, even if final interpretation is different from that of a commercial business.

The IRR is the rate at which the NPV is zero. In Table 7.4 it approximates to 23 per cent at the end of year 3. Manual calculation uses trial and error, so it is much simpler to put the data into a spreadsheet program, which also uses trial and error but gives the answer in seconds.

Sensitivity analysis asks sensible questions, and reruns the analysis with the variables the questions inspire, eg what if the capital costs were 10 per cent higher, what if sales volumes were as forecast but price were higher (or lower) or what if the pre-production period were extended by a year?

We hope that this chapter has done enough to illustrate the importance of numerical analysis in many types of decisions, and have reinforced the views expressed in the preceding chapter that accounting is much more than a legal necessity. It is vital for the success of the charity.

REFERENCE

Parker, RH (ed) (1984) *Macmillan Dictionary of Accounting*, Macmillan, London

8

Marketing: basic concepts

The word 'marketing' often has a connotation from which many in the UK third sector instinctively shrink. Is this because of an association of marketing with selling, and particularly with the 'hard sell'? We hope to show that this is an erroneous view, and that a sensible approach to marketing is beneficial and essential.

Marketing is inextricably linked with fund-raising although this is not its only purpose. In this chapter we will describe the basic concepts of marketing in the context of a number of its uses in voluntary organizations, and including public relations and publicity. The chapter following will look closely at various aspects of fund-raising, including some more specific applications of marketing concepts to this end.

There is of course an enormous difference in the application of marketing concepts between a charity like Henley Management College, which is effectively a form of business, and one like the Royal National Lifeboat Institution, whose services are free. In between these extremes there are numerous variations. To try to cope with these wide differences we will describe two marketing models: 1) a business model, which we will take first because it is a good vehicle for thinking about the concepts, although we know that in its present form it is not helpful to voluntary organizations that have no business activities; 2) a model derived from this, which will fit many more organizations, although again it will not cover every charity. However, we believe that any organization will be able to derive a model from the concepts to suit its own operations.

Among the differences are the various organizations and people that the voluntary organization has to reach and in some way influence: customers/members, providers of funds, volunteers, clients or beneficiaries, and sometimes other stakeholder organizations.

THE BUSINESS APPROACH TO MARKETING

'The primary purpose of every business is to stay in business, and to do that you have to get and keep customers. This is usually interpreted to mean that you have to sell what you have... this just isn't so' (Levitt, 1968).

Figure 8.1 illustrates the classic approach to marketing used in business. There are many charities where some form of business activity falls within the charitable purpose. Examples are the training programmes run by the Directory of Social Change and the Society of Genealogists, which in each case relate to only a part of the charitable purpose, and organizations such as a number of the colleges whose commercial activities lie close to the heart of why they exist. Of course the stakeholders of a charity or other voluntary organization are not shareholders, and the motivation is not profit, but nevertheless the business model is still relevant. There are also many charities that own non-charitable trading companies, which are in business, and these should operate accordingly.

Marketing requires information, analysis and creative thinking, but not necessarily in this order. It begins with the customer, and the model indicates that assessments of customer needs lead to the marketing strategies that are developed (the interrelationship of the *market* and *marketing mix* boxes). These strategies have an effect on the market, although unfortunately not always giving the wanted result, which in turn feeds back more information to consider in relation to the strategy. We have used a traditional market share approach, which may be unrealistic for small organizations, although the idea of measuring performance against a target is valid for any business activity.

The *market* box of the model suggests a number of points of information that it is desirable to have about the market, although the importance of each point will vary with the type of market. There are obvious vast differences between consumer and industrial markets, and within each of these headings depending on the nature of the product. In consumer markets there are big differences between

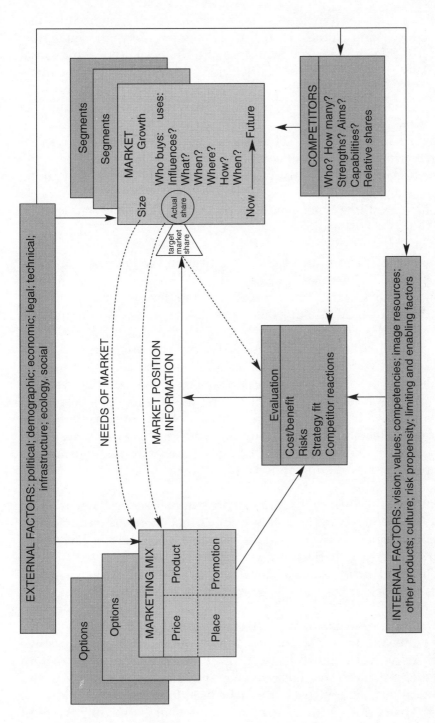

Figure 8.1 *Basic marketing model*

capital purchases like houses and furniture, staple commodities like basic foods and clothes, luxury items like jewellery, and intangible services like hairdressers, insurance and financial advice. Industrial markets are subject to a similarly wide spread of variety. The question, 'Who buys?', meaning in this context who in the organization makes the buying decision, assumes great importance in industrial markets.

In the model the market is shown as made up of a variety of different segments, and of course these may be many more than the two we have used for illustration. Identifying the niches is often the route to success.

There are three other boxes on the model that show factors that will influence the choice of marketing strategy:

- External factors affect the organization, competitors and the market. We met these in Chapter 3.
- In all markets there are competitors, and the box lists a number of things to think about when considering these. The underlying issue is how to make our product or service more attractive to our chosen market segment than the competitive offerings.
- Internal factors will also affect what is possible. These may be limitations of the governing documents, the resources available and the level of risks, which may affect what can be offered and how it is offered. The culture of the organization may restrict choices further. Limiting and enabling factors are the strengths and weaknesses that make it easier or harder to adopt a particular marketing option.

Elements of the marketing strategy are summarized in the marketing mix box. What is immediately clear is that there are innumerable options about how the offering is assembled, both within each of the four Ps listed and in the interplay between them.

The four Ps approach was developed over 40 years ago. It is not the only way of thinking about the marketing mix, but it has stood the test of time.

Price means what it says. It is concerned with terms of trade, discounts and price promotions. It may, of course, be an aggressive element of marketing strategy. It may be used to change the pattern of order purchase size, thus reducing unit sales, order processing and physical distribution costs. It may be used to increase the volume of sales: Henry Ford with his cars provided what is probably the most well-known example of this strategy in practice. And of course different price strategies may be applied to the various segments of a particular market (usually with some modification of one or more of the other Ps). Because it is such an obvious element of strategy, it is often wrongly used by organizations that slash prices to meet competition rather than making changes to the other factors to make the offering more acceptable to the market.

Product is the next of the four Ps. This element covers the intangible aspects of a product as well as its physical characteristics. The tangible aspects include the shape and composition of the product itself, and the way in which it basically sets out to give satisfaction to its consumers. This would cover the design and finish of furniture, the taste and dietary value of a convenience food, the formulation of a toilet preparation or the curative benefit of a pharmaceutical.

Closely allied to these characteristics are the packaging and size of unit offered for sale. Packaging is of the utmost importance in the marketing of many items. With an industrial product the main problem might be to package in a way that gives the most convenience to the user; with a grocery product the shape and appeal of the package may be a vehicle to advertise special offers and promotions, which may be the deciding element in the attraction of a purchaser. Packaging as a means of preserving goods from damage and storing them until sold is often second in importance to packaging as an active element of sales promotion. There is also a cost aspect attached to each additional package or size of unit marketed: each additional item brings extra charges for financing inventories and storage, as well as possibly adding to direct production costs. The reduction of variety can often be an important method of planning for improved returns.

From packaging it is natural to turn one's thoughts to branding. This element covers such items as the marketing of brands to appeal to the various segments of the market, policy for the production of 'own label' products for others, and whether the company brings out families of brands or creates a new brand for each product. Although branding is a product choice, it is usually closely allied to promotion to establish awareness of the brand and a positive image for it.

The intangible aspects of product strategy cover those items that the organization offers to purchasers as an inducement to buy, for example the terms of credit it is prepared to give, any particular guarantees attached to the product, a special delivery service, or free after-sales servicing of appliances. With electrical goods or motor cars, the widespread availability of service and repair shops might be a highly attractive intangible to the prospective customer.

Place is a term that calls for a little stretching of the imagination, and would be better translated as distribution (except that this word does not begin with 'P'). The heading covers the channel of distribution chosen to get the products from the manufacturer to the consumer. Attention to this aspect of strategy ensures that the organization takes full advantage of any opportunity to innovate, for by pioneering a new method of distribution it may be possible to change the nature of the market.

In planning distribution strategy, an organization might well set different brand share targets for each of the alternative outlet types: it might aim for different penetration levels for each outlet. And, of course, the other elements of strategy, price, promotion and even product can be designed to help give effect to the chosen distribution strategy.

The remaining of our four Ps is *promotion*. This covers numerous activities in addition to the mass advertising that immediately springs to mind. Under this heading we would include merchandising, sales promotion and point-of-sale activities, sampling and general product public relations. Selling also comes under this heading. There are many variables to choose from in relation to the types of promotion used, the weights assigned to each and the way in which the product image is put across. The forward-looking organization will not have a static approach and will find considerable opportunity for development and improvement.

There is one important box in Figure 8.1 that we have not yet discussed: *evaluation*. As we have seen, a marketing strategy begins with decisions about which markets and segments to target and then becomes a choice between many options. These have cost and benefit implications that need to be examined; the risks may vary, and likely competitor reactions need to be considered. The marketing strategy also has to fit with the general strategy of the organization.

Two of the fund-raising situations where business marketing concepts are important are shops and contracts.

Shops

The growth of large out-of-town shopping centres has meant that many towns have surplus shopping units in town centres. Property owners do not like empty shops, which project a run-down air, and frequently let shops out to charities at favourable rents. This has been one of the reasons for the very rapid growth of charity shops.

This expansion by over 105 charities has led to overcapacity, and many are struggling. The NSPCC, Relate and World Vision UK have decided to pull out of retail activities, and presumably the two big cancer charities that recently merged will be rationalizing their networks. Of the 10 largest charity shopping chains, eight saw their profits fall in 2000. Even some of the largest have not been exempt: Oxfam, which has 829 shops, saw its profits fall by nearly a quarter. Recent legislation has meant that the resale of electrical goods and upholstered furniture is now more difficult. It is also possible that a few years of high employment have reduced the appeal of the ubiquitous purveyors of second-hand goods. There has also been a steady increase in competition from car boot sales.

Typically charity second-hand shops have relied on location rather than promotion to inform the market, have not given a great deal of attention to the ambience of the shop, have priced at what the local market will bear and have given little attention to identifying the market segments they are serving. National Trust gift shops, which sell new goods, put much more attention into the selection and design of the products, and their pricing. There is a brand-image consistency not found in the traditional shop selling second-hand goods.

However, there are different ways of marketing the same types of second-hand goods. Triad, which has just been going for three years, has had an enlivening impact on this sector. Thousands of items of clothing are donated every week, and are sorted in a very large warehouse in the west of London. Clothes from 700 clothes banks based all over the country are brought here every week.

They are sorted on a production line. Those items not considered saleable are sold as rags, worth £85 for every ton. The rest are sorted again into designer clothing, quality clothing, vintage, family fashion and other categories. They are then directed to an appropriate store that specializes in these items, thus targeting specific segments of the market, where the style of the outlet and the way it is staffed are adjusted to the needs of the segment. Triad is now ranked 25th in the profit league of charity shops. (As noted in Chapter 3, Oxfam has moved into a targeted approach by bringing some specialization to its chain of shops.) All this is marketing.

Pause for reflection

Use Figure 8.1 to contrast the marketing strategy of Triad with that of the many more-traditional second-hand shops. Are there other options for charity shops that might be worth examining? Why do you think the charity movement has been so slow to move from its traditional pattern?

There were 240 charity shops that closed in 2001, 120 more than in the previous year, but there is scope for those that identify and carefully target viable market segments. The key to success is a well-thought-out marketing strategy.

Contracts

Recent changes in political philosophy have meant the public sector has become increasingly aware it is not necessarily as effective at doing some things as the other sectors. This ranges from the privatization of the utilities through to the local authorities that contract out services like waste collection. It has been a major shift in the way society is run. Who would have imagined state schools or prisons would be let out to private firms to run under contract? Often these firms are profit-making organizations run like any other business.

However, there are a number of areas where voluntary organizations play a key role. For example, much of the income of overseas aid organizations comes from large contracts running for several years from national and international governments and their agencies. The Woodland Trust has management contracts for some Forestry Commission woodlands, and the Royal Society for Nature Conservation administers funds and manages projects under the Landfill Tax Credit Scheme. Social services subcontract parcels of work. The contract procedure can be rigorous, to ensure best value for money and enable a monitoring process that can ensure quality. Sometimes this can be galling for the charity, which may well not only be very cost-effective but have a higher standard than the council, which is now overseeing the contract, ever maintained.

Marketing this sort of service or activity is very different to consumer marketing. Assuming the market intelligence has been undertaken, so that the organization is aware of impending opportunities, the first hurdle is to get on the bid list. The concept of buyer's risk becomes important, and it is worth trying to think of the issue from this point of view. Can you satisfy a buyer that you have the capability and resources to handle this type of contract? How can you demonstrate this? What would the consequences be for the buyer if you were to fail to perform to the right time and quality? How can you allay these fears? The big advantage is that there are relatively few buyer organizations facing each organization, so it is possible to get to know them very well and to build up strong relationships.

Promotional activity is likely to be personal selling and relationship building, although prospects are improved when the organization has a strong image. There has to be care in defining what the product is and ensuring that it can be delivered, and it can be difficult to decide the price to quote: the worst error is to quote a fixed price for an open-ended assignment where the scope of the task is not fully known. It is also sometimes harder than it appears to reach a common understanding about what is really wanted, and the project will fail unless time is spent on this issue before a bid is prepared.

There is much to think about before deciding to try to obtain this type of work. It can be time-consuming and costly to bid for such contracts, and the charity must determine whether the cost of bidding makes the contract uneconomic. The provision of statistics for supervision purposes can cause bureaucracy and add to operating costs.

These are not the only problems. A charity may grow rapidly from such large contracts and become dependent on them. This is not unlike a business becoming dependent on sales to a big buyer like Marks & Spencer. This dependence can undermine the rightful and necessary independence and freedom a charity should have from politics or other pressures.

There is also a danger that workers in the public sector feel they are being undercut by 'free' volunteers. The converse is also possible. Volunteers may resent working free for the taxpayer, and object to the form filling that a government contract may necessarily bring.

At the time of writing, the Treasury was completing a study on the role of charities in the provision of services, the outcome of which could have significance for charities.

Pause for reflection

Before reading further, jot down the elements of the marketing model that you think contain principles relevant to the non-business activities of your organization, under the headings of fundraising, volunteers and making connections with potential clients/customers.

ADAPTING MARKETING CONCEPTS TO 'NON-BUSINESS' ACTIVITIES

There are many elements of the business model that are not relevant to many voluntary organizations. Figure 8.2 provides a basic model for organizations where the business model does not fit. For space reasons we have had to leave off the evaluation box, but decisions of course should be carefully costed and evaluated before they are made. Competition also disappears from Figure 8.2 because, excepting those who come under the business model, most voluntary organizations, and particularly charities, do not compete: they cooperate. There is one exception, in that all who seek donations from the public are in a sense in competition with other charities. This becomes more than an abstract consideration when several charities choose the same period to hold street or door-to-door collections. We have experienced as many as three in one week, but even worse was the occasion when there were two in one evening!

The five central boxes show the organization and some of the things to be considered under the marketing options headings. Voluntary organizations have to obtain resources; our model shows two types of resources that require marketing attention, funds and volunteers, but of course there are others. Resources are applied to various activities: the output of the organizations. We have shown two types of output in the diagram: what might be called the deliverables or the services provided and campaigning to change situations. It is the answers to the questions, in the context of the internal capabilities shown in the centre box, that enable marketing context to be identified and the best options chosen.

Let us try to bring this model to life with an imaginary new charity. Imagine an influential person who has become concerned about the

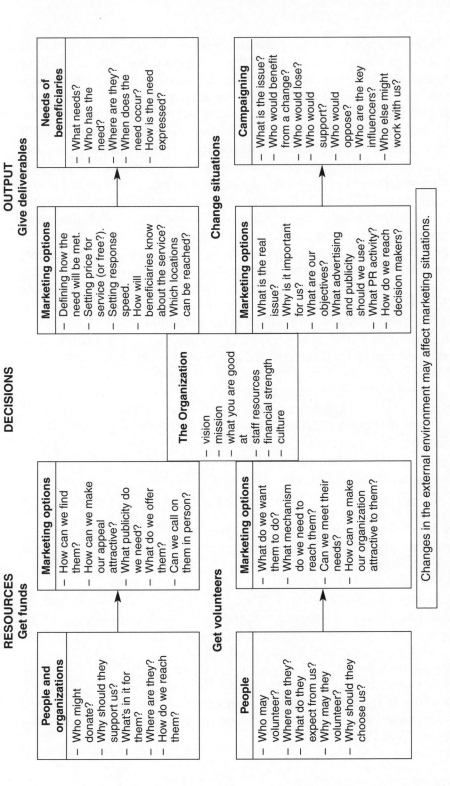

RESOURCES
Get funds

DECISIONS

OUTPUT
Give deliverables

People and organizations

– Who might donate?
– Why should they support us?
– What's in it for them?
– Where are they?
– How do we reach them?

Marketing options

– How can we find them?
– How can we make our appeal attractive?
– What publicity do we need?
– What do we offer them?
– Can we call on them in person?

The Organization

– vision
– mission
– what you are good at
– staff resources
– financial strength
– culture

Marketing options

– Defining how the need will be met.
– Setting price for service (or free?).
– Setting response speed.
– How will beneficiaries know about the service?
– Which locations can be reached?

Needs of beneficiaries

– What needs?
– Who has the need?
– Where are they?
– When does the need occur?
– How is the need expressed?

Get volunteers

Change situations

People

– Who may volunteer?
– Where are they?
– What do they expect from us?
– Why may they volunteer?
– Why should they choose us?

Marketing options

– What do we want them to do?
– What mechanism do we need to reach them?
– Can we meet their needs?
– How can we make our organization attractive to them?

Marketing options

– What is the real issue?
– Why is it important for us?
– What are our objectives?
– What advertising and publicity should we use?
– What PR activity?
– How do we reach decision makers?

Campaigning

– What is the issue?
– Who would benefit from a change?
– Who would lose?
– Who would support?
– Who would oppose?
– Who are the key influencers?
– Who else might work with us?

Changes in the external environment may affect marketing situations.

Figure 8.2 *Four marketing situations: a basic model*

number of underprivileged children in a local area. This person feels that the problem is so important that something has to be done about it, and the initiative is taken to bring together a number of like-minded people to consider how to address it. From this meeting the beginnings of a vision emerge, of what might be done, with an idea crystallizing that what is needed is a number of multi-ethnic youth clubs and homework clubs across the area for the younger teenagers. From this it is possible to determine how these would operate and what specific resources would be needed to begin to turn the vision into action. (This will be familiar ground to those who read Chapter 2.) Let us assume that an organization is now set up, with the intention of implementing the embryo plan. However, it is obvious that the resources that can be raised depend on what the organization intends to do, and what can be done depends on the resources raised.

The first three needs are funds, volunteers and premises. The chances of success for each is enhanced if there is clarity about the cause, the detailed way in which the organization is trying to make a difference and why this is expected to help the situation. Here the reputation of individual trustees can be important, as it builds confidence into an otherwise unknown organization.

For each of these three resource categories some thought should be given to who might help, why, what is in it for them and the best ways of making contact. Potential donors should be prioritized: for example, large businesses that operate locally in the area might be willing to donate because it is a local charity that benefits families of their employees. Small area businesses like shops may make small donations because the initiative may reduce crime in their immediate vicinity. How each potential donor is approached is initially a matter of exploiting all the contacts the charity can muster, and as far as possible should be done through personal visits. However, local press articles can ease contact, so public relations (PR) should form a part of the marketing effort.

Volunteers can be reached through local press and radio stories, by leafleting certain streets, direct approaches to schools and appeals for help to the employees of donor businesses. Again it is not just the cause that will capture imagination but the specific roles that volunteers are needed for. The coach for a planned football team is likely to be a very different person from the disc jockey for disco evenings. Again it is the same questions. Who might help? How can we best reach them? What can we offer them (in terms of satisfaction)? Why should they choose us?

Let us assume that initial funds are raised, we have found premises and we are able to open our first club. Here is a different marketing issue. Firstly the benefits of attending have to be expressed differently. Teenagers will hardly turn up unless they think it is going to be fun and different; explaining the social benefits to the community in a way that inspired the donors is unlikely to fire their enthusiasm. The specifics that are offered at the youth club have to be carefully thought out in relation to the needs of the 'market'. At an earlier stage we may have tried some focus group research to find what is important to the target teenagers. We need to think of ways of letting the target members know that we have something they will enjoy. It may be that we need to leaflet houses again, or get the support of schools to publicize that we are open. If we have premises of our own we may create a PR event by having an open day and persuading the local press to attend. We may also have to consider whether a charge is made for any of the things that go on at the club: even if membership is free, do we sell refreshments?

This little illustration is full of marketing decisions, without which the vision could never become a reality. The real issue is to take time to think everything through, to ensure that the best possible decisions are made. In each category we looked at, ultimate success depends on correctly identifying the target market and then finding cost-effective ways of reaching it.

The marketing effort of many voluntary organizations is often badly misplaced, as the target market has been badly thought through, or is confused. The clearer the definition of whom you need to aim at, the more cost-effective your marketing effort is likely to be. There may, of course, be more than one target, requiring different strategies. But the key marketing thinking is to identify and respond to what is seen as important by the various target markets, rather than assuming we know and designing a marketing approach based entirely on our own opinions and experiences.

PUBLIC RELATIONS

Public relations, like marketing, often has a bad name. This may sound absurd, but derives from the public's perception that it is linked to sleaze and that its practitioners depend on expensive lunches! The reality is very different. Everyone is 'perceived' – or has an 'image'. Nearly every organization has some 'visibility'. The ques-

tion is whether it is positive and helpful to the organization, or negative and harmful to the organization, in the execution of its mission.
Does your image help or hinder you?

Pause for reflection

What do you think the general image is of your organization?
How do you know? Does it need improving? How would you
ensure that if it is appropriate it is maintained?

A four-step approach

By PR we mean the publicity a charity gets for which it has not
directly paid, as opposed to advertising when space is purchased for
a known price (per second of airtime, or single column inch in the
press). Typically it is about encouraging the media to write or talk to
or about your organization at no direct cost to you. The word 'direct'
cost is used, because there may be a significant cost in having a PR
department or individual whose role is to facilitate the best exposure
in the media of favourable material about your organization.

How do you set about it, and where do you start?

Step 1

There is a need to define your objectives. What do you want from the
PR? Is it more donors, more volunteers, ensuring that clients are
aware of how the organization can help them, persuading the
government to enact new legislation, or is it to promote the broad
concept on which the whole organization's existence is based (eg
prevention of cruelty to animals)? It is a common failing to initiate a
PR programme before thinking through carefully what it is expected
to achieve and what the priorities are. As the saying goes, 'Having
lost sight of our objectives, we redoubled our efforts.'

Step 2

Determine your target audience. If you are raising funds, are you
aiming at any group of people in particular? Is it perhaps boards of
directors, politicians, solicitors who help people making their wills,
or is it the general population who hopefully will give generously in
the next flag-day appeal?

Step 3

You must then decide what is the message or image you wish to get across. What needs to be projected to the relevant people to get them to do the right thing? Press stories rarely give a telephone number of an organization, but you can usually get a name into the article. If you post out copies of the article, be sure that the covering note includes full contact details.

What makes the charity interesting? Is it local, national or international news? Can it be linked to ongoing general news at the time, such as a local drought or a food poisoning scare? Can it be linked with advantage to a well-known figure, be it a pop star, sportsperson or even a politician? When using such a link it is essential to realize that you first have to persuade the media to carry the story, and through this to reach your chosen audience. What will interest a national newspaper usually will not interest a local one, although both may include the people you are trying to reach. What excites you may not be seen as newsworthy by the journalist with whom you are dealing. The more you can tailor your needs to his or her needs, the more likely you are to build up a relationship that will help you get more published.

Pause for reflection

Ask your friends who are unconnected to the charity what it is that they could find interesting (or boring). Write down in a short sentence what are the three key messages you want to get across. Do not lose sight of your objectives. Which newspapers are the right ones to carry the story? Why should they want to publish it?

Think through the implications of what you are saying and how it will affect the range of persons linked to you – trustees, volunteers, staff, donors, clients etc. The Prince's Trust – Business has as one of its objectives a priority to help young offenders. An article about this got wide coverage. Imagine, however, the impact it had on a law-abiding client: he was selling his cleaning services to banks and his clients then assumed he must have a criminal record.

Remember that however carefully you draft a press statement or choose your words during an interview, it is the journalist who will write them up, and an editor may slash large chunks of the story to make it fit the available space. Most journalists would feel insulted if you were to ask to approve the article they write, and would decline anyway because it is their article, not yours. Every story needs an angle to make it interesting, and you are in competition with every other piece of news that has reached your chosen media.

Step 4

You then need to select the media you want to take your message. It may be a waste of time and effort to seek to get mentions of your charity on television unless some unique item of general news generates interest. If this happens, it is important to have someone available who can speak for or represent the charity. The chairperson or chief executive may be the most appropriate person, though sometimes there is someone else who may be more skilled or experienced.

Getting your organization known in the media as one that 'has a view' and can express it clearly can be a great advantage, but this usually takes time before it bears fruit. Whoever is the spokesperson must be very carefully briefed and prepared in advance. Organizations like Age Concern have reached a point where they have key people who are seen as expert sources by journalists, and who are consulted when the journalist has an article to write that touches on their speciality. We have always found that journalists on the quality papers play fair, and the name of the organization will appear in the article if it has provided help. As many voluntary organizations will be working in a specific subject area, it is not too difficult to get to know all the journalists who are specialists in that area.

Many voluntary organizations have a greater appeal to regional or specialist programmes and newspapers, so it is useful to get to know the editors or reporters who count.

Radio has become a much easier and often more appropriate medium for voluntary organizations. There are countless local radio programmes always searching for an extra local angle. They are usually very public-spirited and cooperative. In addition the average trustee or senior manager of a voluntary organization, who may have little experience of media interviews, will find speaking on the radio, where notes can be used, far less intimidating.

It is important to build up a list of media contacts. They can be contacted in advance, and perhaps fed with routine news to get them aware and interested in you. Then when you have a big story you want to get across, your mailing list is up to date and ready for immediate use.

Organizing for PR

Someone in the charity should be assigned to be responsible for public relations. In large charities this will be a professional with staff, and there may be a contract with a PR firm for some of the execution of policy. For most small charities this will be a trustee or director.

The board should:

1. Determine what is the underlying message and image the charity wishes to project.
2. Establish how the message will be projected.
3. Decide whether the charity will do anything specifically to make news, eg stage an open day or call a press conference.
4. Agree who will do what. This will include:
    - Who will be the spokesperson, in particular who will be responsible for spotting an event, or item of news, concerning the operation of the charity, which can be used with advantage to draw attention to the charity, eg the 100,000th delivery of meals on wheels, or a trustee getting a New Year Honour for work for the charity.
    - Who will follow up on the news, collecting all the relevant information and facts, and drafting a press release.
    - Who will be responsible for 'cultivating' or getting to know the appropriate media editors and journalists.
    - Whether it is possible for someone to develop a reputation as an expert on a particular subject, so that journalists make use of this facility.
5. Determine how the PR activity will be monitored. At a routine level this may include reviewing the press and assembling appropriate cuttings for review by the trustees. Unless the organization is prepared to take and scan every newspaper or listen to every radio and TV broadcast, full coverage can only be obtained if a specialist agency is used to monitor what appears.
6. Decide whether the organization needs to plan in advance for a crisis, if it works in a controversial or highly sensitive field. The slogan 'Expect the unexpected' is a good one. Something goes wrong; someone is hurt; the media get hold of it; the charity must respond quickly. There must be an understanding in advance on who can say what, and what message has to be cleared in advance by the chairperson or CEO. Time is often of the essence, and it is vital that the charity is able to respond quickly, relevantly and with one voice.

Voluntary organizations that have a local network have an advantage and a disadvantage. The Ramblers' Association obtains local as well as national press articles because it has an area and group organization that can remain in touch with the local media, and be aware when there is something local to publicize. However, it all has to be kept in order through a policy document and rules about who does what. The downside would be if the local organization went 'off message' about a national issue, such as an area press officer giving a personal opinion instead of the Association's view. This could easily happen, as with such a large network of local officers it is inevitable that not everyone knows the up-to-date central view of a particular issue, and not all members may support this view.

Planning PR policy and actions

PR policy must be planned in advance and should be seen as a potential tool to help the charity to fulfil its function. It cannot be used effectively without this element of thinking.

PR of necessity has to be reactive, because a news story may be initiated by a journalist, or the opportunity to publicize may come about because of something happening outside the organization that makes a particular story newsworthy. It should also be proactive and generate publicity.

One method we have found useful in planning PR, and which may be used in conjunction with other promotional activities, is a simple matrix. Across the top we identify all the key targets we want to reach, and down the side we identify the various ways in which they may be reached, blanking out the cells where the method is inappropriate. This gives a series of cells with a valid target and a possible means of reaching it, within which we can indicate priorities or other useful information.

Although PR will never know in advance everything that is newsworthy, there is a great deal that can be scheduled and keyed into the matrix. For example, the organization may know some months ahead the date a new service is to be launched, when the annual report will be available or when a survey will be completed, which may give newsworthy information. Where there appears to be an impending shortage of newsworthy information, the PR activity can set about collecting material from throughout the organization, in the form of case studies and examples. From all of this a schedule of planned activity can be produced, although room must be left for the unexpected.

There is always a danger that PR is used by an individual for self-aggrandizement or self-promotion. However, the opposite may also be the case. Those most appropriate as spokespeople, or who could best be interviewed, do not come forward for fear that colleagues in the charity will think they are only massaging their egos. The second situation is, in practice, more common. Part of the planning of PR might be to give training to such people to build confidence and capability.

It is up to the trustees to look around and determine who will be the best person to project the image of the charity. Some will find a solution by making the PR totally impersonal. Continuity may be unbroken, internal politics may not be stirred and no colleague is offended. This must depend on the circumstances.

On balance the media prefer to be able to quote or interview someone who becomes known or who is an established name. Such an individual may be seen as an expert or specialist in this field to the added benefit of the charity.

Handling the media

An executive who has never had to handle the media may be daunted by the prospect. This is not inevitable. The most important thing is to plan, organize in advance and avoid being taken unprepared. This may mean a member of your organization should draw up a list of names and addresses of key contacts. Try to get to know them before any special event, a launch or a crisis arises.

When you are to be interviewed by a journalist, anticipate the likely questions and prepare your answers. Have back-up statistics to rebuff difficult questions. Make sure your response is positive: 'half-full rather than half-empty'.

With radio, go into the interview clear in your own mind what message(s) you want to get across. Get them across by providing them as answers to what is asked. When an interviewer asks a question the listener often forgets exactly what the original question was, provided the response is really interesting.

With television, a live programme may be daunting but is safer than one that is made in advance. It prevents a news editor screening a reworded question to the one you were actually asked. It also avoids your response becoming dated by the time the programme is screened.

With the media there may be times when you have inadvertently given wrong information, or the journalist made a mistake. If criticized unfairly, you should be allowed the right to reply. Often these hiccups can be turned to your advantage.

As an alternative, use the letter page of the newspaper. Sometimes it is possible to stir up a lively debate and from this turn adversity to triumph with much increased exposure.

With the serious press, you can have reasonable trust in the integrity of the specialist journalists with whom you may deal. If you want to tell something off the record, to ensure that he or she understands the background to something, you can do this, but make sure that the journalist knows when this passage starts and finishes. It is better to explain anything off the record before the interview begins, to avoid confusion, and better still not to have to do it at all. Do not deliver juicy pieces of scandal in off-the-record remarks: all this may do is point the journalist to another story that he or she may work on using other sources. Be fair to the journalists: they are coming to you because they have to write news stories, so do not expect them to write something if you cry 'Confidential' to every question you are asked, or expect them to work up something interesting when you have really told them nothing at all. If this happens you will have a hard job to get the journalist to come next time.

Press releases

Decide whether you are giving an exclusive story to a journalist or offering it to everyone. By 'exclusive' is meant a time advantage, in that you will give the journalist an opportunity to publish his or her story before issuing a general press release. This can be good for both parties. It may be far better to have a well-positioned fairly long story in one target newspaper than to obtain a tiny filler paragraph in all of them.

If you do decide to issue a press release, remember that it is a starting point for many media stories. If well written it will greatly increase the probability that it will be used. Media personnel are always in a rush to meet deadlines, and in this way you can make it easy for them. Usually a journalist will handle many of them every day. The speed with which you inspire a journalist's interest is a critical factor between whether he or she bins it or reads it to the end. There is an expertise to writing good press releases.

If asked to write about an event, anyone not used to writing a release will write it in a logical sequence, starting with the background and emphasizing which part of the event was the most important from his or her standpoint. Perhaps it will even end with a 'punch line'.

With press releases the first two or three sentences are all-important, and unless they excite interest and attention the reader or the journalist moves on. So the human interest, the punch line, may need to come at the start. The sequence of elements of news often does not need to follow in a chronological order but in descending order of interest. So get the key message you want to get across somehow into the start. There is always the likelihood the sub-editor will skim down your releases and use red pen to cross out the balance once he or she gets bored! So it is important to get into what is left the key message you need to get across.

It is often a good policy to add an 'editor's note' to a press release. This can be a précis about the organization with facts, figures and names, which a journalist may use if the story really excites his or her interest.

Such a note should name who should be contacted for further information. Addresses, phone numbers, fax and e-mail for each individual should be tabled. Remember that the media work round the week and clock. After-hours and weekend numbers may also need to be added.

Publicity material

Leaflets and newsletters

Many charities will find the need to produce publicity material that can be handed out. Again the first question is 'Why do you want it, how is it to be used and to whom is it directed?' Something to be left with a civil servant concerned with subcontracting may be different to what is needed to show major donors, corporate sponsors or private individuals. Then again such material may be valuable as a support to staff morale or the recruitment of staff or volunteers. At the other end the material to be read by those you hope will benefit from the charity may well need a totally different emphasis.

The question will then be whether you need different material for different audiences, or whether you can design something that will meet many different occasions and audiences. If you try this, will it be such a compromise that it does not meet the interests of any one group?

Typically the material needed for major donors or someone prepared to give you subcontract work will not be time-sensitive.

That for staff or beneficiaries will need to be more relevant to what is happening right now. This material will be much more related to pictures of people doing things, rather than facts, figures and history.

The design and writing of this material needs to be done professionally. Printers often end up doing the design by default, but a specialist will usually do a better job. Beware of the taste of those who judge the proposed design. One charity involved with inner city homelessness was anxious to project the depth of despair and need of the client base. The cover picture of its brochure was so dark and miserable that prospective donors instinctively put it on one side and did not open the front cover.

Pictures

The saying 'A picture is worth a thousand words' is often very true. It is important to have a photographer to cover events you wish to be reported in the press. Equally it is advisable to build a stock of photographs that can be handed to the media. This may mean ensuring you have photographs of the charity in action, perhaps involving a known location or means of transport. It is vital that members of staff and their clients are in pictures to humanize the story.

Photographs of the chairperson, chief executive, local manager or the person who is being interviewed should be available. If a client or staff member has achieved something of note then that person's photograph should be available to complement the news item. Such photographs must be of a quality appropriate for media use. These types of photographs can also boost staff or client morale when they see themselves in print.

The unstaffed publicity stand

The unstaffed publicity stand, if well designed and supported by literature, can be useful for certain organizations, particularly those with a local connection. The local groups of one multi-area charity regularly use such methods, for example by arrangement with local libraries, where they are able to set up the stand for a period of several days at a time. Membership applications are frequently generated from this activity, partly because there is a local contact telephone number in addition to that of the headquarters.

Web sites

The benefit of having a Web site on the Internet is becoming rapidly more obvious, especially when targeting the young. A great advantage is the amount of material that can be presented and browsed through at leisure. Callers can quickly focus on what particular information interests them. Voluntary organizations with a national network will find this especially useful. A Web site can, of course, be quickly and cheaply updated, as opposed to printed material, and it is important that a Web site is regularly updated.

Increasingly, voluntary organizations are using Web sites to enable downloading of the annual report and accounts, the results of a review of strategy, and the latest news and press statements. In addition it is a convenient way of distributing free information produced by the organization, such as the helpful material made available by the cancer charities. Distribution costs for many free publicity items can be reduced if they are put on the Web site in a downloadable form. However, a Web site will not be accessed by everyone you want to reach, and it is usually a supplement to rather than a replacement of the traditional methods.

Although a simple Web site is not expensive to establish and maintain, the lack of sophistication of the site makes it unsuitable for all but the smallest voluntary organizations. Large Web sites that contain significant amounts of information can be costly (although costs will be much reduced if there is skilled volunteer support to build and maintain it). When the Web site is also used for collecting payments, whether for services provided or for donations, it has to be secure, and this increases costs further.

The scope for giving donations on the Internet has greatly increased. Of course it is always possible to use a Web site to solicit donations to be paid by post, but this loses immediacy compared to the opportunity to make a credit card payment there and then. But extreme care must be taken over security, as without a guarantee that the payment part of the site is secure few people would make payments this way.

A Web site has to be managed, which means that someone has to be appointed as Webmaster (such a role is sometimes suitable for a volunteer) to ensure that the policy is maintained and that the site is frequently updated and periodically modernized. There needs to be a control over what is put on the Web site. The number of hits the Web site attracts is a useful statistic to monitor, as well as the number of downloads of material. It is also worth monitoring what other organizations are doing. This medium is changing so quickly that what is good and up to date today may be old hat next year. Is that important to you?

You also need to get the Web site registered with as many search engines as possible. When we researched various charities for this book we tended to use the links in the Charity Commission register or links in umbrella organizations covering the voluntary sector, but the more usual route where someone is unsure of the Web address of the organization, or even its name, is to use a search engine.

TO BE CONTINUED

In this chapter we have looked at what we might term a 'tool kit' for marketing, and explored it in different contexts. In the next chapter we will go deeper into various aspects of fund-raising, and will also look at the difference in concept between the rolling, ongoing activity and the one-off appeal.

REFERENCE

Levitt, T (1968) *Innovation in Marketing*, Pan, London

9

Marketing and fund-raising

Two aspects of fund-raising, Web sites and trading activities, were discussed in the previous chapter. Here we will explore a wide range of fund-raising activities, looking at both regular rolling actions and special one-off appeals. We conclude with a discussion of grants, which may lie outside any specific marketing activity.

ROLLING MARKETING CAMPAIGNS COMPARED TO SPECIAL APPEALS

There are two very different types of marketing campaigns. The first is the ongoing rolling programme. This is the norm when you need a regular supply of volunteers or customers. It is also the norm when you are fund-raising for the regular requirements of the organization.

Some charities, such as Action Research, exist in order to raise money and award it to medical research. This is 'ongoing', year after year, month after month. From time to time a charity may need to make a special appeal, perhaps to raise capital for new buildings or equipment, or for a new initiative that needs start-up funding.

Case study 9.1: Action Research

Background

Action Research celebrated its 50th anniversary in 2002. The use of Paddington Bear as its logo has been very effective in raising awareness. The charity has assets of £14 million, of which £8 million are committed and £6 million uncommitted reserves. The latter are needed to cover one year of operating costs, three years of the cost of research training fellowships, and a contingency fund.

The mission of the charity is to fund university and hospital-based medical research. There is a focus on unborn children, babies and children. A proportion is also given to fund research into a variety of medical problems of adults and the elderly. It does not fund heart, cancer or AIDS research, as it is felt there are plenty of other charities that are dedicated to these areas.

The annual income is £4.5 million, of which £2.8 million comes from regional and central funds. Legacies are impossible to forecast accurately, but they typically run at £500,000 a year. Recently this rose to £900,000. The cost of fund-raising has risen and now comes to £2.3 million a year. Within this cost is £500,000 for PR and associated costs.

Issues

It is significant that even for a comparatively well-known, respected and established charity the cost of fund-raising is high. In the last 10 years the cost of fund-raising has risen steadily from 30 to 60 per cent. Action is in hand to get this down to 45 per cent within two years.

The amount people give is not elastic, and charities must compete to increase their 'share of the available cake'. In 2001 there was a fall in the stock market, well-noted redundancies, the outbreak of foot and mouth disease, a general election and the events of 11 September. Each event like these can cause nervousness and reticence to donate more generously.

The amount that should be spent on publicity is very difficult to gauge. How it should be directed is also contentious. The publicity aim of Action Research is to increase awareness amongst their potential donors. Posters at railway stations in London and the radio station Classic FM appear to have been effective.

The establishment of a Web site has proven very worthwhile, as a high percentage of those who access it are potential donors.

It is perhaps surprising that the Charity Commission has been keen to see Action Research spend some of its investment assets. The Commission is not anxious to see charities build up a large investment income, but wants them to depend more on what they can raise annually.

Although the marketing principles are the same, the management issues of the one-off appeal are different. The appeal requires the talent of the sprinter, as opposed to that of the long-distance runner. Sprinters and marathon runners both act in the same basic way, but their style and planning will vary.

The two approaches should not be confused. The parish church that every two years has a 'special appeal' for parishioners to increase their annual covenant will soon find their supporters 'battle weary'. Such special efforts become less and less effective.

THE ROLLING MARKETING CAMPAIGN

Who is your target audience?

The group of people you need to address will determine where you need to place your message. For example, if you are looking for retired millionaires to donate large funds, then advertisements in the popular dailies may well be counter-productive. If, however, your aim is to encourage more ex-service personnel to help you with an appeal to run ex-service personnel hostels, then perhaps an approach through local ex-service personnel clubs would be appropriate.

Where you place your message will largely depend on the resources you have at your disposal and the cost-effectiveness of any expenditure. Perhaps you have no funds available and must rely on personal one-to-one appeals to friends. Could this be where trustees and patrons might help? Perhaps you should bear this in mind when you are selecting these people.

Expenditure on paid advertisements is rarely affordable by the very small charities. The question to be answered is 'How cost-effective is it?' As the effect of advertising is usually cumulative, this is often difficult to answer. It is also liable to attract criticism if precious funds are 'wasted' on advertisements whose return cannot be confidently identified.

An alternative to paid advertisements is the reference to your charity in a positive light in the editorial copy of the media. This is when you need help from someone with a knowledge of PR. Large organizations will need professional help. However, many small charities may find a volunteer with appropriate experience. Perhaps a retired journalist or someone involved professionally in marketing might be prepared to take on the responsibility for this.

What is your message?

The message you want to put over will be affected by whom you are aiming it at. For example, a Church of England parish church needing to raise more funds is likely to focus on the church members within the parish. In many parishes these people may feel they are already giving as much as they can.

However, beyond the faithful there may be very many more people who rarely go to church and give nothing. They may, however, be proud of their local church and not want it to fall into disrepair or become empty. They may vaguely hope that when their teenage daughter marries she will have a white wedding in this church – vicar permitting. A wider appeal may well bring in many donors.

Although the underlying message may be the same, it may be written differently if it is directed at church members, all the people within the parish boundary or all the people within the whole town. And it may be different again if it is aimed selectively at different groups within these definitions. An appeal to local businesses will be couched differently from an appeal to individual church members. The issue to consider is what will motivate the target groups and how they will be persuaded.

Here we can see a quite separate set of motivations that may need to be awakened, and a message designed to appeal to them. The question is: do we know what motivates people to give, to sponsor, to volunteer or to ask for help? Do not take for granted that you know the answer. Later on, we write about why corporations give time, money and their prestige. Here we should consider issues beyond just 'because the charity is a good cause'. Why should they give to your particular charity when there are many hundreds of other charities clamouring for their support?

Pause for reflection

Write down a few succinct points to show why you believe that a particular group of persons should give to your organization. (This is a good discipline in a real situation.)

Not all giving is for the highest of altruistic motives. It may be that the donor, whether corporate or individual, wishes to be seen as associated with a well-respected charity or identified with some important person in that charity. The motivation may be to project a good public image or to assuage a guilty conscience. The motivation will matter if someone with less-than-ideal motives is seen to be closely associated with a particular voluntary organization and brings discredit to it.

One new charity was anxious to have a prestige president. It was quite well connected, and made several approaches to ideal individuals. Each one, because of a very successful career, was too busy and declined. The embarrassment came when several well-known executives put their names forward or let it be known they would be happy to fill this role. Unfortunately, for one reason or another, they were unsuitable and could have damaged the image of the educational charity. In the event the vacancy was left open for many years until the right person became available.

What is needed is to talk to different groups of people who do donate or support the charity and get from them in discussion the real reasons for their support. This needs to be sensitively and carefully done, as the charity is unlikely to be able to commission original motivational research into the response to their appeals.

What printed material is needed?

Image is projected by the material a voluntary organization produces, whether it is a mailshot to households, a report on a critical issue, a letterhead or a publication. It looks more professional if all the material has the same style and appearance. Often an organization will use different typefaces to spell its name, the logo will not be consistent and the general appearance makes the effort look amateurish and undeserving of support. Fortunately today, thanks to the personal computer, it is possible for even the smallest voluntary organization to produce consistent, high-quality material in-house, although it is better if someone with design skills is involved in setting up the basic ground rules.

When preparing printed material it is useful to design it in such a way that it can be used in a variety of situations, such as handouts to visitors, direct mail or supporting material to support a request from a major corporation. The material should be able to 'stand alone' when used outside direct mail situations. This means ensuring that the charity address and telephone number, e-mail address and Web site are clearly visible. If possible, the name (and possibly a photograph) of someone the caller can speak to will increase the likelihood of the material paying off.

A certain amount of background information about the charity is necessary to generate interest and ensure credibility. However, do not assume everyone will be as fascinated as you may be about your founders, your history or what the charity did in the 19th century. Ensure the emphasis is on the output: the benefits the charity brings. Make it cheerful, and ensure a number of people see it in the proof stage and express an honest opinion. Typically a charity will not have many people who know professionally what makes a good brochure. However, avoid one situation where the chairman of a small charity went to immense personal trouble to design a brochure. To avoid hurting his feelings the board members felt they could not say it was terrible. The result was a disaster and a waste of money.

Try to personalize the material with names and photographs of your staff or customers (or case histories with disguised names if there are issues of confidentiality). If relevant, strike a local identity. There is a lot to be said for giving the name of someone people can ask for. This gives inexperienced callers a sense of reassurance. Naming members of staff can have drawbacks. Staff may leave or individuals may be harassed by unsuitable calls. In business this is sometimes overcome by inventing a fictitious name that all the staff know. Calls for this name are put through to the correct member of staff who operates and answers to that name for the day, or as long as he or she is operating in this role. Such names can last for years and years. The whole theme is to make the organization friendly and not intimidating to phone.

Make it clear what you want respondents to do

It is important that the message is clear about what it is you want those who wish to respond to your appeal to do. Is it to come to an open day, to write a cheque or to phone you? Think this through, and reread your leaflets or any other form of publicity to see whether this is clear. Is it obvious where someone should write to or to whom they should make out a cheque? If you want people to phone you, is it clear where they phone? Often people are apprehensive of phoning an organization they do not know. Ensure when they ring your organization, even at lunchtime, that the phone is quickly answered in a friendly way and competently handled. Ensure messages are handled efficiently and your organization has a discipline about phoning back. A good image projected by printed material can be destroyed by the first contact a potential donor has with the organization: often this is by telephone.

What alternative approaches to marketing should be adopted?

In all marketing activities there has to be a 'vehicle' by which your message is delivered. This is an immense subject, and new approaches are being developed all the time. The charity field in particular has been full of innovative approaches to 'get at' those people who it is thought are most likely to help. This may be in cash or kind. There are four main groups (in addition to those discussed in the previous chapter): 1) high-value donations; 2) private individual donations; 3) events and attractions; 4) purchased services.

High-value donations

We discuss four ongoing categories of high-value donations in the following sections, with two others, grants and lottery grants, which have some very different characteristics, being left to later in the chapter.

High net worth individuals

This is a term frequently used in the financial services industry for an identifiable group of rich individuals. Most are tabled in many direct mail lists, which it is possible to buy. For many charities this is neither necessary nor desirable. Inevitably those on these lists are swamped with appeals, and hence a further appeal is likely to fall on deaf ears. Nevertheless, where members of a charity, or its friends, know rich persons, it may well pay to make individual approaches. This is time-consuming. Much will depend on the strength of the link to the rich person, and the tact and persuasion of the individual making the approach.

There is often an added advantage in winning the support of wealthy individuals. They may have achieved their wealth through inheritance, or professional or political success, or through the medium of sport or entertainment. Such persons can give credibility, stature or glamour. They may also be in a position of influence that leads to support from corporations, trusts, foundations or even government grants. In project funding such people play a particularly important role.

Legacies

The saying goes 'You have to speculate to accumulate'. This is especially true when you mount a campaign to encourage people to put your charity in their will. Obviously the results are not immediately apparent, and hence any resource put into this activity must initially be an act of faith. Anyone needing quick results, or hoping in the short term to measure the pay-off, should not go down this path.

One fallacy is the belief that wills take a very long time to lead to payment of a legacy. The truth is a little different. The average time between a charity's name being put in a will and it being implemented is only five years. It seems that those knowing their days are numbered are more likely to review their will and be conducive to nominating a charity for a gift.

Table 1.4 showed that some 6 per cent of the income of the top 2,950 charities comes from legacies. For many small charities this may be an unlikely source, but it is not restricted to the big charities. However, some people want to know a little more about a charity before they write it into their wills, and charities that make it hard or impossible to obtain copies of their annual reports may cut themselves off from this source of income.

The Royal National Lifeboat Institution (RNLI) depends heavily on their remarkable income from legacies. Naturally there is a nervousness as to whether such a flow will continue over many years. This has led to action to prevent overdependence on any one source of funds and to take action to spread the risks and diversify the fundraising.

Case study 9.2: Royal National Lifeboat Institution

The RNLI has an enviable reputation for being the best-run charity in Britain. It is therefore worthwhile to understand a little of how it has built up this reputation and how it tackles some of the issues it now faces.

Since its foundation in 1824 it has carefully guarded its independence and since the middle of the 19th century has declined the offer of central government funds. Lifeboat stations today remain part of the local community, with many families having helped staff the lifeboats for generations.

Only 20 per cent of the crews come from a nautical background, and women have been included in the crews since the 1960s. There is a retirement age of 45 for the crews of the in-shore lifeboats, and 55 for the all-weather crews. Great importance is attached to the volunteer ethos, and the phrase 'the nobility of the cause' still expresses an attitude that pervades the service. It is a point of pride never to charge anyone for the services they perform.

The RNLI has one full-time crew based on the isolated Spurn Point on the Humber. The typical all-weather boat has only one full-time paid member, the mechanic who is charged with the day-to-day maintenance of the boat. The decision to launch the boat is vested in the station honorary secretary or deputy, not the coxswain. The latter selects his crew for each 'shout' from those available at the time of the launch.

In view of the long and honourable history of the RNLI, it is perhaps not surprising that up to 71 per cent of the annual income (£68.5 million) comes from legacies. In fact, only £27 million or 28 per cent comes from fund-raising activities. This includes the famous flag-day appeals. The balance of £1.5 million comes from trading activities.

Though non-legacy fund-raising is a success, it is interesting to note that even the RNLI does not come by this money without a lot of hard work. No fewer than 192 full-time fund-raisers are needed. The Institute knows that even after 178 years it still has to invest heavily in fund-raising, and in 2001 this had an annual budget of £9.3 million.

This level of effort reflects that a large legacy income is no cause to relax, for it could so easily lead to a loss of vitality. This issue is taken very seriously. Indeed there is a fear that this heavy dependence on legacies may reflect the attitude of the older generation. The RNLI, therefore, has to ensure that it maintains its support from future generations.

This has encouraged the RNLI to take an interest in providing a beach life-guard service. It is hoped that young people will become familiar with the RNLI and from their early experience continue to support it in future years. With wise caution it has undertaken several pilot studies, and carefully moni-tored the outcome. These have been part-funded by appropriate local author-ities, with which the RNLI has a clear-cut contract. These lifeguards, often young graduates, provide a very different 'glamour' image to the traditional much older crews who staff the lifeboats. This could provide a clash of culture and difference of attitude if it was not sensitively handled. Growth in this field is strictly controlled, and very high standards have to be established and main-tained.

Because of the inherent dangers in sea rescue it is not surprising that rigorous attention is given to crew training. Lifeboat crews want excellent training, and the divisional inspector monitors the standards achieved. In addi-tion there is a realization that we all live in a litigious world. The RNLI must be able to demonstrate that crews are adequately trained. This is one of the reasons why the Institution is investing in the lifeboat college alongside its headquarters in Poole. It is hoped that a recognized qualification will be granted that will have a 'market value' to the recipients. On the same site there will be a wave tank, logistics centre, boat facility and visitors centre.

This charity brings out a number of lessons:

- Firstly, it does not rest on its laurels or the security of its present funding. It refuses to run the risk of being dependent on the public sector. The

Institution is also taking a long-term view of its income and field of endeavour.

● Secondly, it is determined to remain driven by a noble volunteer ethos with a local identity.

● Thirdly, other than legacies, fund-raising does not come easily or cheaply. It is hard work.

● Fourthly, the importance of staff training means that, increasingly, it will be essential for staff to be developed to a recognized professional standard. The charity must be known for quality and competence, and not accept lower standards from crews just because they are volunteers.

Corporations

Social responsibility, and attention to the corporate image has led to a considerable increase in the way corporations make outright gifts of money or goods and services in kind to charities. Though some of it is due to the genuine goodwill of the directors, much of it today is based on hard-nosed business decisions. A well-directed policy on giving donations to charities can play a significant role in building corporate image. For corporations it is money well spent if they have thought through whom they will give to, how it will be given and how they will exploit the goodwill and publicity generated.

For one large city business the choice of which particular charity was best able to help them centred on how often and for how long senior partners would be able to meet influential trustees. The milk of human kindness was not on the agenda!

What is important is to tailor the corporate approach to the individual company. What the charity does and how it is exposed to the public are of great importance, and must be a match to the needs of the donor. This is not to say that the charity should change its way. It is simply to point out that one charity will appeal to one company and another charity to another. Wilson's report (1993) on how and why companies give to charities confirms this point.

United Biscuits had, for example, a very active corporate philanthropic budget and programme. It actively sought to help the local communities where its factories were located. In particular it helped young persons to get jobs when there were redundancies. Subsequently it sought to purchase a biscuit factory in Hungary, which was overstaffed and which the government wished to privatize. The payback came when the Hungarian government accepted the lower bid from United Biscuits because of the proven philanthropic approach the company operated, which would be particularly relevant if the company implemented the expected redundancies.

Case study 9.3: A day in the life of a corporate manager (community appeals) – the National Society for the Prevention of Cruelty to Children (NSPCC)

What does a corporate fund-raiser actually do? We asked one to describe a typical day:

I get straight to work dealing with the actions from meetings with corporate supporters. One company which has a large staff base is planning a varied programme of employee fund-raising starting with a payroll giving campaign so I e-mail him some support materials. The other wants to set up a sales promotion whereby they will give a donation to the NSPCC for each product they sell. The latter requires a written agreement between the company and the charity so I amend our standard contract and e-mail it to the lawyer for checking. This takes time but I am confident that the promotion will more than cover the costs we incur in staff time setting it up. Halfway through my assistant calls with details of the post, which includes a large cheque we were expecting, and I add to my list of things to do that we need to arrange a cheque presentation and do a press release. Towards the end of the morning I check and answer my e-mails, which usually come in thick and fast from all parts of the organization and supporters too!

In the afternoon I work on one of my key longer-term objectives, which is to set up a number of business groups in Berkshire. I have some good contacts there so can avoid cold calling. Key to the success of the business groups is volunteer leadership so I draw up a short list of contacts at director level or above who might be able to help me and start writing to a few to see if they will meet with me. I point out briefly what the benefits are of involvement for the groups, such as networking, increased profile and focused community involvement. Although companies these days may be motivated to help the community out of a sense of philanthropy, what they decide to do needs to have good business reasons to justify it – it's not enough just to say we need help.

A crucial motivating factor though in the first instance is having a good case for support so I ring a colleague in children's services to request up-to-date information on how many children the local project aims to help and how much that will cost, as I will need this for face-to-face meetings with potential volunteers.

Finally, I prepare for a meeting I have tomorrow with the marketing director of a company that wants to support us. I read through the research I have on the company and make notes of things I want to cover and questions I want to ask. It's important I am clear about his objectives but in case he's not sure how to proceed I have a few ideas myself. I pull out relevant documents I need to take with me, put them in my briefcase ready for tomorrow.

Pause for reflection

What lessons can you draw from the NSPCC case study that might be applicable to your organization? What other ideas does it stimulate?

An alternative to cash can be goods and services in kind. This can often be easier for a local executive to authorize, especially if the company is the subsidiary of a foreign company. For example, empty offices could be made available at a nominal or peppercorn rent. The use of boardrooms, or conference or training facilities can often be given at no cost, but results in a big saving to the charity that is in need of them.

A merchant bank in the City of London offered to meet all the printing needs of a charity for a three-year period. The bank needed the facility to be on immediate call for urgent work. This meant that for much of the time it was underutilized. It really incurred little extra cost to render a most valuable service to this charity.

Is corporate sponsorship a possible alternative? Sponsorship is big business, and much of it is sports-related, where players or machines carry corporate logos. Companies also are often willing to sponsor a charity for a particular fund-raising event, for example at an agricultural show. Because such an endeavour may be at considerable risk from the weather or some other uncontrollable event, the charity may be unable to participate unless it can find a business to underwrite participation in the event. In most cases the business will gain publicity, with a strong chance of having to pay out nothing.

In all these events the charity should be as helpful as possible to the sponsor. This should not mean that the corporate logo is allowed to smother the identity of the charity. However, a good corporate sponsor can add to the credibility of a small charity, and hence their interests can be mutual.

Media appeals

Do not forget the media, which can help many charities. Comic Relief and the ITV telethon programmes have continued to raise many millions. 'The Week's Good Cause' on the radio still has a considerable pulling appeal. It is worth finding the policy of your local media. Typically your local radio and newspapers will, during the course of a year, make a point of championing several local charities. Do not be defeatist, as 'Nothing ventured, nothing gained', and an approach can be very worthwhile.

Private individual donations

Recent years have seen a remarkable number of new ways of easing money from prospective donors. Charities need to be aware of taxation changes and of new, often electronic ways money can be donated, and be ready to exploit them. The following sections detail some different ways.

Deed of covenant

The deed of covenant has been around a long time. The donor promises to donate a given sum for a specific or indefinite period. In the past the commitment was for a specified period, and there were small problems if the donation was cancelled within the specified period. For this reason people were often fearful of committing themselves beyond the one year. There is no longer this problem, and hence it is useful to allay this old fear.

The advantage is that the charity can get the income tax paid refunded, which greatly enhances the value of the gift. This is, of course, assuming the donor is an income tax payer. It does however involve the charity in a certain amount of administration. This is to ensure the annual donation is paid, and the income tax is recovered. Although inflation has fallen in recent years, it is still a factor. It is therefore important to ensure that donors are encouraged to increase their donations periodically. This may be easiest to do when the charity is a membership organization, like the many family history societies.

Gift Aid

Gift Aid allows a charity to reclaim the basic rate of tax on a donation from individuals. It does not matter how small the donation is. The charity must write to the Inland Revenue to register for tax purposes, get a declaration from the donor to confirm he or she is a UK taxpayer, and claim the tax back, either manually, by using a computer software package or by using an organization such as the Charities Aid Foundation (CAF).

Gift Aid gives a tax break to those who pay tax at the higher rate of 40 per cent (taxable income to exceed £29,400 for the tax year 2001–02). Suppose such a taxpayer made a Gift Aid donation of £78 net. Tax reclaimed is £22 and therefore the taxable income is reduced by £100. This taxpayer would then see his or her tax bill reduced by £100 × (40 – 22) per cent = £18.

Payroll giving

A direct deduction from an employee's pay cheque has recently become quite popular (see the NSPCC case study). A company may be keen to encourage staff to make donations as part of their civic duty. However, people change jobs with increasing frequency, and this can lead to a considerable administrative task. If a donor makes a gift of £100 then that is what the charity receives. A sum of £100 is deducted from the gross earnings and so the net cost to the donor is either £78 or £60, depending on the donor's highest tax band. It is essential, therefore, to get the donors to 'gross up' their donations.

One disadvantage is that some employers contract out the work to agencies that charge for this service, which is deducted from the payment to the charity (one agency charges 3.75 per cent.)

Giving shares

With the increased share ownership this should become of increased importance. A 40 per cent taxpayer can give a charity £10,000 at a cost of £6,000 to him- or herself. This does not attract capital gains tax to the donor. (The Inland Revenue has produced a useful guide, IR 178.) Organizations such as CAF and Sharegift provide schemes specifically designed to help charities with the administration.

Charities Aid Foundation

CAF runs a number of schemes that enable donors to spread their giving in any way they wish. The most popular scheme is to donate a monthly sum to CAF, for distribution to whichever charities, for whichever amount, the donor deems fit. Often a sum is available that accumulates as the amounts passed to named charities is less than the sum put aside every month. The donor is then in a position to draw sums from this 'pot' and donate them to any charity he or she may happen to wish on the spur of the moment. Charities can, with advantage, ensure knowledge of their own activities are well known to CAF staff.

It is also possible to give via charities' own Web sites, so it is worthwhile for charities to register their details with the CAF. CAF charge donors 4 per cent of the gross amount (3 per cent to CAF and 1 per cent to NCVO) to maintain the account.

Credit card giving

The days of cash in the pocket or a ready chequebook have declined. When people wish to give, it is now so much easier to phone, give a credit card number and the deed is done. Charities should be geared up to handle calls that may arise at any time – possibly from an appeal or a mention on the TV or radio.

If you are fortunate in having an appeal in the national media, it may be sensible to engage an organization that is geared to handle a large number of phone calls at a specific time. They are geared up for this, whereas you are unlikely to have the required number of trained staff to cope.

Membership subscriptions

There is a wide variety of ways of encouraging individuals to support an organization in return for some recognition. For example, an individual can become a 'member' by paying an annual subscription. This, however, will normally assume the member gets in return some advantage from subscription, although in some cases this will be minimal. There can be complications when membership depends on being seen as 'good value for money', instead of a continuing association with the organization. The Strategic Planning Society is perceived as a professional society, although a registered charity, and will only retain its members if they see value in belonging. The Society cannot claim the tax back on membership, as relief is given by the Inland Revenue to the member: membership is considered to be a deductible expense. For most charities members are a means to an end, rather than the end itself. An advantage of having a membership base is that it brings a measure of stability to the annual income and, if members agree to pay by direct debit, administrative costs are reduced. It also gives an address list of supporters.

Sponsorship

The sponsorship of individuals to achieve something (such as run a marathon) has grown rapidly in recent years. It involves people of all ages seeking the support of friends. This has the added benefit of giving the performers an added motivation to achieve their goals. It is also a way of getting the cause of the charity discussed by a wide range of individuals.

Flag days

Flag days have been a very traditional approach to fund-raising.

They involve an army of collectors, and subsequent administration. Collections like this are governed by specific legislation, are strictly controlled and are restricted to charities. Older charities hang on to their regular slot in the year. New charities may find it very difficult to get in on the schedule of flag days, which is usually carefully regulated. It may be very much easier to do it on a local basis, at least as a start.

Events and attractions

The aim of these activities is to draw crowds to the organization, perhaps to sell goods, entertain or just generate goodwill. In all these types of events there is a good opportunity to get the organization's message across. What the message is, and how it can be effectively presented, must be given careful thought if the opportunity is not to be wasted.

Attendance at public events and shows

An alternative to an open day on your own property is to take a stand at some event. This may be a local fair or even a large event like an agricultural show. The bigger the event, the greater the likely cost. The cost of the site and the marquee will occur every year you attend. Mention has already been made that these are costs you might get a sponsor to meet. What you put in your stand in terms of display is likely to be a one-off cost.

Bringing your organization to life and then getting passers-by motivated needs a lot of skill. The outcome needs to be carefully evaluated. Is the cost in terms of money and time well spent? Would another activity be more cost-effective?

If a voluntary organization has been doing the same thing year after year it may take courage to try something new. However, a good rule is to experiment and check the results. How to do this at minimum expense is an issue, but getting into a rut and believing there is only one form of marketing activity must surely be wrong.

Take into account the number of person hours that are needed to set up the display and staff the stand. Shows are open for long hours, and you may well need two shifts to cover each day. Seek answers to how your stand is perceived by your target audience. What proportion of those who pass by stop or even notice you? What sort of impact do the staff on your stand give? Has anyone given them any briefing and tips on how to work on the stand? Do they need training?

A badly staffed stand can be counter-productive, as the poor impression given can last a long time. However, a stand attracting the target audience can be very worthwhile if the potential opportunities are grasped.

Recently at an agricultural show a charity manager was on a stand coaching a new member of staff on the value of trying to find something out about each person visiting the stand. Noticing an elderly gentleman had wandered into the marquee, he said, 'Now let's see what we can find out!' In the relaxed discussion that followed it turned out the man had just sold the business he had spent his life building up for £34 million. He had no children, was a widower and was musing where he would direct his energies in his new retirement. Here was an opportunity to introduce him on the stand to volunteers, as well as some of the beneficiaries.

Sponsorship of private events

Mention has been made of the need to find ways of attracting sponsors, and that this will become much easier if a potential sponsor can see the way it will benefit him or her. One such way is for the sponsor to fund some event that his or her customers, staff and friends can attend (and take the best seats).

This can take quite a lot of organizing, as there is a need to match the sponsor to the type of event that would interest him or her. This could be a sporting event, a theatre, a dinner etc. Golf matches, especially if celebrities are involved, can be very popular and profitable. A night at a theatre is likely to be easier in a provincial town, especially if there is a popular move to support this theatre. A sponsor who can underwrite a big dinner in a unique location, like a castle, can enable a very attractive event.

Such events cannot be undertaken lightly. The way you will sell the tickets and what will generate the big audience draw must be carefully thought out. Typically it cannot be undertaken by a charity if there is risk of financial failure. This is where a local business may be able to help provide a financial guarantee. The event may end up as an enjoyable evening, at no cost to the sponsor and with a lot of good publicity for all concerned.

Open days at charity premises

When a charity has a physical presence, a school, a hospice, a home etc that it can show to people, this can be the most productive opportunity for fund-raising. People do not want to give money to some nebulous concept. They want to give to something that is tangible, and that they can touch or see. It is not putting money at risk, can show donations are put to good use, can encourage staff and volunteers, and should encourage beneficiaries. It can also be a good way of fostering relations with the local community.

These events should be carefully orchestrated. If possible some variety should be added to the programme, rather than exactly the same format occurring every year. It is often worth attempting to get a local newsworthy figure to open the proceedings. This will add to the attendance and ensure coverage in the local media.

It may be difficult to decide who is an appropriate person to ask. A pop star may be fine if it is sheer attendance figures you want, or if you are putting up stalls to sell something at a profit. It may, however, project the wrong image and attract inappropriate types of visitors. Similarly, an elderly person of great stature may be wrong if it is the young you want to attract.

Open days can be used to raise money by selling products and refreshments, and as a way of encouraging people to donate their money and/or time. The possibility of forming a group, 'Friends of ABC Charity', through an annual membership may also present itself at such an event. These occasions may also be a way of identifying possible volunteers who can be followed up after the event.

Private meetings and lunches

Most charities find that a small number of people can have a quite disproportionate impact on the fortunes of the organization. These may include: senior executives and trustees of corporations and trusts; high net worth individuals; civil servants granting contracts or permits; national and local politicians; media controllers and journalists; opinion formers in all shapes and guises; stars from the sport and entertainment industry.

Trustees and senior charity executives need to identify who is important for their particular organization, get to know them and seek to influence their views and attitudes. Often this involves networking, and some trustees may be better at this than others. Charities should find ways of getting such an identified group to know more about the organization and the benefits it provides.

Open days, previously referred to, can be such a way. Simple lunches or in the evening a small reception can be another. Done on a regular basis a network of friends in high and key places can be very valuable. Avoid too many being invited at the same time. Ensure each key individual is spoken to personally and handled as a VIP. This is much easier when the charity has a physical presence and can show guests the charity in action.

Purchased services

Voluntary organizations tend to be short of money. Indeed if they are not, then perhaps the sights of the trustees are too low! Fund-raising is often very expensive. The recurring question is 'What is the most cost-effective marketing approach?' There are situations where it is money well spent to buy such services. This includes press, TV and radio, direct mail and market research. Although some may be beyond the financial reach of many charities, there is always the possibility of getting sponsorship from a corporate donor, to enable something worthwhile to be done.

Press, TV and radio

Only the larger charities are likely to have the resources and operation to justify and pay for press and TV. However, local radio is much cheaper, and paying for a small amount of advertising will often encourage a local radio station to give free airtime to some of your news releases.

If money is to be spent, then much careful attention must be given to the exact coverage of the particular media. This must match the profile of your target audience as closely as possible to avoid wastage. Measurement of audiences is not just overall numbers but their geographical location, gender, age, job and/or income, ethnic group and sometimes the target life cycle position of the reader/ viewer (for example, single adults, newly married, married with children, retired).

The advertising departments of most publishers and broadcasters can provide information on the number of people they reach and the profiles of those people. With television and radio, this may vary by times of day and particular programmes.

Getting the correct profile has a direct bearing on the chances of success. It is important to remember whom you are aiming at – is it the donor, the volunteer or a prospective beneficiary?

Posters

A really large hoarding will rarely be used by a charity except possibly to indicate a specific nearby location, such as a soup kitchen.

The cost of printing small numbers of posters can be very high per sheet, and the best locations are unlikely to be available.

However, small A4-size posters can be cheap to produce, and can often be placed free of charge on noticeboards, in homes, in shop windows etc.

Direct mail

Everyone groans at the pile of junk mail that drops on the doormat. Even if most direct mail is thrown away, in practice it is often the cumulative impact that brings results. After the third and fourth shot the message or image starts to sink in and do its work. However, it requires perseverance and it may be some time before direct mail can recover its cost.

Expertise in advertising, graphics and direct mail is essential. The message that appeals to an executive inside the organization may be totally irrelevant for the target market, but without expert help this may not be perceived.

Success also depends on careful attention to lists. The message has to get to the right target with as little wastage as possible. But buying lists can itself be expensive, and the number of times they can be used is restricted.

Direct mail requires a lot of volunteer work, unless an outside service is used that has automated equipment.

Market research

Business organizations often spend large sums of money researching their market. This can vary from determining what people want to buy and what they think of the organization (the image) to what reaction they have to its advertising and marketing activities: in fact all the things shown in the market box of Figure 8.1. Voluntary organizations also need to know how they are perceived and whether marketing effort could be made more cost-effective. None but the largest charities are likely to have big budgets for this activity. However, there are some useful lower-cost options.

One approach can be to interest a local business school or even a sixth form college to do a local exercise. As an alternative it may be possible to run your own panels or focus groups. Getting a disparate variety of people to sit round and discuss such issues as giving, generosity and then the image of the organization may bring out some home truths. It can be very enlightening. If the results are heard verbally at first hand it is better than reading a tactfully written report written by outsiders.

A note of caution is in order. The answers from good research can be highly productive and very worthwhile. However, cut-price or amateur research badly done can provide wrong answers and lead to bad decisions. It is better to find a volunteer with marketing research experience.

THE ONE-OFF SPECIAL PROJECTS CAMPAIGN

The rolling campaign enables management to develop, improve and finesse their marketing approach over time. The one-off campaign for a capital project is far more time-sensitive. Though there can be a certain amount of flexibility, there is normally a fixed period of time by which a specific sum of money is to be raised. If funds are not forthcoming and the stated target is not reached, the campaign is deemed to have failed. You cannot have two bites at the cherry. Relaunching a failed campaign is usually very difficult.

So what are the important differences?

1. *Selection of the chairperson of the appeal.* A special appeal needs its own chairperson, but this appointment must not conflict with the chairperson of the charity itself. The selection, or perhaps persuasion, of the appeals chairperson is of critical importance, as one duty will be to set the scene for big and critically important donors. It is an active role, and the person selected should be experienced in working with the media. The person appointed has to be credible, which means having a current reputation rather than one that has waned or has yet to be developed.

   There is also a case for appointing a patron or president who 'blesses' the campaign. This ideally might be royalty, a lord lieutenant or a member of parliament. If the organization already has a patron, he or she may be in a position to fill this role.

2. *The appointment of the treasurer.* A special appeal for funds normally requires a volunteer who is the identifiable treasurer, perhaps a local bank manager. There should be a separate bank account for the appeal. Donations for the appeal must be kept separately from the routine funds that the organization may receive.

3. *The appointment of a campaign manager.* An appeal of a significant size will need one person to be in total charge and carry full responsibility for the overall and smooth running of all aspects of the campaign. This person must have the authority needed to carry out this function. The person might be a fund-raising consultant especially brought in for the duration of the task, or a member of staff who is good at motivating people on a project. In either case the role must be carefully defined to empower the person without removing the overall authority of the trustees.

4. *Fund-raising consultant.* The pros and cons of hiring a fund-raising consultant are often debated. The realistic target to be met needs to be substantial to justify the cost. When funds are very limited such consultants can be drawn in with only a limited remit, perhaps advising on key initial policy issues. Choosing a consultant who will suit your charity, with the personalities involved, is important. Take into account the nature of your campaign and seek someone who has worked in the same field as the particular charity. It is an advantage if it is someone who is known and it is an added advantage if it is someone who will be sure to get backing, but the trustees have to be careful that there is a proper selection process and that the assignment is not given to a friend without ensuring that the appointment is appropriate and value for money.

5. *Seed money.* It is not possible to run a major campaign without costs. A special campaign usually seeks for funds for a definable purpose, which means that the funds received have to be ring-fenced and cannot be spent for another purpose. It follows that 'seed money' is needed in order to finance the appeal. This may come from general funds, or even better is if a donor can be found to provide the funds to enable the campaign to take off.

6. *Establish a target.* Establishing a clear target is important. Avoid the chairperson setting it too low to ensure he or she can claim the campaign succeeded. It is better to undershoot a £5 million appeal by £1 million than to set a target of £3 million and only raise £3.5 million.

7. *Research into prospective major donors.* Research is needed to identify those potential donors who are most likely to give you substantial sums. The focus should be on high net worth individuals, trusts, foundations, livery companies and corporations. Highlight from reference books those individuals and organizations that express a particular interest in your type of work.

The next step is to find a way of networking your contacts to get, if possible, a direct introduction to the potential donor, or the decision maker in an organization. 'Time spent on reconnaissance is seldom wasted' is an old military saying and is very apt in this phase of the operation.

8. *What is in it for the donor?* People like to believe that all donations are given in a spirit of altruism. The truth is that very many donors would like to get recognition and appreciation, and attention should be paid to what can be done for the donor. The campaign might include the need to purchase a new ambulance. A gift of an appropriate amount might ensure the name of the donor is placed on the door of the vehicle.

A private donor might give a sum that could fund a building, which could be named after a recently deceased spouse or child. A self-made person might wish to have a scholarship named after him or her, aimed at the underprivileged young person. After all, the new Oxford University college of management is named after an important Saudi citizen.

There are also examples where more modest contributions are sought from a larger number of donors. The courtyard of the replica of the original Globe Theatre in London is covered with small flagstones, each bearing the name of the person who had 'bought' the stone, at a price that was considerably more than that at which a similar stone could have been obtained at a builders' yard. We can claim to have walked all over some of our friends!

9. *What is the message of the appeal?* Attention should now be given to preparing the case. Why is this appeal needed, why now and why your organization and not some other? What would happen if you did not succeed? Why are you special and unique? What benefits do you bring to society and/or specifically to the neighbourhood?

A slogan and/or a logo can be an advantage. And there needs to be a promotional description of the appeal. The help of an advertising copywriter and/or a graphic artist can ensure a more professional approach.

When appropriate to the purpose of the appeal, it helps to humanize it with pictures and case studies of those who stand to benefit and those who have benefited from the current activities of the organization.

Seek to sell the end result, such as the patients who recovered or the unemployed now running their own business. Show the old science laboratory at the school today and a sketch of what is needed to teach students to compete in the market tomorrow.

10. *Who can be notable supporters?* Now seek to line up notable supporters. These may be local figures who are respected and are in the public eye (perhaps a major employer, a noted writer or artist) as well as sports personalities and entertainers. You may need someone to open a fête or other event, or want to use the picture of someone colourful on a brochure or magazine, or obtain endorsements to be incorporated in an appeals pamphlet.

11. *The involvement of local organizations.* Enrol local organizations in the campaign. If you give help to the homeless, can companies in the local construction industry help? If it is a medical charity, can a local pharmaceutical company become a supporter? Equally it may be important to line up potential support from local organizations of goodwill. These might include the Rotary, the churches, the Women's Institute or the Scout/Guide movement. Some local organizations may be able to offer help in kind, such as the services of a professional copywriter or graphics artist, or the printing of materials.

12. *Going public.* It is only after you have got the big donors signed up, when perhaps two-thirds of the target has been achieved, that you should go to the general public. All too frequently the campaign chairperson is impatient and assumes the main funds will come from the public. Sadly this is all too often a mistake. Patience, planning and preparing the groundwork are the secret to the successful running of a one-off appeal.

13. *After completion.* It is important to remember at the end of a successful campaign to show appreciation for everyone's support and hard work. This might be a reception or just a letter, but it is the thought that counts. Thank the chairperson as well as the person who makes the tea.

GRANTS

Although the general image of the organization may be helpful, grants are obtained by direct application. They are possibly the only sources of funds where success is not influenced by the quality of marketing effort.

Trusts, foundations and livery companies

There are about 8,800 independent grant-making trusts and foundations in the UK, according to the Association of Charitable Foundations (ACF). Most exist only to make grants to deserving causes, and give about £2 billion a year to registered charities, universities and religious organizations. About 70 per cent give in the health and welfare fields, 30 per cent to arts and recreation and 9 per cent to causes related to religion.

Though the Wellcome Trust, which funds medical research, is well known, the general public have little awareness of most of the trusts in Britain. Some are very large, while others give away only a few thousand pounds each year.

The ACF publishes a useful guide to applying for a grant from a trust or foundation. Our summary draws from the points made in this document:

- *Research the trusts.* Guides and directories to the major trusts are published by the Directory of Social Change and these make a useful starting point. Each trust or foundation has specific subjects of interest, and frequently a defined geographical area of activity. National trusts may make a grant to a local organization, but a local trust cannot make grants outside its defined area. Activity and geography will reduce the 8,800 trusts to a much smaller number that might be prepared to help, and the resultant number may be reduced further by the size of the grant you are seeking. There is no point in asking a small trust for a grant that is beyond its scale of operation, and similarly the largest trusts will not be interested in very small grants.

  From all this analysis, it should be possible to prepare a short list of possible donors. The next stage should be to contact the organizations on the list to obtain any literature that they have, and an application form if the trust requires it.

- *Write the application.* There is a step before you begin to write the application, which is fully to define the project, including preparation of carefully thought-through budgets.

  The ACF suggests that the main letter should be no more than two pages long, and should not be overloaded with attachments. The submission should cover:

- The purpose of the work to be funded – who it will help and how, what is distinctive about it, what will be achieved if a grant is given (and perhaps what will not be achieved if a grant is not given).
- A budget for the project. Work out your needs carefully. Don't economise on essentials, such as training or unavoidable overhead costs.
- Ask for a specific sum of money. If necessary say you are seeking a contribution of £X towards a total budget of £Y, and that you hope to raise the rest from other sources which you specify. Do not simply say you are a worthwhile organization and desperately need funds.
- Your name, address and telephone number – oh yes, people do forget.

(ACF, 2002)

Include a copy of your latest annual report and accounts.

● *Etiquette*. Allow plenty of time for an application to be processed (some trusts employ no full-time staff), and most have more applications than they can make grants to. Do not try to make contact by telephone, unless a phone number is given in the directory. If none is given it means that phone calls are not welcome. Follow the lead of the trust: if they want you to call on them they will ask, and if they want to visit your premises (usually a good sign) they will make the suggestion. If possible find out what they want to cover if they do ask to visit, so that you can have the right people on hand, and any extra information that might be needed.

If you are given a grant be meticulous in following any conditions, including periodic reports. Even if there are no conditions, and a cheque arrives, do not forget to write to say thank you. Apparently many charities do not do this. Inform the trust early if any problems arise with the project. Let them know when it is completed, share with them any good publicity received and give them information about what the results of the project have been. The trusts and foundations exist to achieve something through other registered charities, and not just to provide money. The best thing you can do in return for the grant is to run an efficient and successful project, and to enable the trust to see the benefits it has brought.

There are also 100 City of London livery companies. The 12 'chief' companies are well endowed, and all have well-organized systems to allocate their charitable funds.

Lottery grants

The Lottery is a relative newcomer to the British charity scene, and numerous grants have already been made. The good causes money is split into a number of funds. We will concentrate on the Community Fund (originally called the National Lottery Charities Board). In 2001 this fund received 18,817 applications for grants totalling just over £1 billion, and gave 9,724 grants totalling £374.5 million. Lottery income is declining, which means that this fund has less to distribute each year. The community fund administers four grants programmes:

- *The main grants programme* is for projects that 'help people who are unable to play a full part in economic, social and community life'. The fund wants to support complex long-term projects, particularly if they help to prevent or reduce disadvantage.
- *The programme for grants for projects costing up to £60,000* has the same aims as the main programme, but has a simpler application procedure.
- *Research grants* are given for high-quality medical research and social research to promote well-being. The current priority of the programme is social inclusion, with projects to benefit young and old people, those from black and minority ethnic groups, and those with learning difficulties.
- *The international grants programme* targets development projects that address the causes of poverty and inequality.

Awards for All is a separate fund related to the Lottery, and is for grants of between £500 and £5,000. It targets small groups involved in arts, sports, heritage and community projects.

With giving on such a large scale, it is inevitable that the application for a grant is highly formal. It must be assembled with great care, and advice sought on how best to proceed, to maximize your chance of success. It is worth seeking advice from a charity that has been successful (there are long lists of them in the annual report of the Community Fund, see www.community-fund.org.uk). Application forms are required and can be obtained from the Fund.

Grants are not restricted to registered charities, but the organization must:

- Be independently established for charitable, benevolent or philanthropic purposes.
- Have a constitution or set of rules, defining its aims, objectives and operational procedures.

- Have a bank or building society account which requires at least two signatures on each cheque.
- Be able to provide a copy of its most recent approved and signed accounts.

Those given grants will, of course, be expected to report progress regularly, with a clear indication of what is being achieved and the extent to which the project is on time and to budget. It is important that an organization assigns responsibility for this and sets procedures for the monitoring process.

REFERENCES

Association of Charitable Foundations (ACF) (2002) *Applying to a Charitable Trust or Foundation*, ACF, London

Wilson, A (1993) *Corporate Giving: A research report on how and why companies give to charities*, Action Research, Horsham

10

Rationalization, consolidation and closure

There are several problems of change or scale that a voluntary organization can run into, some of which can be fatal. Two of the case studies we have included in other chapters illustrate how organizations can adapt to changing needs: both the Coram Family and the Royal Philanthropic Society had to reinvent themselves. In both cases this was because the circumstances had changed and it was no longer relevant to continue operating in the old manner.

Unfortunately voluntary organizations can also become insolvent and, although they can sometimes be saved, they may also have to be dissolved and, if a charity, removed from the register. There are technical differences between incorporated and unincorporated bodies, particularly in relation to the responsibilities and potential liability of trustees, but the general advice is similar, and largely covered in the chapters on accounting. It is to manage the organization in such a way that there is early warning of the signs of financial problems, and to take remedial action to avoid insolvency. In some cases this may result in a recovery plan; in others it may be prudent to dissolve the organization before it runs into serious difficulties. Charity Commission (2000) gives useful advice to charities facing insolvency, which also has some relevance for other voluntary organizations.

A voluntary organization may fail because in some way it was misconceived and carried the seeds of failure from the beginning.

Case study 10.1: Home Finders' Fund

(Note: the name of the charity is disguised.)

This is the story of a charity that was started in the early 90s and failed. It has been wound up with its assets passed to another charity. There are many lessons to learn from the reasons it failed and why it never should have been started.

An elderly, highly respected and well-connected figure was involved with the problems of homelessness especially in London. He had the idea of starting a new charity whose focus was to develop innovative ideas on how to combat homelessness. By running 'pilot studies' and proving their viability others might adopt the ideas and develop them on a bigger scale.

He gathered around him seven highly competent, like-minded people from different professional backgrounds. All totally endorsed the ideas of the founder, and were very knowledgeable in different aspects of the social, economic, medical and local planning problems connected to housing. Though most were retired, all already had very heavy charitable commitments. Their homes were widely dispersed across the home counties, so meetings were held in London. This was 'neutral territory' but involved everyone in a lot of travel.

Sums of money were raised through personal connections and direct mail to corporations, and the Lottery funded one project. However, fund-raising campaigns were run amateurishly, and there was an expensive brochure, the design of which broke every rule in PR. Sadly those who knew it was terrible simply did not have the time themselves to get the design changed, and did not want to appear to criticize the well-meaning work of the founder.

A series of projects was mounted, staffed by paid freelance individuals chosen for the assignment. However, there was inadequate, and sometimes no, supervision or control. There was no follow-up, and hence the quality of the end result was very questionable. Because of this there was no resultant publicity, and fund-raising became more difficult.

The founder's health was failing fast, and he sadly died. The meetings were inconclusive, so fewer and fewer made the special journey to London. Those who were left realized there was no future for this charity. One of the trustees knew a charity with comparable ultimate objectives, and the remaining assets were passed over to it.

This is a charity that failed in what it sought to do, and failed to survive. There are many lessons to be learnt:

- It is not sufficient to have a well-meaning board of trustees. There was no one to provide the professional management. The trustees all already had too much on. As all lived a long way apart it meant a lot of time to travel to attend meetings. A human camaraderie did not develop. They gave immense goodwill and would give wise counsel. However, at the end of the day no one could make the commitment to roll up their sleeves and get down to implementing details themselves. A battle is not won by famous retired generals! An army needs young lieutenants and a sergeant major, not to mention a few privates. To get any organization started, if it is not well funded, means that the founders have got to have the personal energy, drive and commitment, and have supporters who can do some of the donkey work.

- There was insufficient 'seed' money to establish the basic administration.
- There was inadequate supervision of projects. No one had the time or commitment. Had they produced well-documented results it is certain greater funding would have followed.
- There was inadequate effort put into effecting a merger. The trustees were all only too anxious to get this responsibility off their backs.

This is a tale of well-meaning individuals who simply had not thought through what was involved, and assumed that everyone else would do the hard work. Starting a charity is hard work!

Small voluntary organizations can be effective when their scale fits the tasks they set out to perform. Many of the family history charities fulfil their roles adequately without needing to become very large. Local playgroups, many of which will not be registered charities, may do better by remaining minnows than by expanding. But there are other organizations that are too small to fulfil their charitable purpose adequately, or are slightly out of tune with the needs of the clients they serve, or have outlived their initial purpose. Others may be well intentioned, but cannot muster the resources to enable them to afford proper facilities and a nucleus of paid staff.

Previous chapters emphasized the need for vision and for a strategy to meet the future. For many organizations there comes a time when they need to consider the need for a fundamental restructuring of the operation. The choice may be between mediocrity and superior performance, or in some cases between a new direction and dissolution. Some will start to query whether they are able to carry on, or indeed are justified in doing so. One theme of this chapter is restructuring.

Sometimes restructuring is an inadequate solution, and a better way forward is to merge with another similar organization. This is not a solution that is considered as often as it might be in charities, and the recent merger between two large cancer charities is a notable exception. A merger may result from strength, because both parties, although succeeding, realize that more could be achieved.

It is also an option for those that are either faltering or just too small to make much difference. The initiative may be to combine with one or more other small charities, or to approach a prospering, well-run charity, with a view to being absorbed.

The converse of this may be when a charity seeks to absorb other charities that are going through difficult times or have lost a sense of direction. The voluntary sector cannot share the hunger for aggressive acquisition, which is typical of business, but this should not rule out ways of improving performance through initiating discussions for a merger when this is in the interests of both organizations and their stakeholders.

The second topic of the chapter is merger and variations on this theme, with particular emphasis on the small struggling charities.

RESTRUCTURING

There comes a time in the history of an organization when it is felt that tinkering with management and policies is insufficient, and more radical changes are needed.

We live in a fast-changing world. Society, politics and economics are never static. Medicine, IT and other technologies are evolving rapidly. What was right for one decade may be wrong for another. Trustees should take heart from the case histories of the Royal Philanthropic Society and the Children's Trust. Dramatic changes were needed, and the trustees had the foresight, courage and drive to restructure and make today's charities much more relevant and dynamic than ever before.

Case study 10.2: The Children's Trust, Tadworth Court

Background

This Trust is an excellent example of what vigorous protests, a dedicated effort and inspired leadership can build. The original Tadworth Court Children's Hospital was stripped of its assets (very valuable land) and was scheduled to be closed down. The main building was in a sad state of repair, while the high-quality care and treatment of the children took place in a collection of inadequate buildings such as Portakabins throughout the grounds. It is now being turned into a world-class centre for the most severely disabled children in society.

History

Tadworth Court is the administrative centre of the Children's Trust. It was originally a magnificent manor house near Epsom. From 1927 to 1983 it was an offshoot of Great Ormond Street Children's Hospital. The NHS in an effort to raise funds and reduce costs sold 40 acres of the site for housing development, and planned to close the Tadworth operation.

There was however a noisy protest. With the support from the parents of patients, the staff and several national charities, efforts were made to continue.

The treatment provided

The Children's Trust now serves children with exceptional needs: those with profound disabilities, injured in accidents or affected by degenerative and disabling conditions. Typically this involves brain damage and/or sensory deprivation.

The care provided involves a rehabilitation unit, and a respite care service to give carers a break. There is also a school, outreach nursing care and a continuing care for children with life-limiting conditions.

Approximately 70 children are being looked after at any one time. The paid staff number around the 300 mark.

Financial background

The Trust has invested in a professionally run, energetic fund-raising campaign. This has enabled a substantial loan to be paid off, and a very ambitious capital programme to be implemented. This included replacing the maze of Portakabins with high-quality, purpose-built school buildings, a research centre and three residential care homes. It included the purchase of a lot of impressive special equipment needed to handle children with severe handicaps.

The Trust recently had a grant of £2.1 million to handle the repair liabilities associated with the listed main building. This is now a centre for very seriously disabled children, who can be treated in the best purpose-built facility in the country.

Management issues

Against this background of successful fund-raising and investment, a number of management issues are apparent:

● The funding of day-to-day costs comes from a combination of income from the NHS and payments from the local authority education and social services budgets. However, the cost of one child is at least £90,000 a year. It is natural that many authorities should baulk at such a heavy expenditure, which usually they are legally obliged to make available. This therefore often leads to endless negotiations, often on a case-by-case basis.

261

- There is often an inherent danger that some new public sector policy or theory will undermine the relationship between these three fund providers and the service provider.
- It is pleasing to note that the board has made a policy decision to allocate a portion of the sum raised annually by donations towards supplementing the day-to-day costs of providing the quality of care needed by such severely handicapped children. This currently is running at £0.5 million a year.
- There is a special department that coordinates the recruitment, training and deployment of volunteers. There are 300 regular volunteers whose weekly support represents the equivalent of 17 full-time staff. This alone is worth approximately £0.25 million a year. Significantly the chief executive emphasized the view that it was vital not to treat volunteers as second-class citizens, but to value and respect their contribution.
- The relationship with the three fund providers is complex. At the same time they are both customers and competitors. The NHS is also the biggest supplier of skilled labour (nurses and therapists) and hence greatly influences the pay rates for the staff, which is by far the greatest component of overall costs.
- One small item of the public relations programme includes inviting to a simple lunch a few who might give particular support to the charity. At Tadworth there is much to be shown, and the lunch provides a useful opportunity for networking. When a charity has something for prospective supporters to see, the advantage of them seeing the charity in action at first hand is considerable. Prospective donors like to see that there is a big 'bang for their buck'.

Conclusion

The remarkable spirit that pervaded this charity has been succinctly summarized in the last paragraph of the chairman, Sir Brian Hill's, annual report, which says: 'For our achievements and in the tasks ahead, I thank our staff for their professionalism, our donors for their generosity, our volunteers for their dedication, and above all, the children for enriching our lives and giving us the motivation.'

When the subject of rationalization is raised the first question to be asked is 'Why?' What objectives will a reorganization be designed to achieve? Are there problems that present policies are not addressing successfully? Do not be content with generalities; be specific, and face up to the issues that worry people. Is it a matter of inappropriate individuals? Is it the objectives of the charity that may no longer be as relevant as the day they were first written and so need to be redefined? Is the whole style of operating no longer appropriate?

New objectives or specific problems should be written down and discussed. Do not sweep problem issues under the carpet in the hope they will be forgotten. They fester. The worst possible scenario is to enter into a restructuring without all trustees and management reaching an understanding of why it is being done and what it is all about. Unfortunately any change can easily run into the internal politics of the trustees or management. The obstacles need to be faced, sorted out and resolved early on. Entrenched views of long-serving trustees or managers need to be handled with immense tact. Burying them is unlikely to be a valid solution.

The next step is to analyse what the options are. What alternative courses of action are open to you? Do not have change for change's sake, but do not shrink from radical thoughts or creative thinking.

Consider the risks involved. Will those who fund the charity be disenchanted? Will they pull out, and leave you worse off? To what extent should you be beholden to your benefactors? This can be a very difficult issue to resolve. Or would your donors be encouraged to give more if they felt you had become more active and fore-sighted?

Beware of the rumour that slips out to staff, particularly if the restructuring involves redundancy or other changes that will affect them. Word gets around and can cause problems if this happens before decisions have been made and issues fully worked out. It is natural that job security is a very sensitive subject, and people want to know ahead of time if their own job is not going to be safe.

One problem is that in periods of insecurity people look around in the job market 'just in case'. Inevitably the best staff are the quickest to get job offers. Key managers may have been taken for granted and paid below the market rate. The reverse can also be inevitable. Staff you might most want to leave are the ones who find getting a new job the hardest, and hence hang on to a job they have.

Bear in mind that key staff who leave may take very many months to replace. This period is regularly underestimated. The converse is also true. Staff you need to lose may prove very expensive to make redundant.

Thinking through staff implications will need to be done in strict confidence. The timing of who is told what, who is reassured, and when, needs to be carefully planned. However, as soon as it is possible staff should be told officially, so that unfounded rumours do not start and so that every person knows how he or she will be affected. There should be a complete exposure of the benefits to the organization, as well as the effect on individuals. Anyone whose job is seriously affected, either for better or for worse, should be told immediately. It is bad for morale to have a general announcement at the end of a day, so that everyone has to go home without knowing his or her own situation. Similarly it is extremely bad to announce who will leave in an open meeting, unless these people have already been told individually.

Haphazard news filtering out, and wrong deductions drawn from it, can do immense, needless harm to staff morale. It can end up being expensive if staff you intend to keep do not wait around to be told.

The financial implications of restructuring must be given a high priority, in particular if there is the danger that a hiccup in fund-raising may generate a cash flow crisis. The Charity Commission tends to discourage charities from sitting on underutilized assets. This can produce something of a dilemma. Trustees may feel that property the charity owns gives them a financial reserve and sense of security. The question that may need to be faced is whether sitting on an underutilized asset is in the best long-term interests of the customer.

However, restructuring may lead to a surplus of property – some rented, some owned. Knowing how quickly one can move on leases may be very relevant. With surplus property that has a long lease, consider subletting provided the lease allows it. However, there is a risk with subletting, as the main lessee does not lose responsibility for fulfilling the terms of the lease, and there will be continuing financial risks.

The essence is to move as quickly as possible to avoid assets lying idle for long.

Consider quickly the effect restructuring will have on your systems in general and your management controls in particular. It is likely that many managers will be doing slightly different jobs – ones they are not familiar with. Control information in the early days may be critical, but may be different from the information that has been produced hitherto. Figure 3.4 and its supporting discussion in Chapter 3 may be helpful as a guide to what should be considered.

Do not take your volunteers for granted. They can vote with their feet more quickly than anyone else. It may have taken years to build up a team. Badly treated, they can wither away very quickly. Determine how the change will affect them and what can be done about it. Remember that there may be a close friendship between a volunteer and a member of staff affected by the change, and a disaffected employee may cause a disaffected volunteer. The golden rule with volunteers is to show your appreciation for all they do and not to take them for granted.

The charity exists for the benefit of its customers. How will any restructuring benefit them? Are the benefits they get going to be increased, are they going to be given a better service or is it just that the service will be made more cost-effective? Will more resources be released and coordination within the charity improved? Look at the restructuring from the viewpoint of the 'coalface'. What will be improved? If nothing, why are you considering the upheaval?

If you are considering a major change of policy, consider whether it is possible to run a pilot project. Implement your new ideas on a small local scale and see the result. Did you make mistakes, and can you do it better? Having seen the outcome of your new policies, is the restructuring worthwhile? Have the benefits been realized? Are they worth the upheaval and likely dislocation? Many will say the charity does not have the time for the luxury of a pilot study. This may be true. However, the best answer is to think ahead and not wait for policy changes to be a matter of urgency or desperation. By planning ahead and seeing the likely need for change, the time may be available to run some experiments. In this way, when the need arises and you must change, you have the background of knowledge and experiments to be confident the changes you propose are workable and effective.

Pilot studies may help to avoid the danger of the trustees and senior management being remote from the actual sharp end. Nothing destroys the credibility, goodwill and confidence in the board and senior management than a great plan being handed down that is unrealistic and bound to fail. It is essential that those with an up-to-date knowledge of the reality are involved at an early stage of any restructuring plan.

Management restructuring should be thought through in depth. It will involve the jobs and careers of people. The plans will need to be made in some detail, so that when they are announced the changes can be implemented swiftly. Those executives you want to keep can be told very quickly. Those whose jobs are safe but whose role will change must be enthused that their new responsibilities will be satisfying and worthy of their track record.

Those whose jobs will disappear also need to be told as quickly as possible, but in a way that is sensitive, humane and legally correct.

This work is very time-consuming. It is essential to give it high priority if restructuring is not going to cause a fall in motivation and resentment even with those who stay. It can cause much ill will for the charity if those who are let go feel they have been badly handled.

Case study 10.3: Problems in a division

One major charity, which we will not name, found only one of its five divisions broke even, while the rest ran at a loss. Sources of the original funding were declining, and recourse was made to accepting public sector contracts. This resulted in further initiatives and it was hoped that synergy would be generated by bringing them all together under one command. One can fully understand the logic that led to these steps being taken. However, they were not thought through, and were implemented without an understanding of the real situation in the field. They bore little resemblance to the real interests of the customer. There are a number of pitfalls that should have been avoided:

● The plethora of new initiatives caused the organization to lose focus, and a failure to give adequate attention to the one service at which it really excelled.
● Volunteers found that government contracts equalled bureaucracy. Paperwork and justification of what they were doing grew. Volunteers complained they wanted to help customers and not satisfy civil servants. They also felt they were now fulfilling a government contract, unpaid. Had they not already paid their taxes, so why should the government get work done on the cheap by their free labour?
● Although staff had been told the organization would be restructured at a meeting before Christmas, the concepts of the new structure were not unveiled for three months. Many staff were still unsure of their future even after the new structure was meant to be working.
● There was no evidence that synergy, which was held to be vital between services, could actually be generated. Staff in new positions were implementing new policies with no idea of the implication of what they were doing.
● The new field structure showed head office to be totally out of touch with the realities of the local scene. Here decisions were made about services delivered to the customer. The senior management of the organization were shown to be alarmingly ignorant. They were applying a civil-servant-type solution to an essentially business situation.
● This was sad because the volunteers played a major role in the delivery of services, and had had massive goodwill towards senior management.

THE PROBLEM OF SMALL AND STRUGGLING CHARITIES

No charity has a licence to go on for ever. The original role for which it was founded may be no longer relevant in present circumstances. This book has tried to highlight several charities that have successfully made a dramatic change of direction. There are others in today's world (where every organization is fighting for the customers' or donors' money) for which the future is bleak and the question of whether they can remain solvent is very real. For some, there may be no option but to close while there are still funds available to meet the need to cover the cost of closing down (including redundancy pay for any paid staff the charity employs, obligations under leases and payments due under contracts with suppliers). This part of the chapter considers the position of these small and struggling charities.

There are 42,000 charities with an annual income of less than £1,000. Some are start-ups, which are vibrant and will become tomorrow's giants with efficient, clear leadership and direction. There are, however, many others that for various reasons are unable to fulfil their expectations. The problem may be lack of leadership, a poor sense of direction or inability to muster enough funds, and because of such problems they are struggling. Possibly the founders have died, and because of lack of adequate succession, and changes in society, they have 'run out of steam'. They may not be efficiently deploying their assets to further the original objectives.

There are others that have grown, appear successful and yet have not developed the financial controls needed. One day they awake in horror to discover that their growth has led to a cash flow that will not sustain their viability. Nationally, these thousands of charities collectively include a considerable resource that is not usefully being deployed in the best interests of society and there are still thousands even when we exclude those charities where the optimum size is to be small.

A significant proportion of this group will have trustees and directors who do not have the time, the skill and/or the commitment to revitalize the charity, and do not know what to do. They have not faced up to issues such as:

● Should the charity be closed down?
● With whom could/should they merge?

- Who among the trustees will initiate and undertake the negotiations?
- What are the legal complications and costs?

In many cases the result is that year after year nothing gets done, and the organization just drifts.

There is a case that can be made for a new type of organization in the UK charity field that can act like a marriage broker. In the hard world of commerce, that organization is a merchant bank! Obviously no profit-making organization is likely to take on such a role in the voluntary sector. What can be done and who can play this role? The unfortunate reality is that there is no political capital for the government or a politician to pursue the cause of this sector of the charity field. The Charity Commission itself, in the absence of any political push, is most unlikely to be interested.

Firstly, their main concern is to oversee the few hundred really major charities that make up most of the charity field. The Commission staff can be shown to be effectively and efficiently employed when dealing with many millions. They have neither the staff nor the budget to consider the tiddlers.

Secondly, if they were to take a proactive role in bringing the small charities together, they could be placed in a conflict-of-interest situation. If their key role is to supervise the charity field, they cannot be part of any direct action for which they might be liable.

MERGERS

The efficiency of the capitalist system of the Western world is, in theory, based on the premise that profits attract greater reward and investment. Those who fail to use their assets efficiently or effectively do not raise further funds. Companies gain or lose market share and profits in proportion to their competitive ability to meet the needs of their customers. Thus resources of society are channelled to the most successful, those meeting the demands of the market place.

The economic implications and outcome of this are seen in the stock market, and the mergers and acquisitions, friendly and hostile, that are seen in the newspaper every day. Negotiations for such events may be tortuous, tedious and require a lot of skill and effort by merchant banks, lawyers and brokers. However, there is at least one clear measurement available – the share price. Will the owners of one company accept a particular price from another to hand over ownership? Certainly there are likely to be issues of staff job security and countless other considerations, but the underlying economic fact of the share price is the ultimate arbitrator.

Directors not earning their corn are replaced with others who have the required expertise and drive. Directors of failed companies lose their jobs. Those who make a success get rich! This is the jungle, the survival of the fittest.

With charities, trustees are not working for personal financial reward, and there are no owners in the accepted sense of the word. Charities do not have a share price, cost structures may be misleading and inter-charity comparisons may be very dangerous. There is no equivalent to the financial services industry seeking to stimulate (for their own reward) an acquisition or merger. Published information about the performance of charities is scarce and often misleading.

Many in the charity field would thank their lucky stars that they are not in the business world. The very words 'takeover' and 'acquisition' are seen as pariah words and even in the business world an acquisition is often inaccurately called a merger because it is less emotive.

A small number of mergers do take place between charities, but these represent only a small glitch in the overall scene. Some would say this preserves the true spirit of organizations founded and funded at least initially on good will and staffed in part with volunteers who work for no financial advantage.

There are, however, two sides to this situation.

Firstly, can highly competently run charities meeting a real need attract adequate funds to play the role society would wish them to fill? How do they attract capital and fund cash needs of an expanding organization? Does too much depend on the special skills of fundraisers and the whims of those in a position to donate or allocate large sums of money? Though many do find a way to grow, many are stunted by a chronic undercapitalization, low-paid staff and a board of trustees who do not have the skill or motivation to rise to the challenge and develop the full latent potential of the charity.

Secondly, though well-run charities may have difficulties in growing, there are many badly run charities that survive a very long time. Even many successful charities may find they are locked into a situation where the potential is never realized. Often assets are badly invested or underutilized. The historical needs a charity was set up to meet may have been overtaken by events.

These two situations are not in the interests of society. While it is important to seek to retain the spirit and goodwill of the charity sector, ways must be found to ensure: 1) that well-run and directed charities meeting an important need are able to expand; and 2) that charities beyond their sell-by date and whose assets are underutilized are absorbed by other charities with a similar charitable purpose that will give better direction to policy and ensure assets are put to more effective use.

At present there is a very imperfect legal, social and management environment, which inhibits merger as a solution. Although the Charity Commission says it is now legally possible, there are still formidable difficulties that mitigate the extent to which charities can join up, consolidate or merge.

What should a charity do when it feels the need and wants to justify seeking to merge with another, possibly one that is bigger, better off financially and managerially stronger? Or what issues face a charity considering absorbing a smaller and/or less successful charity in their mutual interests and those of society at large?

Is there a need to relinquish the charity's independence?

Society needs an environment where those with vision, drive and perhaps resources can found a charity. Typically these start off small, are led by friends, are underfunded and fight for survival. The best ideas, best management and the best funded will survive and grow and become the Wellcome Trust of tomorrow. From small acorns, large oak trees grow. However, there are many that for a variety of reasons have outlived their role as independent organizations. These will include:

● Charities whose trustees have grown old and lost their energy and enthusiasm, while their expertise or contacts may be out of date. Will boards find new trustees and retire those no longer able to keep up?

● Charities whose trustees and paid executives have had a brilliant start. They have been very entrepreneurial, and the charity has grown. Now, however, the problems and responsibilities they encounter are out of all recognition to the early days. Will the chief executive whose energy and devotion have made the success grow with the job, or stand aside and allow a newcomer to come and take over the job? These are human issues of great sensitivity.

- Charities without the foresight to bring in specialist skills, which may seem very expensive. They may, however, become essential as the operation becomes more complex.
- Charities that have lost or are unable to update their sense of vision. The needs of customers may have changed, and what the charity set out to do may no longer seem so relevant or necessary. This can be a particular problem when the charity is founded on a major legacy from one person who stipulated exactly how the charity should operate and whom it should serve.
- Charities that largely depend on public sector contracts, commit themselves to a specific level of production in their workshops or, for example, run an operation overseas. They may be bearing a level of risk that is disproportionate to their present size.
- Charities whose financial and management systems have become inadequate because of the charities' greatly increased scale. The trustees and executives may not realize that they do not know the true state of affairs! Sometimes growth gives the illusion of success, but within it may lie the seeds of bankruptcy. This can come from overtrading to the point where needs for cash cannot be met.

Avoid continually putting off the initiation of a search for a partner. Financial and management reporting may perhaps have always been slow, and now is running late. Suddenly trustees find they have a crisis on their hands. They are unprepared, and panic leads to hasty action. Years of good work are dissipated, and everyone is the loser.

The question that needs to be asked is why more charities are not seeking some form of merger. There appear to be six main reasons:

1. Provided the charity is not going bankrupt there can be a strong motivation to do nothing. The pride and reputation of the trustees may be at stake, and the result is that the charity just shrinks and continues on a little while longer. Finding a merger partner may be time-consuming, and trustees may not know where to start. Effecting a merger can involve a lot of extra work. Who is to do it?
2. Older management may well want a quiet life and prefer to sit tight. Any merger may threaten job security. Younger management may see career prospects decline. They may hurry to find new pastures.
3. The legal issues can be daunting. To sort them out speculatively may be difficult to justify at a time when money is short.

4. Typically there are few charities that want to take on another in difficulties.
5. The lack of, and the presentation of, data make searching for a merger partner difficult. Whom it may be worth approaching needs to be researched.
6. Unlike business, the penalty for doing nothing is small. The reward for taking action may be unpopularity.

Would your charitable objectives be better and/or more quickly attained by absorbing other charities?

The first question for trustees to ask themselves is whether they want to grow (or grow faster) and if so why. In business terms it is usually in order to make more profits. In a charity the reasons for growth may be more difficult to pinpoint or admit. Perhaps there will be a fear that to grow too fast is likely to impair quality.

Here are some of the main reasons for growth:

● The mission of the charity to help certain people or do some good is fulfilled the more this is achieved.
● A wider/deeper service may be provided, eg to extend the age, geographical spread or range of services offered. It is assumed that any partner brought in will be offering a complementary, rather than a competitive, function.
● Synergy may be created by merging management functions that can be brought together. For example, there may be savings in merging the activities of fund-raising, IT and HRM.
● Ability to spread the cost of expensive, skilled specialists (eg law, tax etc).
● Ability to assume greater risks.
● Greater attraction to important donors, foundations or the general public.
● Increased ability to bid for larger contracts.

Against this should be weighed the danger of:

● being financially overextended;
● key management being overextended and taking their eye off the ball;
● entering a field of activities that the trustees and management do not understand;

- becoming overdependent on key contracts;
- losing focus and sight of the charity's original purpose.

In merger negotiations try to think dispassionately about the motivation and attitude of all those individuals who will be party to the decision. Who will be against the merger and why? How could their objections be overcome? What do the individual trustees on both sides want? Is it to retire, retain identity, get the charity to grow in stature or simply for the charity to do a bigger and better job?

Care should be taken to consider the viewpoint of donors, staff, volunteers and customers. None should be taken for granted.

Points from the world of business: steps that should be taken in a merger of organizations

1. *Underlying strategy.* What strategy is the merger trying to fulfil? Why do we want to make it?
2. *Identify acquisition target.* What are our criteria for a merger partner? Which organizations might we target?
3. *Open negotiations.* Discuss the possibility with the most likely targets, working down the list in order of preference.
4. *Organize finance.* If prospects look good, assess the finance needed and organize the sources of finance. This would not be an issue in the charity sector, other than providing funds for any costs that would be involved in bringing two organizations together.
5. *Plan post-acquisition implementation.* At an early stage plan the steps that will be taken once the merger is complete. In a charity merger this could be done jointly by the two organizations before any merger takes place. Ensure that a budget is set to cover the costs of post-acquisition work, including marketing, restructuring and the costs of new systems.
6. *Due diligence.* Ensure that there is full understanding by each organization of the other. This is partly financial (different accounting systems, contingent liabilities, extent of obligations), but should include HRM and IT. Understand how each charity serves its customer base: what is similar about them and what is different?
7. *Finalize deal.* Conclude the legal details, and ensure that the necessary steps are taken in terms of the governing docu-

---

ments, and that all contractual and statutory matters are dealt with.

8. *Implement post-acquisition plan.* Make the merger work. This always takes more time than expected, and requires concentrated effort for a period. Ensure that all the expected benefits of the merger are obtained.

In business, before an acquisition or merger is undertaken, a process of due diligence is needed. This involves an examination of the organization being acquired so that surprises do not arise after the legal documents have been signed. Depending on the size and complexity of the merger, something similar needs to be undertaken in a charity situation.

A thorough financial analysis will, of course, be essential. The compatibility of financial reporting and IT may well produce problems. Equally, attention to the legal complexities will need to be given a high priority. These two issues are the most likely to generate the biggest stumbling blocks.

Trustees and executives need to think through how a new charity will be absorbed and fitted into the management of the wider operation. People are the key. Individuals, be they trustees, staff or volunteers, may well need to adjust and take on new roles. This needs to be thought through in some detail before a decision to merge goes through. Do not overlook the problems of the two organizations having different conditions of employment, differing pension schemes and even differing car allowances!

Be sensitive to the culture and style of the two organizations. Perhaps one has been run in an autocratic style, while with the other a more democratic style has reigned. If staff find it difficult to adjust it can become a major source of friction and misunderstanding.

In very many business deals it is said that two companies have merged as equals. Key and top appointments may appear to be carefully and fairly balanced between the two parties. Do not believe it! Either from the start or over time, one of the original organizations will become the dominant partner. Bear this in mind.

Realize that negotiating mergers and making them work take time. Consider the time capacity of your trustees and management who may be involved. It is easy to allow your own charity to lose momentum when senior managers need to spend a lot of their time on the business of another charity. Loss of focus can easily occur, and is only discovered after it happens.

Remember that in the end it is people who make the merger successful. Human attributes of goodwill, trust, respect, enthusiasm and drive are the active ingredients. Do not neglect the time needed to cement relationships at all levels. It pays off.

Case study 10.4: Enabling Partnership

An exceptionally interesting initiative has been made by the Enham Trust in Hampshire. They were in the fortunate position of having generated surplus funds. It came to the attention of Enham trustees that a well-known and respected charity, RADAR, were getting into serious financial difficulties. The idea was floated that the Enham Trust might help RADAR with these problems and help them realize their full potential. The question was how.

At the outset the key aim was the retention of RADAR's name with maximum independence to campaign hard for disabled people. The initial concept involved the creation of an umbrella charity, with Enham Trust and RADAR becoming equal subsidiaries. However, the Enham Trust is a Registered Social Landlord (RSL) and cannot be a subsidiary of an organization that is not an RSL, and it would not have been possible to register the new organization as an RSL.

To overcome this difficulty it was decided to change the name of the Enham Trust to 'Enabling Partnership'. By the use of an internal 'Chinese wall' the direct service provision would continue under the brand name Enham, and retain the logo previously developed for the Enham Trust. A board of management with delegated powers was created to oversee the strategic direction of Enham and to maintain the direct service provision. The opportunity was also taken to allow user representation to occur. Four of the committee members of the board of management are directly elected by the users of the services.

The board of trustees of the Enabling Partnership retain overall responsibility for the whole charity and ultimately the whole group. They have defined their role as giving policy and strategic direction, and delegating powers to professional managers. As a founder member, RADAR may appoint up to three of its trustees to serve on the Enabling Partnership's board of trustees. Equally the Enabling Partnership board may appoint up to three of its trustees to serve on RADAR's board. However, care has been taken to ensure the arrangement does not reduce the number of RADAR trustees who are directly elected by RADAR members.

Becoming a subsidiary required RADAR to amend its articles of association. In theory the Enabling Partnership could exercise powers that would give it control of the RADAR board of trustees. However, an intra-group agreement defines the roles and responsibilities of the Enabling Partnership and RADAR.

In this the Enabling Partnership pledges only to exercise its reserve powers in extremis.

Work was also needed to address RADAR's financial situation. This was achieved by setting up a medium-term loan facility that would allow RADAR to draw down funds as agreed in its budget. The generous terms included:

● The loan was not callable.
● The loan was subordinate to all other creditors.
● There was a clause that allowed the already low rate of interest to be waived.
● There was no time limit for repayment.

Practical implications

The intra-group agreement envisages that other charities may care to join the group structure. The arrangement allows member charities to keep their unique identity and operate autonomously. This is subject only to agreeing annually a business plan and budget. The interchange of trustees should ensure that the future direction is mutually beneficial. However, unlike a merger where one or both parties disappear, the group structure allows for the possibility that a member charity may leave. This must be mutually agreed by all member charities to be in the best interests of the member charity and the group.

The holding company seeks to develop synergy by providing support in financial management, and management controls, together with general administration. It also provides a centralized service covering:

● fund-raising;
● marketing and PR;
● IT and payroll;
● HR.

This seems a very generous and creative initiative only possible because both charities were committed to helping the disabled. It will not be a surprise to learn that other charities have quickly queued up to join what some might see as an overgenerous gravy train. The Federation of Shopmobility and Holiday Care are both in an advanced stage of getting final agreement, while several more have initiated the joining process.

Enham does not see itself as providing a temporary bout of intensive care before a sick charity goes off again to do its own thing. It is hoped that a true family of charities all focusing on helping disabled people will prosper and help each other.

A measure of the vision, leadership, tact and professional expertise that has been displayed is contained in a letter recently written to the Enham chief executive by a RADAR trustee:

May I take this opportunity to say how encouraged I am by the working relationship which is evolving between the EP and RADAR. I believe that a mutual confidence and respect is rapidly replacing the caution (even suspicion) which was characteristic of the negotiation period. Whether or not RADAR's predicament was avoidable, it was very humiliating and inevitably resulted in a rather prickly defensiveness: by contrast, we can now see the partnership in action, both at trustee and management levels. We all know that securing RADAR's financial viability remains a daunting challenge, but one which is now visibly shared.

Acceptance of new partners

The Enabling Partnership is not prepared to take on any lame-duck charity. These must develop policies that will get themselves out of their problems. Many charities have approached them in some difficulties, and their problems usually arise from one of two deficiencies: 1) inadequate financial and management controls – management and trustees are simply unaware of the true state of the charity; or 2) issues becoming more complex as a charity grows – trustees and management do not have the expertise themselves, and feel they cannot afford to buy in the necessary skills.

The future of the Enabling Partnership

One can speculate on whether such an agreement is likely to be sustainable. Leadership, personalities and conditions change. Human attributes of pride, ambition and backing the home side can destroy the strongest partnership. The bait of an advantageous loan from Enham is unlikely to be regularly available. In theory one charity, in a similar manner, should in the long term provide support for a sister subsidiary. Will this in practice be likely to happen?

When trustees of a chain of subsidiaries on the Enham holding company board need to set priorities and allocate scarce resources, will they act in the common interest? Will they see themselves as delegates, there to fight their own corner? Will policy decisions – unpopular with one subsidiary – be accepted by all the trustees of that subsidiary, who may feel their interests are being neglected?

Will the subsidiaries take the benefits while they have problems, and get out the moment they in turn are expected to make a contribution to the common good? Will the benefits of synergy, management expertise and administrative systems bind the family of charities together into a permanent cohesive whole? One hopes it will go beyond being a happy honeymoon, and that it will not end in a divorce when the going gets tough!

Notes on the parties involved

The Enham Trust

The Trust was founded in 1918 to serve ex-servicemen and TB sufferers. Over time it has focused on assisting physically disabled people, having approximately 100 customers in full care with a similar number in part care and in their local village. The goal of the programmes is geared to progression to open employment.

There is major attention given to assessment with three weeks being the average length of stay for such a programme. There is also a strong emphasis on paid commercial work. This ranges from horticulture to light assembly. A major furniture plant on site has recently been sold, but will continue to provide employment.

Much of the accommodation is excellent, and the training facilities amongst the most advanced in the world. The income comes 18 per cent from grants, 33 per cent from accommodation and care services, 32 per cent from trading and the rest from other sources. The total comes to £8.9 million a year. Appeal costs run at only 1 per cent. Trading expenses represent 64 per cent, with accommodation and care services taking 34 per cent.

Joint Ventures with the Prince's Trust (focused on self-employment) and The Shaw Trust (placement services) have been recent initiatives. Such joint endeavours are perceived as being of increasing importance.

Royal Association for Disability and Rehabilitation (RADAR)

London-based and employing 33 staff, it has an income of £1.46 million and in 1999/2000 had a deficit of £230,000. There are two commercial arms. One produces a publication for the disabled, and sells advertising space. This made a significant surplus. The other, RADAR Consultancy, was set up in 1995 to sell access audits and training skills in support of the Disability Discrimination Act.

RADAR trustees voted unanimously in favour of joining the Enabling Partnership.

The National Federation of Shopmobility UK (NFSUK)

The Federation supports 260 local shop mobility schemes throughout the UK with training, advice, practical guidelines and policy development. In 2000 the income of the organization was £142,000. Local shop schemes are self-funding. They are either charitable bodies in their own right or are established by the local authority. The Enabling Partnership will offer NFSUK an opportunity to undergo a process of revitalization and modernization.

The trustees of NFSUK have approved a motion to take the Federation into the Partnership agreement, and await a final membership vote on the proposal.

Holiday Care of Horley

Holiday Care is an information service helping the handicapped, disabled and elderly. It provides data on holidays, accommodation and respite care. Information is also available on transport and equipment both in the UK and overseas.

ACHIEVING A CHANGE THROUGH CUSTODIAN AND MANAGEMENT TRUSTEES

(Rule 12 of the Public Trustee Rules 1912 and as amended operational guidance OG 39 A1 and A2 Custodian trustees; operational guidance OG B1 and B2 Management trustees)

If a charity is seeking ways to operate in close partnership or share services with others, it may be worth considering the operation of Rule 12. It is a little-known approach, and involves appointing a custodian trustee as described by the operational guidance notes referred to above. Very simply any charity can appoint a custodian trustee. A range of corporations can act as custodian trustees, including limited companies, health authorities, local authorities and others. A corporation must be empowered by its constitution to undertake trust business, be registered under the Companies Act 1948 and have a capital of not less than £250,000.

The custodian trustee holds the title to all the property (land, shares etc) of the charity. It is not involved in the day-to-day management of the charity. This is undertaken by the management trustees.

The advantage is that the custodian trustee is perceived to have a perpetual existence, and hence the title to the property never has to be reinvested in a new trustee. Custodian trustees give an added measure of security for the property of the charity. Charities may also benefit from the advice, knowledge and experience of their custodian trustee. Could this perhaps be developed, in the future, along the lines of the support the Enham Enabling Partnership provides?

The disadvantage of having a custodian trustee can be:

- There may be a charge for the services.
- The role may be confused with the management trustee.
- It may cause difficulties in the charity's investment management.

It does not need great vision to see how this could be a simple way of gathering together a group of charities. Legally they retain their individual management control. Gradually over time, as mutual confidence builds up, the custodian trustee starts to act in a more proactive manner. Beginning with advice, it may later provide services similar to those provided by the Enham Trust. This could be a voluntary and incremental approach with each charity retaining its identity and management control.

This is an approach widely used by, but not confined to, the Church of England. Their central board of finance and regional diocesan boards of finance act in the custodian roles for trusts and charities connected to the church.

REFERENCE

Charity Commission (2000) *Managing Financial Difficulties and Insolvency in Charities*, Charity Commission, Taunton

11

Epilogue: the future

The longer-term future of a charity may be related to the longer-term trends in a society, the country, the culture and the economic environment in which the charity will operate. There is an old saying that a person who uses a crystal ball ends up eating ground glass. It is therefore not the intention to make forecasts but to raise issues that might impinge on the charity scene over the next few decades. This can affect the policy direction a charity moves to over time.

RETIREMENT AGE, LIFE EXPECTATION AND PHYSICAL FITNESS

The trend that we are all living longer and remaining fitter to a greater age has a positive potential for charities. A shorter working week may also enable those in work more time to devote to unpaid volunteering.

Balanced against this is the trend of people to enter careers at an older age and have interruptions through retraining and redundancies. Overall there is a likely need to work longer to build up a pension for a comfortable retirement. Employers are unlikely to give long-term career contracts to anyone but the most vital executive or specialist. Hence there will be fewer examples of executives being seconded or paid off to retire in their early 50s. Such people have been available to be re-employed by charities at a relatively low salary. This has often been a vital source of staff for charities. Will greater fitness lead to an increased playing of sport? Will relatively low travel costs encourage people to spend more of their retirement overseas or in second homes? These factors may have the effect of curtailing the number of people prepared to devote a considerable amount of their time to charitable work.

THE ATTITUDES TOWARDS VOLUNTEERING AND PERSONAL DONATIONS

Perhaps one of the key issues is whether social attitudes to volunteering and giving will change for better or worse. In a survey, one-third said that volunteering was no longer relevant. Will the socialism of state provision (which tends to pervade the EU at present) be balanced against the pressure for the population to become more self-sufficient, providing for and looking after themselves? As a higher proportion of the incomes of some charities becomes more dependent on public sector funding, will there be an increased reluctance of taxpayers to donate and put in effort without financial reward on what was public sector paid work?

Will public sector funding and the need for accountability lead to a greater use of league tables of performance, and the accoutrements of bureaucracy? One cannot blame the civil servant wanting to ensure that public money is well spent, and that value for money is gained. However, the resultant paperwork can discourage the enthusiastic amateur spirit that traditionally has played a major role in attracting volunteers. 'I'm here to help individuals, and not to fill in forms' is a cry that already is heard, and that is very damaging to the volunteer ethos.

Charities will need to provide professional standards to fulfil public sector contracts. There will be a fear of litigation, which will lead to the need for volunteers to be properly trained and qualified (eg to take a party of children on a canoe trip).

Significantly, a recent British Social Attitudes annual survey by the National Centre for Social Research found that nearly two-thirds of people felt we relied too much on volunteers. In particular the older age groups felt society needed more professionals and should not depend so much on the volunteering ethos. However, the survey found many people wanted to improve their skills and get a qualification, although others will not wish to be involved. When those not volunteering were asked if they would like to get involved, significantly 37 per cent said they would, but when asked what would help them get started they replied that making it easier to approach the charity would help. There will of course always be an honourable role for those who sell flags, provide teas or arrange hospital flowers. This fundamental attitude of goodwill, and the sociability that flows, is unlikely to diminish.

At present 2.4 per cent of the population are involved in the voluntary sector. This is five times the percentage in Germany, eight times the percentage in Japan and half as much again as the percentage in the United States. Have we reached saturation?

The lesson from all these conflicting pressures is perhaps not to take the goodwill of people for granted. If volunteers need to be recruited and retained, at whatever level, they will need to be cultivated, encouraged and sincerely shown appreciation. Will a higher living standard and a greater personal disposable income lead to greater generosity? Perhaps the answer lies in being able to compete with the pull of other attractions in the battle to get a share of people's expenditure. Perhaps those who strike the right note, make the right appeal and tug on the right heartstrings will prosper, while others will find the role gets harder and harder. Is there not a need for greater professionalism in the advertising, PR and marketing that charities undertake?

HIGHER-CALIBRE STAFF AND PROFESSIONALISM NEEDED

Recent years have seen a great increase in the professionalism and equally the salaries of the chief executive and his or her staff. However, there is a long way to go before salaries in the charity field compare with those in the outside world. Maybe the spirit of idealism will always lead people to work for less than in the open market. However, in the United States there is a greater willingness to pay good salaries, for they see it is a false economy not to have top-quality staff. As the saying goes, 'If you pay peanuts, you will get monkeys'.

Nowadays it is quite common to hear of people intent on making a career in the charity field. It is certainly vital that the sector attracts high-quality, forward-thinking people in an economic, social and legalistic environment that changes ever more rapidly. This issue of trying to run a viable, efficient charity with the need for high-quality skills is likely to become bigger. Perhaps the slogan 'Runs like a business, but feels like a charity' is a good one, which should be followed.

One of the side effects of this is the discrepancy that is likely to develop between, for example, the pension of the chairperson of the trustees and the salary of his or her CEO. The former will be carrying the greatly increased legal responsibility, and may have found it much harder to build up a good pension. This could produce an invidious position.

A MORE LITIGIOUS, TECHNICAL AND BUREAUCRATIC SOCIETY

There is a strong move to make trustees more responsible, and this is coupled with the trend towards a more litigious society. This will put greater pressure on trustees, who may be less willing to serve. It is also likely there will be a trend to make organizations bigger. This often is partly because of the need to be able to carry risk or to have greater specialist skills in-house. The move of the state to seek a third way to get not-for-profit organizations to run contracts will lead to the need for greater accountability. The scale and complexity of issues will probably lead to the need for greater expertise from trustees.

Smaller charities are likely to find the hiring in of expensive expertise particularly onerous. This will be one of the many pressures leading to the need to work closely with other charities to cut costs by sharing common services and expertise.

STRUCTURE OF THE THIRD SECTOR

While many organizations find there is often a great advantage to growing and increasing in size, and there will always be room for innovation and start-ups, there is a danger that a large number of charities will fall between the two positions. They may be too small to survive economic pressures, if they are below an economic size. What makes an economic size will be open to much argument.

All these factors are likely to lead to a greater need to merge. An alternative will be a greatly increased fashion of partnership agreements, either formal or informal. Perhaps there will be a greater divergence between the large, professional, well-funded charity undertaking a major role with public sector contracts, and the small enthusiastic band of amateur volunteers still 'doing their bit'.

IMPROVING THE VIABILITY OF THE SECTOR

The Enham Trust's partnership agreement, and the use of custodian trustees suggest ways of helping smaller charities to become more professional. Both approaches may need to be modified and developed for different circumstances.

What is needed is the broker role mentioned in Chapter 10, to fulfil in the voluntary sector some of the intelligence and introductory tasks that merchant bankers undertake in the commercial world. Part of the role would be to identify and bring together organizations that might link up to their mutual advantage. It would also guide organizations on the legal issues and the steps that have to be taken, without large legal fees. In an ideal world such link-ups would enable a charity to:

- retain its identity while sharing professional skills with other organizations, or moving to a full merger if it wanted to, for financial or other reasons;
- be linked to a custodian, or holding organization, which would have a strategic objective to build synergies between different charities;
- ensure that it would be able to work more closely together with other charities on an incremental and voluntary basis;
- remain true to its founding objectives and the sector it was set up to serve;
- have confidence that there would be sensitivity to the human issues involved at the staff, volunteer and customer level.

It is not unrealistic to hope that the Charity Commission would look positively on such an organization or organizations, and encourage the mass of tiny charities to consider talking to such a body.

It is hoped that this would help to 'tidy up' the tail-end of the charity field, and ensure assets are wisely invested and efficiently deployed. It would enhance the image of the charity field by reducing the number of failing or ineffective charities, and enabling trustees to make more effective use of funds and assets.

Useful information

BOOKS AND REPORTS

The letters at the end of each entry show whether the book is written specifically for the voluntary sector (V) or is a general book (G) that has some interest for the sector.

Accounting and taxation

Randall, A (1995) *Charities and Taxation*, ICSA, London (V)

Randall, A (2001) *The ICSA Guide to Charity Accounting*, ICSA, London (V)

Sargeant, A and McKenzie, J (1998) *Benchmarking Charity Costs*, Charities Aid Foundation, West Malling (V)

Wise, D (1995) *Performance Management for Charities*, ICSA, London (V)

Wise, D (1998) *Accounting and Finance for Charities*, ICSA, London (V)

Administration/management

Courtney, R (1996) *Managing Voluntary Organisations*, ICSA, London (V)

Doven, R and Ellis, F (1995) *Fairness in Funding: An equal opportunities guide for grant makers*, Association of Charitable Foundations, London (V)

Hedley, R and Rochester, C (1993) *Good Grant Making: A practical guide*, Association of Charitable Foundations, London (V)

Hudson, M (1995) *Managing without Profit*, Penguin, London (V)

Leatherdale, M (1998) *How to Run a Charity*, ICSA, London (V)

Robson, P (1997) *Consumerism or Democracy? User involvement in the control of voluntary organisations*, Policy Press, Bristol (V)

Scottish Council for Voluntary Organisations (SCVO) (1999) *The Big Picture: A framework for quality improvement in all voluntary organisations*, SCVO, Edinburgh (V)

Change management

Hussey, D (1998) *How To Be Better at Managing Change*, Kogan Page, London (G)

Hussey, D (2000) *How to Manage Organisational Change*, 2nd edn, Kogan Page, London (G)

McHugh, M (2001) *Managing Change: Regenerating business*, CIM, Cookham (G)

Pendlebury, J, Grouard, B and Meston, F (1998) *Successful Change Management*, Wiley, Chichester (G)

Directories

Directory of Social Change, *Guide to the Major Trusts*, Directory of Social Change, London (V)

Directory of Social Change, *The International Development Directory*, Directory of Social Change, London (V)

Fitzherbert, L and Richards, G (2001) *Directory of Grant Making Trusts: A guide to the major trusts 2001/2002*, Vol 1, Directory of Social Change, London (see also Walker, 2001) (V)

SCVO (2000) *The Directory of Scottish Grant Making Trusts*, SCVO (only available electronically, with updates) (V)

SCVO (2001) *Directory of National Voluntary Organisations in Scotland*, SCVO, Edinburgh (V)

Walker, L (2001) *Directory of Grant Making Trusts: A guide to the major trusts 2001/2002*, Vol 2, Directory of Social Change, London (see also Fitzherbert and Richards, 2001) (V)

Fund-raising

Alford, M (1992) *Charity Appeals: The complete guide to success*, Dent, London (V)

Canning, A (1999) *A Practical Guide to Fundraising and Public Relations*, ICSA, London (V)

Palmer, D (1998) *Monitoring and Evaluation: A practical guide for grant making trusts*, Association of Charitable Foundations, London (V)

SCVO (1995) *The Scottish Code of Fundraising Practice*, SCVO, Edinburgh (V)

SCVO (2001) *How to Raise Funds: A guide for Scottish voluntary organisations*, SCVO, Edinburgh (V)

SCVO (2001) *Organising an Event*, SCVO, Edinburgh (V)

Human resources

Burnett, J (2001) *Managing People in Charities*, 2nd edn, ICSA, London (V)

Hussey, DE (2002) *Business Driven HRM*, 2nd edn, Wiley, Chichester (G)

Information technology

Harris, I and Mainelli, M (2001) *Information Technology for the Not for Profit Sector*, ICSA, London (V)

Law

Croner (2001) *A to Z Essentials: Charities Management Handbook*, Croner, Kingston upon Thames (V)

SCVO (2001) *Guide to Constitutions and Charitable Status*, SCVO, Edinburgh (V)

Marketing

Ali, M (2001) *The New DIY Guide to Marketing*, ICSA, London (V)

Bruce, I (1998) *Successful Charity Marketing*, ICSA, London (V)

Murray, A (2001) *Teach Yourself Public Relations*, Teach Yourself Books, London (G)

Sargeant, A (1999) *Marketing Management for Nonprofit Organisations*, Oxford University Press, Oxford (V)

White, J (1991) *How to Understand and Manage Public Relations*, Random Business Books, London

Planning

Hussey, D (1998) *Strategic Management, from Theory to Implementation*, 4th edn, Butterworth-Heinemann, Oxford (G)

Hussey, D (1999) *Strategy and Planning: A manager's guide*, 5th edn, Wiley, Chichester (G)

Taylor, M (2001) *Project Management for the Not for Profit Sector*, ICSA, London (V)

Loose-leaf with update services

Croner, *Financial Reporting for Charities*, Croner, Kingston upon Thames

Croner, *Management of Voluntary Organisations*, Croner, Kingston upon Thames

Reason, J, *The Charities Manual*, ICSA, London

Research and statistics: the voluntary sector

Charities Aid Foundation (CAF) (2000) *Dimensions 2000*, 4 vols, CAF, West Malling

Pharoah, C (1997) *A Delicate Balance*, CAF, West Malling

Sargeant, A and Kaehler, J (1998) *Benchmarking Charity Costs*, CAF, West Malling

SCVO (1999) *Working in the Voluntary Sector: A report to map the voluntary sector workforce and its training needs in Scotland*, SCVO, Edinburgh

SCVO (2000) *Scotland's Third Lottery Report*, SCVO, Edinburgh

SCVO (2001) *Learning at the Top*, SCVO, Edinburgh

Walker, C and Pharoah, C (2000) *Making Time for Charity*, CAF, West Malling

Walker, C et al (2002) *A Lot of Give: Trends in charitable giving for the 21st century*, CAF, West Malling

JOURNALS

Charity Finance (Charity Finance Directors' Group)

Chartered Secretary (Institute of Chartered Secretaries and Administrators)

Corporate Citizen (Directory of Social Research)

International Journal of Non-Profit and Voluntary Sector Marketing (Henry Stewart Publications)

NICVA News (Northern Ireland Council for Voluntary Associations)
Research Quarterly (National Council for Voluntary Organisations)
Scope (Northern Ireland Council for Voluntary Associations)
Third Force News (Scottish Council for Voluntary Organisations)
Trust & Foundation News (Association of Charitable Foundations)
Trust Monitor (Directory of Social Research)
Voluntary Action (Institute for Volunteering Research)

ADDRESSES

Our aim is to provide a few important addresses. The brief descriptions given are focused on some points that we feel are particularly helpful, and do not attempt to describe the whole range of activities of each organization. Similarly the aims of each are summarized. Where known we have also given Web site addresses.

Association of Charitable Foundations
2 Plough Yard
Shoreditch High Street
London EC2A 3LP
www.acf.org.uk
Aims: Promoting good practice among trusts and foundations, and educating the public about them.
Services: Books and reports, journal, research.
Information: Overall facts and figures about grants given by foundations; publications.

Awards for All
Application has to be made to the appropriate region. To find out where you fit, telephone 0845 600 2040, or visit www.awardsforall. org.uk.
Aims: A Lottery-related fund providing grants for small community projects.
Services: Grants in the range of £500 to £5,000.

Centre for Institutional Studies
University of East London
Maryland House
Wembley Park Road
London E15 1ET
Tel: (020) 8223 4290
Fax: (020) 8223 4298
www.uel.ac.uk
Aims: A problem-solving approach to public and community services. Seeks to involve people and communities.
Services: Research, consultancy and teaching; a partner in the Institute for Volunteering Research.
Information: Research studies.

Centre for Voluntary Sector Research
Henley Management College
Greenlands
Henley on Thames
Oxfordshire RG9 3AU
Tel: (01491) 571454
Fax: (01491) 571635
www.henleymc.ac.uk
Aims: Enhancing the relevance of academic work to professional practice.
Services: Research, publications, conferences, voluntary sector specialization within Henley Management College research degrees.
Information: Publications list, abstracts from the *International Journal of Non-Profit and Voluntary Sector Marketing*.

Charities Aid Foundation
Headquarters:
Kings Hill
West Malling
Kent ME19 4TA
Tel: (01732) 520000
Fax: (01732) 520001
www.caf.org.uk
Aims: To do all in its power to ensure that charitable giving to charities is robust and effective.
Services: Various support services for charities.
Information: Up-to-date research, statistics and other information about the sector.

Charities Evaluation Services
4 Coldbath Square
London EC1R 5HL
Tel: (020) 7713 5722
www.ces-vol.org.uk
Aims: Helping to improve the efficiency and effectiveness of chari-
table organizations.
Services: Consultancy, advice, training and publications.
Information: Publishes two series of books related to its aims.

Charity Commission
(The three offices of the Commission each cover a specific number of
counties. Information about the scope of each can be obtained by tele-
phoning 0870 333 0123 – which is the same for all – or from the Web
site.)
London office:
Harmsworth House
Bouverie Street
London EC4Y 8DP
Fax: (020) 7674 2300
Liverpool office:
2nd Floor
20 Kings Parade
Queens Dock
Liverpool L3 4DQ
Fax: (0151) 703 1555
Taunton office:
Woodfield House
Tangier
Taunton
Somerset TA1 4BL
Fax: (01823) 345003
Aims: To give the public confidence in the integrity of charity.
Services: 1. To ensure that charities in England and Wales are able
to operate for their proper purposes within an effective
legal, accounting and governance framework.
2. To improve the governance, accountability, efficiency
and effectiveness of charities in England and Wales.
3. To identify and deal with abuse and poor practices in
England and Wales.

Information: An extensive range of publications about the legal and financial issues of charities, the register of charities, statistics of charities in England and Wales.

Charity Finance Directors' Group
Camelford House
87–89 Albert Embankment
London SE1 7TP
Tel: (020) 7793 1400
e-mail: mail@cfdg.org.uk
www.cfdg.org.uk
Aims: Helping charities to manage their accounting, finance and related functions.
Services: Sharing knowledge of good practice and finding solutions to problems.
Information: Publishes a number of briefing papers.

Community Fund
St Vincent House
16 Suffolk Street
London SW1Y 4NL
Tel: (020) 7747 5299
Fax: (020) 7747 5347
www.community-fund.org.uk
Aims: Help meet the needs of those at greatest disadvantage in society.
Services: Distribution of National Lottery money to voluntary organizations.
Information: Statistics of awards made.

Companies House
England and Wales:
Central Library, Chamberlain Square, Birmingham B3 3HQ
Tel: 0870 333 3636
Crown Way, Cardiff, CF14 3UZ
Tel: (029) 2038 8588
25 Queen St, Leeds, LS1 2TW
Tel: 0870 333 3636
21 Bloomsbury St, London, WC1B 3XD
Tel: 0870 333 3636
Fax: (029) 2038 0900

75 Mosley St, Manchester, M2 2HR
Tel: 0870 333 3636
Scotland:
37 Castle Terrace, Edinburgh, EH1 2EB
Tel: 0870 333 3636
www.companies-house.gov.uk

Croner CCH Ltd
140 London Road
Kingston upon Thames
Surrey KT2 6SR
Tel: (020) 8547 3333
Fax: (020) 8547 2637
www. croner.cch.co.org.uk
Services: Subscription service providing legal and financial information for charities.

Directory of Social Change
(Also has an office in Liverpool)
24 Stephenson Way
London NW1 2DP
Tel: (020) 7391 4900
www.dsc.org.uk
Aims: To promote social change by helping voluntary and community organizations.
Services: Research and publishing, training courses, conferences, an annual charity fair, encouraging voluntary groups to network and share information, campaigning to promote the voluntary sector, bookshop.
Information: On fund-raising, management, communication, finance and the law, largely through training and publishing.

Inland Revenue
England, Wales and Northern Ireland charity tax enquiries:
IR Charities (Repayments)
St John's House
Merton Road
Bootle
Merseyside L69 9BB
Tel: (0151) 472 6036/6037
Fax: (0151) 472 6268/6060
www.inlandrevenue.gov.uk

Northern Ireland charity registration:
FICO (charity title)
St John's House
Merton Road
Bootle
Merseyside L69 9BB
Tel: (0151) 472 6036/6037
Fax: (0151) 472 6268/6060
Scottish charity registration and repayments to charities:
IR Charities
Meldrum House
15 Drumsheugh Gardens
Edinburgh EH3 7UL
Tel: (0131) 777 4040
Fax: (0131) 777 4045

Institute of Fundraising
Market Towers
Nine Elms Lane
London SW8 5NQ
Tel: (020) 7687 2806
www.institute-of-fundraising.org.uk
Aims: A membership organization aimed at promoting the highest standards of fund-raising.
Services: Training, networking and dissemination of best practice.
Information: Publications include codes of practice for various aspects of fund-raising.

Institute for Volunteering Research
Regent's Wharf
8 All Saints Street
London N1 9RL
Tel: (020) 7520 8900
Fax: (020) 7520 8910
www.ivr.org.uk
Aims: To stimulate and contribute to education and training on volunteering, through disseminating research and sharing information.
Services: Research consultancy and evaluation, undertaking and commissioning research.
Information: Facts and figures about volunteering; research findings.

National Centre for Social Research
35 Northampton Square
London
EC1V 0AX
Tel: (020) 7250 1866
Fax: (020) 7250 1524
www.natcen.ac.uk
Aims: Social research to provide information on a wide range of social policy issues.
Services: Original research, including long-running surveys such as the British Crime Survey and Family Resources Survey; seminars.
Information: Facts and figures about a wide range of social issues. Reports may be purchased.

National Council for Voluntary Organisations
Regent's Wharf
8 All Saints Street
London N1 9RL
Tel: (020) 7713 6161
Fax: (020) 7713 6300
www.ncvo-vol.org.uk
Aims: To help voluntary organizations to achieve high standards of practice and effectiveness.
Services: Events, legal services, research.
Information: Briefing papers on legal matters, research, other publications.

National Lottery (Lotto)
The Lottery does not distribute the money raised for good causes, although its Web site (www.national-lottery.co.uk) provides a short summary of the distribution organizations, and links to Web sites. The distribution bodies are listed here. Those marked * are entered in more detail under their own names.
*Awards for All (www.awardsforall.org.uk)
The Arts Council
* Community Fund (www.community-fund.org.uk)
Heritage Lottery Fund (www.hlf.org.uk)
* New Opportunities Fund (www.nof.org.uk)
Sport England

New Opportunities Fund
Dacre House
19 Dacre Street
London SW1H 0DH
Tel: 0845 000 0121
www.nof.org.uk
Aims: A distributor of Lottery funds, giving grants to health, education and environmental projects across the UK.
Services: Grants for projects to meet certain defined purposes.

Northern Ireland Council for Voluntary Organisations
61 Duncairn Gardens
Belfast BT15 2GB
Tel: (028) 9087 7777
Fax: (028) 9087 7799
www.nicva.org
Aims: Support, training, information and networking opportunities for voluntary organizations.
Services: Library, advice, training events, conference facilities, 'incubation' officers for two to three years for start-ups.
Information: Fact sheets on legal issues, journal and newsletter.

Scottish Charities Office
Crown Office
25 Chambers Street
Edinburgh EH1 1LA
Tel: (0131) 226 2626
Fax: (0131) 226 6912
Aims: Regulation of registered charities.

Scottish Council for Voluntary Organisations
(Also has offices in Glasgow and Inverness)
18/19 Claremont Crescent
Edinburgh EH7 4QD
Tel: (0131) 556 3882
Fax: (0131) 556 0279
www.scvo.org.uk
Aims: Promoting the voluntary sector in Scotland, and helping to improve its effectiveness and capacity.
Services: Events, seminars, research and publications.
Information: Research into the voluntary sector in Scotland.

South Bank University
Southwark Campus
103 Borough Road
London SE1 0AA
Tel: (020) 7815 7852
Fax: (020) 7815 7865
Services: Various courses in charity management, including the ICSA
Certificate in Charity Management.

THE AUTHORS

David Hussey and Robert Perrin welcome feedback from their
readers and can be contacted at the addresses below:

David Hussey
44 Forestfield
Horsham
West Sussex RH13 6DZ
e-mail: davidhussey@compuserve.com

Robert Perrin
Harlequin house
Hurston Lane
Storrington
West Sussex RH20 4HH
e-mail: robert@perrin.co.uk

Index

References in *italic* indicate figures or tables